Deborah Hicks Midanek
Speaking Out on Governance

M000268473

The Alexandra Lajoux Corporate Governance Series

Edited by
Alexandra Reed Lajoux

Deborah Hicks Midanek

Speaking Out on Governance

What Stakeholders Say About the Revolution

DE GRUYTER

ISBN 978-3-11-066668-7
e-ISBN (PDF) 978-3-11-067000-4
e-ISBN (EPUB) 978-3-11-066670-0
ISSN 2629-8155

Library of Congress Control Number: 2020933716

Bibliographic information published by the Deutsche Nationalbibliothek
The Deutsche Nationalbibliothek lists this publication in the Deutsche Nationalbibliografie;
detailed bibliographic data are available on the Internet at http://dnb.dnb.de.

———

This book is dedicated to the wonderful people who invested their time in speaking with me for its creation; and to the many more who are working hard to improve corporate decision making for the benefit of all.

Contents

About the author

Deborah Hicks Midanek is an independent director, a pioneer in the corporate restructuring industry, a veteran of Wall Street trading floors, and a serial entrepreneur. Widely respected for her turnaround skills, she has diagnosed and remedied problems for over 60 corporations and facilitated the growth of nearly 30 other ventures, including her own. She has been described by the late Fletcher Byrom, chief executive officer of a Fortune 25 company, as a "pure thinker" – quickly gaining a deep understanding of complex problems and demonstrating an extraordinary ability to assimilate conflicting desires and craft lasting solutions.

Deborah has been directly involved in much of the extraordinary innovation that has taken place on Wall Street over the last few decades, and in handling the consequences of its excess. With solid knowledge of capital markets from all points of view and a long record of success in building and rebuilding companies from the bottom up, Deborah focuses on defining transitions as positive processes.

Deborah has served as chairman, lead director, and director as well as committee chair (audit, compensation, governance, special independent) for 23 public and private companies. In her first role as a director, she organized the shareholders of beleaguered Drexel Burnham Lambert Group to achieve recognition by the bankruptcy court and restructured the incumbent board to favor independent directors, whom she recruited and led.

Deborah founded advisory firm Solon Group in 2005 and continues to lead it today. She is a 2011 NACD Board Leadership Fellow, and also a Certified Turnaround Professional, based on career achievement. She has served as chief executive officer of several companies, built and sold her own institutional investment management firm and grew a retail no load mutual fund complex to $1 billion in assets in record time. She joined Drexel to start its interest rate swap (derivatives) function and then led the firm's structured finance department.

Deborah earned her MBA from the Wharton School and an AB from Bryn Mawr College. A frequent writer and speaker on governance, resilience, and leadership, she is deeply involved in promoting entrepreneurship. A New Yorker now living in Mississippi, she is in the middle of a downtown turnaround, renovating and repurposing the 22 19th century commercial row buildings she has acquired.

https://doi.org/10.1515/9783110670004-203

About the series editor

 **Alexandra Reed Lajoux** is Series Editor for Walter De Gruyter, Inc. The series has an emphasis on governance, corporate leadership, and sustainability. Dr. Lajoux is chief knowledge officer emeritus (CKO) at the National Association of Corporate Directors (NACD) and founding principal of Capital Expert Services, LLC (CapEx), a global consultancy providing expert witnesses for legal cases. She has served as editor of *Directors & Boards, Mergers & Acquisitions, Export Today,* and *Director's Monthly,* and has coauthored a series of books on M&A for McGraw-Hill, including *The Art of M&A* and eight spin-off titles on strategy, valuation, financing, structuring, due diligence, integration, bank M&A, and distressed M&A. For Bloomberg/Wiley, she coauthored *Corporate Valuation for Portfolio Investment* with Robert A. G. Monks. Dr. Lajoux serves on the advisory board of Campaigns and Elections, and is a Fellow of the Caux Round Table for Moral Capitalism. She holds a B.A. from Bennington College, a Ph.D. from Princeton University, and an M.B.A. from Loyola University in Maryland. She is an associate member of the American Bar Association.

https://doi.org/10.1515/9783110670004-204

Introduction

Corporate role and responsibility

Never has the role of the corporation been as important in world affairs as it is today. Hence, at no time has effective governance of the corporation been more important. In this book we will look at these tightly linked concepts, through the eyes and minds of a variety of people in leadership roles. It has been an enormous privilege to hear what they have to say. On balance, their views are not just promising but optimistic.

Throughout each interview, though, the sense of urgency is apparent. We have at hand an opportunity for corporations to transform the world as they have done many times in the 400-plus years of their existence. To realize that possibility, there is one thing that is clearly needed: leadership. Leadership that brings the many voices together into a harmonious whole; leadership that is informed not just by the pursuit of profit but by a sense of moral and community purpose. Our corporations must be responsible citizens and lead us all.

Fifty years ago, in a time when the US was floundering for the first time since the end of World War II, Milton Friedman presented the idea that the purpose of the corporation is to earn a profit. Perceived as a radical departure from a more stakeholder-oriented approach at the time, his words took root as investors were being ravaged by the effects of inflation. Shareholder voices and concerns took center stage, and we learned that maximizing total shareholder return was the overarching goal of corporate directors.

Where has that focus on shareholder primacy brought us? It powered what may be an unprecedented period of prosperity, the creation of new products, new jobs, and the opening of new markets. It may also have impeded corporate leaders' ability to think long term and may have widened the real and perceived gap between the haves and the have-nots. It became acceptable, and even admirable, to reduce pension benefits, and to minimize tax burdens by shopping for the most favorable jurisdiction. There is now ample evidence that the maximizing shareholder value paradigm is flawed economically, legally, and socially.

Where is the urgency to change this focus coming from? Multiple factors are coming together. The spreading recognition of climate change and its dangers is frightening us. The size of our institutional investors coupled with the dominance of index-based investing results in quasi-permanent investors who realize that they have no choice but to focus on the sustainability of the companies in their indexed portfolio. Thus, environmental, social, and governance (ESG) issues have been driven to the forefront.

We also have demographic factors at work. Social media and the interconnectedness of the internet have enabled a world in which companies that are not transparent

https://doi.org/10.1515/9783110670004-001

and transmitting values that are easily understood can be bypassed. Whatever label they fly under, people can and do communicate their likes and dislikes instantly, and the impact of these opinions can be amplified in ways far beyond institutional reach. Enough people no longer want to work for, invest in, or buy from companies that are seen to lack strong values beyond maximizing shareholder value; and failing to project such values can be a major risk to corporate well being. Corporate leaders and investors alike have started to recognize that their own long-term success is closely linked to that of their customers, employees, and suppliers, and the community at large. Finally, we have a group of people who have lived through the last 50 years and now have both the time and the wealth to think about how we can collectively try to leave the world a better place than we found it.

Emerging consensus regarding corporate purpose

In 1973, attendees at the Annual Meeting of the nascent World Economic Forum signed the *Davos Manifesto 1973: A Code of Ethics for Business Leaders* which describes a firm's principal responsibilities toward its stakeholders. Somewhat eclipsed by the rise of shareholder primacy but nonetheless compelling, that manifesto is being updated by the new *Davos Manifesto 2020: The Universal Purpose of a Company in the Fourth Industrial Revolution* – designed to ensure that stakeholder capitalism becomes and remains the dominant model. It states that companies should pay their fair share of taxes, show zero tolerance for corruption, uphold human rights throughout their global supply chains, and advocate for a level competitive playing field.

- The purpose of a company is to engage all its stakeholders in shared and sustained value creation. In creating such value, a company serves not only its shareholders, but all its stakeholders – employees, customers, suppliers, local communities, and society at large. The best way to understand and harmonize the divergent interests of all stakeholders is through a shared commitment to policies and decisions that strengthen the long-term prosperity of a company.
    - A company serves its customers by providing a value proposition that best meets their needs. It accepts and supports fair competition and a level playing field. It has zero tolerance for corruption. It keeps the digital ecosystem in which it operates reliable and trustworthy. It makes customers fully aware of the functionality of its products and services, including adverse implications or negative externalities.
    - A company treats its people with dignity and respect. It honors diversity and strives for continuous improvements in working conditions and employee well-being. In a world of rapid change, a company fosters continued employability through ongoing upskilling and reskilling.

- A company considers its suppliers as true partners in value creation. It provides a fair chance to new market entrants. It integrates respect for human rights into the entire supply chain.
- A company serves society at large through its activities, supports the communities in which it works, and pays its fair share of taxes. It ensures the safe, ethical, and efficient use of data. It acts as a steward of the environmental and material universe for future generations. It consciously protects our biosphere and champions a circular, shared, and regenerative economy. It continuously expands the frontiers of knowledge, innovation, and technology to improve people's well-being.
- A company provides its shareholders with a return on investment that considers the incurred entrepreneurial risks and the need for continuous innovation and sustained investments. It responsibly manages near-term, medium-term, and long-term value creation in pursuit of sustainable shareholder returns that do not sacrifice the future for the present.
- A company is more than an economic unit generating wealth. It fulfills human and societal aspirations as part of the broader social system. Performance must be measured not only on the return to shareholders, but also on how it achieves its environmental, social, and good governance objectives. Executive remuneration should reflect stakeholder responsibility.
- A company that has a multinational scope of activities not only serves all those stakeholders who are directly engaged but acts itself as a stakeholder – together with governments and civil society – of our global future. Corporate global citizenship requires a company to harness its core competencies, its entrepreneurship, skills, and relevant resources in collaborative efforts with other companies and stakeholders to improve the state of the world.[1]

Other voices are chiming in along similar lines. In late 2019, the US Business Roundtable, America's most influential business lobbying group, formally embraced stakeholder capitalism with a statement aimed at clarifying the role of business in society. Breaking with long-held views regarding the primacy of serving shareholders, the statement was signed by nearly 200 chief executives, including the leaders of Apple, Pepsi, and Walmart.

> While each of our individual companies serves its own corporate purpose, we share a fundamental commitment to all our stakeholders. We commit to:
>
> Delivering value to our customers. We will further the tradition of American companies leading the way in meeting or exceeding customer expectations.

---

1 *Davos Manifesto 2020: The Universal Purpose of a Company in the Fourth Industrial Revolution,* https://www.weforum.org/agenda/2019/12/davos-manifesto-2020-the-universal-purpose-of-a-company-in-the-fourth-industrial-revolution/

Investing in our employees. This starts with compensating them fairly and providing important benefits. It also includes supporting them through training and education that help develop new skills for a rapidly changing world. We foster diversity and inclusion, dignity, and respect.

Dealing fairly and ethically with our suppliers. We are dedicated to serving as good partners to the other companies, large and small, that help us meet our missions.

Supporting the communities in which we work. We respect the people in our communities and protect the environment by embracing sustainable practices across our businesses.

Generating long-term value for shareholders, who provide the capital that allows companies to invest, grow, and innovate. We are committed to transparency and effective engagement with shareholders.

Each of our stakeholders is essential. We commit to deliver value to all of them, for the future success of our companies, our communities, and our country.[2]

We have also seen the creation and continuing refinement of the New Paradigm for Corporate Governance, developed by the World Economic Forum in conjunction with law firm Wachtell, Lipton, Rosen & Katz. The New Paradigm, discussed in detail in *The Governance Revolution: What Every Board Member Needs to Know, NOW!* sets forth the notion of a partnership between corporations and their investors to focus together on long term value creation.

Frank Bold leads the Purpose of the Corporation Project, which provides a strategic, open-source platform for leading experts and organizations interested in promoting the long-term health and sustainability of publicly listed companies in policymaking and business management. The project hosted a global roundtable series on corporate governance that brought together experts from business, academia, regulators, and civil society to develop new options for corporate governance models, reflected in the *Corporate Governance for a Changing World Report*.

These are lofty ambitions, which require us to build the capacity, strength, and character of our corporate leaders – as individuals and as boards of directors working together to strive to reach them. Corporate failures due to perceived governance weakness litter the landscape and have been amply chronicled. We must do all we can to strengthen governance processes to keep such failures from recurring, and to help boards drive the companies they care for forward. Board service has never been more important and knowing how to both serve and lead is an important set of skills requiring constant improvement.

---

2 Business Roundtable statement, https://opportunity.businessroundtable.org/ourcommitment/

Characteristics of today's corporate board

Before we turn to the interviews, let us review Spencer Stuart's Annual Survey of S&P 500 Boards, to see what today's board looks like.

In the past year, 432 new independent directors joined 492 boards, the most since 2004. Boards on average have roughly 9 independent directors and the percentage of directors who are independent remains at 85%, consistent with the past several years.

Almost one-third of the independent directors are serving on their first outside corporate board. Women account for 46% of new independent directors, up from 17% in 2009, a 171% 10-year change. African American/Black, Hispanic/Latino or Asian represent 23% of new independent directors, compared with 12% in 2014. One out of six new directors are 50 years of age or younger. The number of companies splitting the chair and CEO roles has been increasing for over a decade, and is now at 53%, compared with 37% in 2009.

Average independent director tenure is 8 years, and 65% of boards state that they apply no term limit. Only 27 companies have an explicit term limit, which ranges from 10 to 20 years. Mandatory retirement age is specified by 71% of companies, and age limits continue to inch upward, with 75 the most common age limit. Independent directors on average sit on 2.1 boards. The number of S&P 500 CEOs who do not sit on any outside board continues to increase, currently at 59%, up from 55% in 2018 and 51% a decade ago.

Board evaluations that consider the full board, its committees, and each individual director are conducted by 43% of respondents. Boards average 10.7 members, roughly constant over the last 10 years. The largest board has 18 members and the smallest board has 5 members. Excluding the chair's premium compensation, average director compensation increased to $303,269 from $295,406 in 2018. Stock grants and cash account for 57% and 38%, respectively, for director compensation. The additional fee for an independent chair averages $172,127, received by 98% of such chairs.[3]

The breadth and depth of challenges facing these directors has never been greater, nor have the stakes been more important. Defining the kind of capitalism we want, and organizing our behavior to realize it, may be the most critical question of our era. If we want to sustain our economic system for future generations, we must develop robust answers. More than that, however, we must prepare ourselves and our leaders to execute on such serious commitments.

While the many initiatives aimed at clarifying the role of the corporation indicate increasing attention being paid to improving corporate governance, the functioning of the board of directors, the apex of corporate leadership, remains mysterious and often cloistered. Organizing effective board behavior requires attention, commitment, and shared goals among the parties: corporate boards and management, shareholders, and stakeholders. The interviews that follow open the doors to the boardroom. Taken together they offer a rich tapestry woven of broad and deep experience.

---

3 https://www.spencerstuart.com/-/media/2019/ssbi-2019/us_board_index_2019.pdf

The interviews

We begin our journey with perspective from Myron T. Steele, retired Chief Justice of the Delaware Supreme Court, the bellwether court to many for interpretation of corporate behavior. He offers insight into the value of the flexibility provided by our state chartering system, and its contribution to the vitality and variety of US corporations. Coupled with that, he reminds us of the danger of forcing a one-size-fits-all approach on companies, and draws an analogy between the function of the court and of the corporate board in fostering lively debate that leads to a consistent, clear, and unanimous set of signals for the relevant parties to interpret and follow.

We next hear from Bernard C. Bailey, Ph.D., SE, outgoing CEO of the nonpartisan policy think tank Committee for Economic Development, veteran corporate executive and director who took a sabbatical to complete his doctorate, researching how corporate boards make decisions. He introduces the importance of a concept called procedural justice, which concerns the fairness and the transparency of the processes by which decisions are made. In his view, individual directors must earn the respect of their peers though the value of their contributions. Once respect is established, the kind of trust required to engage in serious and candid discussion can ensue, but none of this can happen if the parties do not believe that procedural justice is employed.

Halla Tómasdóttir, CEO of The B Team, shares with us her conviction that we are in the midst of a "crisis of conformity" which can be addressed by corporate leaders, directors, executives, and boards collectively, who must have two characteristics: humility and courage. The B Team is a global nonprofit initiative co-founded by Sir Richard Branson and Jochen Zeitz that brings together a group of global leaders from business, civil society, and government to catalyze a better way of doing business that prioritizes the wellbeing of people and the planet.

We hear from Carl T. Camden, retired CEO of Kelly Services and founder of iPSE-U.S., working to empower independent workers by giving them a voice in public policy and equal access to benefits. He envisions a new kind of corporation, less dependent on high amounts of capital investment in long term activities. He sees what he calls the tinker toy enterprise, in which teams of experts and capacities can be assembled and disassembled quickly. He also tells a related story about convincing his board to do the right thing in the face of short-term economic loss, and ultimately being rewarded for taking a principled position.

Catherine Allen, CEO of the technology consortium The Santa Fe Group and multi-board director, takes us through her lifelong commitments to working in business while improving public policy and empowering women. She describes the value added to board effectiveness by active questioning and holistic thinking, patterns of action she sees more often in women than in men. She is deeply invested in promoting corporate action based on strong values.

We next turn to Bob Zukis, retired from an international career on the forefront of new product and market development with PwC and now serves as founder and leader of Digital Directors Network. He introduces the eight technology domains that directors should be familiar with and is creating a network of what he calls QTEs, or Qualified Technology Experts. He believes that all boards need at least one QTE. He offers another observation that boards need to think about. Not very long ago, the challenge for a company was to get the workforce to adopt new technologies. Now, he says, end users, whether customers or employees or vendors, are often lapping the company, and the board is not even a party to the conversation.

Anne Sheehan, active now as a corporate director and chairman of the SEC's Investor Advisory Committee, formerly Director of Governance and board member for California State Teachers Retirement System, and board member for California Public Employees Retirement System, reflects on the importance of effective governance by all entities serving as fiduciaries, and especially by public pension fund boards, often populated with a wide cross section of people and experience. She also highlights the communication process between a company, its board, and the institutional investor, stressing the need for as much transparency as possible.

The Honorable Paula Stern is a former US Trade Representative and multi-board director who discusses board pitfalls, namely the frequent formation of elite subgroups that hold and deploy the real power, using the balance of the board members as window dressing. To prevent that from occurring, she cites the value of the strong chairman, who works hard to hear, understand, and bring out the views and concerns of each director. She also brings attention to the interesting question of discerning what has not been discussed but needs to be addressed.

Jane Diplock, AO, former Chairman of the New Zealand Securities Commission, leader of the International Organization of Securities Commissions (IOSCO) during the financial crisis, and multi-board director believes that integrated reporting, of which she is a primary champion, and integrated thinking about corporate behavior provide the basis for the 21st century model. She cautions that corporations that rely on the 19th century Industrial Revolution model of the corporation run the risk of a "Kodak moment" and disappearing. Companies including GE in the US, for example, and Unilever in Europe are looking at their businesses using these tools to consider their short, medium, and long-term prospects, and their sustainability. In addition to directing us to IntegratedReporting.org, Jane suggests we look to the United Nations Sustainable Development Goals, adopted by every country in the world. She believes they offer our best hope for the future.

Next we hear from Roger Martin, just retired from his role as Dean and Institute Director of the Martin Prosperity Institute at the Rotman School of Business at the University of Toronto, cofounder of the major strategy consulting firm Monitor Company, and pioneer of several important concepts including design thinking, which applies design principles to business challenges. He is a prolific writer, strategy advisor, and currently #1 ranked management thinker in the world. In his view, we are frequently not asking the right questions about governance, with the result that great CEOs attract great directors, and weak CEOs attract weak directors, leading to low benefits realized from the board. He suggests that we look for directors who are motivated by a desire to serve the public interest, and further, that "if we're going to have widely held publicly traded companies, we have to honor and revere board members the way we honor and revere judges."

Nell Minow, Vice Chair of ValueEdge Advisors, was cofounder and Director of GMI Ratings, and was Editor and cofounder of its predecessor firm, The Corporate Library, Principal of Lens Investment Management, an investment firm that used shareholder activism to increase the value of underperforming companies. She was also cofounder and served as President of Institutional Shareholder Services, Inc. Nell is direct and specific in her insistence on change. Tired of hearing about the dynamics of buy side and sell side, she demands to know who represents the hold side. Other questions she raises: Why is it that so many companies become sclerotic, become inbred, become hidebound, unable to survive disruption? Why are some of the highest quality people we have so bad at being directors? Hint: her answer has something to do with putting a coffee cup on the head. She suggests that all CEOs must put a significant amount of their net worth into their stock, and not be able to sell until five years after they leave the company. I should mention that she is also an acclaimed movie critic.

Michael Useem, William and Jacalyn Egan Professor of Management and Director, Center for Leadership and Change Management, and Editor, Wharton Leadership Digest, and author, looks at examples of leaders and their courage, citing particularly Larry Merlo, CEO of CVS taking a stand on refusing to sell tobacco products any longer. Merlo was not responding to political or legal pressure, and he could not execute the move by fiat, so he invested a tremendous amount of time talking with all involved to discuss the CVS future. He envisioned it not as a convenience store but as a health services company. Despite incurring substantial financial losses in the short term, he pulled it off by building what Professor Useem called a "coalition of the willing."

Next, we turn to Paul Halpern, an attorney turned private equity investor and Chief Investment Officer for Versa Capital Management LLC. He compares his service on boards of a public company, a nonprofit, and privately held portfolio companies. While he admits that one advantage of the private equity owned company is that the goal is clear, he applies that idea to all enterprises. In his view, boards can have many different purposes, but all members must have a clear understanding as to the particular purpose of each board on which they serve.

Paul Washington is an attorney and Executive Director, ESG Center, The Conference Board; former corporate secretary, Time Warner; former law clerk, United States Supreme Court. Fascinated by constitutional law, Paul looks at corporate governance with a similar lens. Unlike constitutional law in the government sphere, however, he says there is no single authority in corporate governance. The allocation of power and responsibility among shareholders, board, and management is intellectually fascinating, with the SEC, the stock exchanges, investors, and board all exercising different kinds of authority. In addition, the board plays different roles at different times – the board decides, the board oversees, and the board advises. He adds that now the board also engages with investors and with management and other stakeholders. He describes governance as broad and deep, happening at every level of the corporation in a fluid continuum.

This group of thought leaders represents a cross section of professionals, all of whom have played multiple roles in and around the boardroom. The many hats they have worn give them the opportunity to compare and contrast and offer us as their audience both clarity and insight. We hear views from the Delaware bench, from regulators, investors, proxy advisors, executives, board members, policy makers, academics, and activists. Though their comments cover a broad spectrum of subjects, their voices together create largely harmonious music. I hope you enjoy their comments.

Chapter 1
One size does not fit all

Myron T. Steele

Myron T. Steele, former Chief Justice of the Supreme Court of Delaware, is currently a partner at Potter Anderson & Corroon LLP. He served as a judge of the Superior Court and as Vice Chancellor of the Delaware Court of Chancery following 18 years in private litigation practice. He has presided over major corporate litigation and LLC and limited partner governance disputes and writes frequently on issues of corporate document interpretation and corporate governance.

Chief Justice Steele has published over 400 opinions resolving disputes among members of limited liability companies and limited partnerships, and between shareholders and management of both publicly traded and closely held corporations. He speaks and writes frequently on issues of corporate document interpretation and corporate governance.

He has long been ranked by various publications as among the most influential people in corporate governance and in business ethics in addition to being recognized as among the nation's leading lawyers and best judges.

Deborah Midanek: It's a privilege to speak with you. Would you give us some insight into how you became involved doing what you've spent your life doing? What pulled you into the world of the law and then the judiciary?

Myron Steele: I suppose what pulled me into the world of the law is where I went to college, I went to the University of Virginia and had the opportunity there to major in foreign affairs and believed that I would ultimately become an international lawyer. So I went to Virginia Law School, took all the international law courses and then had the huge benefit of having two corporations classes from Ernie Folk, Professor Ernest Folk who taught corporations and corporate finance. In 1967, he was the author of the rewrite of the Delaware General Corporation Law, or the DGCL as it's called.

He had a major influence on me and turned me to thinking about going to Delaware, which was attractive for a number of reasons. My wife was from Maryland so I wouldn't be taking her too far from home. And I was recruited by a law firm in

https://doi.org/10.1515/9783110670004-002

Wilmington, then called Prickett, Ward, Burt & Sanders. Rod Ward's family owned Corporation Services. Corporation Services was the publisher of the new corporation code and had worked closely with Ernie Folk. Ernie Folk was kind enough to recommend me.

Without his recommendation and without his generous grades when I was in his classes, I probably would have never gotten involved in corporate law or understood Delaware's importance. I probably would have gone to a foreign country. As a child, I had lived in Japan and Morocco and I was fascinated with the world.

As time went on, my interests focused on the relationship between the constituencies within the corporation and, ultimately, thinking about corporate governance and its importance and transparency and accountability – all that comes with the judicial oversight that Delaware provides.

After 18 years of private practice, including an extraordinary stint of two years away from the firm on loan to the attorney general's office in which I prosecuted cases, I ended up on the bench.

Deborah Midanek: Were they securities cases that you prosecuted?

Myron Steele: No. Regular criminal prosecution. But the beauty of that was getting comfortable with jury trials at the age of 24. That was very helpful in learning how to interact with people and understand the dynamic of the other side of the law. Ultimately, I ended up on the court of chancery and then I was absorbed for six years in the intricacies of chancery litigation as it applied both to the corporate world and to the chancery's other equity jurisdiction. Then I ended up on the Delaware Supreme Court and then, ultimately, chief justice.

There I had a good deal of interaction with corporate governance and its thought leaders as well as opportunities to speak on the topic over the Sarbanes-Oxley and Dodd-Frank years and the continuing war of the worlds, if I can use the term from H. G. Wells. There is tension between the federal government's approach and state common-law's application of fiduciary duty to what I consider to be the scheme for oversight of directors and all the corporate constituencies with the common-law fiduciary duty overlay.

Deborah Midanek: It's a wonderful answer and very useful. I grew up across the street from Adolf Berle, so I knew that the corporation was a person from a very young age. I just wanted to meet that person.

Myron Steele: You do recognize it's a very schizophrenic person? The corporate entity itself has many minds. It may be a person, but it certainly isn't one person.

Deborah Midanek: That is true. One of the things that's endlessly intriguing about "corporate governance" is its inherent ambiguity. The power of the corporate form adopted in 1602 was remarkable as a capital-raising device capable of transforming the known world, yet what the Dutch did was borrow the guild structure to create the idea of the governing board, which morphed from being a regulatory function into being an operating overseer. That ambiguity is still being resolved now, as we explore the requirements of the job of board member.

Now that you're not on the bench or in that public spotlight quite so much now, is there an aspect of governance and the drama that you find most interesting?

Myron Steele: What has always dominated my thinking is what I've considered to be the pall over governance cast by dysfunctional Washington, DC. I fear that one day someone will wake up and think that the federal government, dysfunctional as it is, may be the best voice and vehicle for implementing one-size-fits-all regulatory demands on what is otherwise the dynamic, as I see it, boardroom. One size clearly doesn't fit all, depending on the business niche of the company, the company culture, the geography, the shareholder base, and so on.

My thinking about regulatory mandates is based on Brandeis' dissent where he described the states as clinical opportunities to experiment in the business world; to try programs that change society and see how they work in a clinical empirically based experience. If it doesn't work, abandon it. If it's doable and successful, export it.

What I feared during what I'll refer to as my "later formative years" working with Sarbanes-Oxley and Dodd-Frank was the political pressure from certain constituencies suggesting to Congress that they could mandate through federal legislation what they believe to constitute good principles of corporate governance. I made any number of speeches suggesting that that is problematic if for no other reason than because it was dominated by political ideology and not by any empirical data. The great reformers, the great progressives, believed that change is the equivalent of progress and betterment when change isn't always related to progress at all, in my view.

I used to refer to it as faith-based corporate governance principles. People just knew that this was better than what currently existed and therefore it had to be mandated by federal regulation. Not tried out by the states with their chartering systems but mandated nationwide, on the theory that, after all, these are nationally traded public companies.

Therefore, what works for General Electric must also work for Revlon. I've never believed that, and I also believe there was no data to support the many mandates that were tried out with Sarbanes-Oxley and Dodd-Frank. Setting a mandatory number of independent directors, separating the chairman and the CEO, eliminating the staggered board; these ideas are not well supported by data. Everyone just knew that they were better for corporate governance.

Of course, the ideas were pushed by ISS, Glass Lewis, and others; largely, institutional stockholders in the public arena. It was almost like the Ten Commandments came down from the mountain and this had to be the way it was. This is exactly how you're going to improve and live your lives. I've never believed in that. I believed in the flexible, contextual discipline of the court system that annunciates common-law principles that have been with us for a long time.

Roman law suggests what constitutes the role of a fiduciary and discusses policing the fiduciary and punishing the fiduciary when they fail. But at the same time, giving reasonable deference to the decision-making of that fiduciary because, after all, those whom the fiduciary serves selected them to be their fiduciary. It is important to give some credence to people's ability to choose who it is that's going to be handling their assets and handling them loyally and with care.

I may have something of a contrarian lack of optimism about the ESG [Environmental, Social, and Governance] movement today because it seems to me that it is virtue-signaling in the same way. But consistent with my view, I do believe that it would benefit corporations to look at community values and the interests of other constituencies; to consider what might be the best thing for them to do for their employees, their stockholders, their directors, their managers or officers. Delaware law has no prohibition against a corporation's board of directors adopting ultimately an ESG concept whether it's the expanded one that people are talking about right now or just environmental, social, and governance change.

What I think hasn't been adequately researched, because I don't think the data is there, is whether these systems will result in long-term improved success for the corporation, or whether they are merely driven by a certain mentality today that short-termism is bad.

It's humorous for a guy who lived through it to look back at the takeover era. At the time, I owned Time Warner stock and was shocked that Time Warner's board was rejecting a $200-plus takeover price for a stock that was in the $60s at the time. I couldn't understand why they would reject it, and then couldn't understand why Chancellor Allen said, "It's perfectly all right to reject it because your duty is owed to the corporation long term," as I interpret his case. He said, "This takeover is inconsistent with what is a thoughtful long-term strategy for enhancing the value of this corporation over time. And you have a corporate culture that you're advancing and has been successful up to this point. Therefore, you haven't breached your fiduciary duty by blocking what is more than double the stock price being offered by a takeover artist that doesn't fit that culture and would ultimately change the entire strategy of your corporation."

One of the beauties of the common-law system based on hindsight review of actions by directors prompted by litigation or by criticism is that a number of our judges over the years have been prolific writers and have advanced the thinking of how corporate governance should work. I've had some wonderfully thoughtful colleagues over the years who have added to the literature considerably by law review articles and speeches that they've made.

It has nonetheless always seemed to me that the greatest threat to what I would consider to be good governance initiatives that meet the goal of long-term success for corporations and their investors and their other constituencies would be a mandated rule-based process where every board, irrespective of their corporation's situation, must follow these rules.

People have said to me over time, "Well, everybody should follow the same rules." My response was, "We're not talking about the rules of the road for drivers of automobiles here." Just because you drive a Jaguar doesn't mean you can drive faster than someone who drives a Fiat on the highway. There are rules for that, but that's not what corporate governance is all about.

The most important factor I think in good governance is stockholder selection of good people to serve on the board. One of the questions that you sent to me asked if I would suggest an example of a board doing a bad job and of a board doing a good job. The poster child for a bad job is Enron. The oddity there, as I think everybody remembers, is that every member of that board was an outstanding individual in the world from which they came. Yet they didn't pay attention to what was going on. Despite ethical rules posted in the boardroom for everyone to follow, they were not providing thoughtful oversight. The most important thing is to have a system that encourages good people to serve on the board, which I still believe to be the root of reliance on the business judgment rule.

As long as you are loyal, as long as you understand your duty of care consisting of the need to develop a thoughtful reasoning process for the decision you make, and you document that process, having spent sufficient time to understand what's going on and to inform yourselves before you make a decision, you shouldn't be shamed if it just turns out to be the wrong decision.

Deborah Midanek: In recent conversations with institutional investors, they are saying the same thing you are. There is no one-size-fits-all, which I found interesting coming from the BlackRock point of view.

Myron Steele: It's always been my belief that the heart and soul of governance is the good people who can be encouraged to serve. In order to create the necessary balance within the accountability system, you have the business judgment rule that allows some freedom to take risk, but you want directors to take thoughtful risk. You don't want them to personally take advantage of the opportunities they have as a fiduciary, yet you do want to incentivize them to work for their corporation and its other constituencies long term.

It's fascinating to me that there's dialog about the other constituencies now beyond just the stockholder; that it's incumbent upon boards now to consider the environment, the social issues, and governance issues, and to have more concern about the welfare of the employee. That strikes me as a return to the Sarbanes-Oxley, Dodd-Frank ideological faith-based approach because I don't think you can legislate that across the board.

But I also don't think Delaware would ever say, "You've breached your fiduciary duty by considering those constituencies, even under circumstances where it might not be as good for today's shareholder when your thought is focused on 20 or

30 years from now and the impact that the corporation is going to have on every-thing around it including everyone who works there over that 20-year period."

Delaware law would accept that. I don't have any question about it even though I'm not around to shape it or participate in shaping it as I used to be. On the other hand, what I'm seriously concerned about is ideology in Washington, DC, conclud-ing that the states aren't moving in that direction fast enough to mandate it, there-fore the feds have to step in and mandate it for everybody everywhere irrespective of their individual situations. That, in my view, is the great threat on the horizon that would disrupt corporate governance through far too much government inter-vention by the politicians that shape policy based on ideology and not on thought-ful empirical evidence.

At the end of the day, it is not so much a legal question, but a social policy question. The question is, does the law get in the way of it, or does the law promote it, or does the law sit back as I think the law ought to do? Considering where the law is today and whether the law should move in a particular direction should be based on facts that support moving in that direction, and that facts should be con-firmed, just like scientific testing.

If it works one time, that doesn't mean anything. It's not proved until it works time and time and time again, over and over. I don't think at this point we're any-where near confident about whether separating the CEO and the chairman of the board or eliminating staggered boards have really had any kind of positive effect on governance. But they were fabulously important to people at one time, which is why I characterize it as faith-based corporate governance.

These people just *know* this is better for the country, better for the corporation, and better for the stockholders. One thing that we as citizens should never overlook is that the ultimate direction this thinking is going in will require the state, meaning the federal government here, the state in political science language, to own all the corporations. How are you going to incentivize people to invest their capital in en-terprises and take risk if they don't believe those enterprises are going to work in a way that's profitable to them?

We created the benefit corporation. For those who want to be social justice war-riors and invest their money there, they can do it in benefit corporations.

Deborah Midanek: Yes, they can. Your comments are music to my ears. But okay, this then begs the question of, "What is the purpose of the public corporation?"

Myron Steele: I think you just articulated it. I've always understood why we, mean-ing current and former Delaware jurists, talk in terms of owing fiduciary duties to the corporation and the stockholders. I think you articulated it perfectly on the mark when you said, "The duty is owed to the corporation and by carrying out that duty to the corporation, you enhance the benefits to stockholders."

And now, in this new era of ESG, you can also implement programs along the way that benefit the corporation because who's to say that corporation isn't benefited when the community in which they work is benefited? Where schools are better as result of what they do, or roads are better as a result of what, when, and how they are built. When their employees are better paid they can have a better lifestyle. That helps the corporation in the long term, too.

But each individual corporation in my view should have the opportunity to make those decisions for themselves. That might entice more investment or higher amounts of equity into the corporation's future, or it may detract. But they should be able to go the way they want to go without having it mandated for them. And only empirical data in my view can overcome my skepticism that a lot of this ESG is virtue-signaling and not really documented by empirical evidence.

Deborah Midanek: I captured a quotation from you in my earlier book about your need to see that empirical evidence before you're going to be willing to take a position on the chairman and CEO debate. People get upset with me when I object that the California legislature is mandating that women now have to be a certain percentage of all boards. Their argument is that the legislature must act because, after all, the companies aren't doing it. To my mind, this is the slippery slope. We do not want the state, that political science state you mentioned, to feel that they have the responsibility to intervene and tell the corporation who or what must be on its board. No.

Myron Steele: We hope that thoughtful people are conditioned, as I think Delaware judges are, not to form an opinion until they have seen all the facts and decided which ones are credible and which are not. What is happening in our world? My law firm has the first woman chairman of a major law firm in Delaware history. We currently have the highest number of women partners.

This isn't happening because somebody jumped up and said, "We need more women in the firm. We need a woman to be chairman." We pick the best people from our associate group and the majority happened to be women all of a sudden. When people understand that that's the way the selection is to be made, people accept it. It has credibility. If we were mandated by the Delaware legislature to have one-third or 40% of our partners to be women, it would be a disaster. In any given year, we might want 100% of our new partners to be women. In another year, maybe one out of three.

But they have credibility when they're clearly picked on their merit. I don't think mandates help women. My wife and I have two daughters. I've been married for 52 years. My older daughter is a Columbia graduate. She's a citizen of both the country of Colombia and the United States. She went to law school, graduated with honors. She is teaching legal writing at Brooklyn Law School right now, but she started off in a New York law firm.

Our younger daughter is a colonel in the United States Army and a West Point graduate. When somebody says to me, "You're just an old male curmudgeon and you don't want to see women progress." Now, they don't really say that, but let's assume they did, hypothetically. I would just point to my own family. My wife runs her own business. Not a big business, but a small one and she loves it and she's successful.

Women get ahead. They're going to get ahead more and more than they did generations ago for sure. So I agree with you. I'm suspicious of ideologically based mandates because it causes resentment that cast a pall over real achievement.

Deborah Midanek: I agree with that. I got a note recently from somebody who heard me speak. Apparently, I said something as incredibly articulate as, "Look, diversity is nature's risk management system. It's not about insisting that X percent of the board members are women, it's about having people on the board who have the vision to see what this company needs." The more different points of view you can bring into that boardroom and have heard, the better off you are. But it's not creating a quota.

Myron Steele: Completely agree with it.

Deborah Midanek: We have talked about Enron as an example of a board doing a bad job. How about a board that does a good job? Can you come up with an example we could look at? Because it's very hard to denote what success is for a board per se.

Myron Steele: What's amazing about that question is it's very difficult to find a board that's doing its job well because it's not reported.

Deborah Midanek: Exactly.

Myron Steele: It's like in the newspaper, a kind deed done by a neighbor is less likely to be reported than the murder in the house next door. So I have every reason to believe if you look at the stock market, that the voters, namely the investors in that world are more pleased than not with the way in which the world of the American economy is progressing right now. There are many boards that are experimenting along the lines of what we've been talking about.

What does a board do when the employees say, "We don't want to work where you've contracted with the federal government to make war-like items or software/ hardware that can be used in war. We don't want you to have a contract with the institution that sells firearms"? How does a board deal with all of that?

I think that credible boards, the ones that are doing a good job are the ones that are discussing all those issues, interacting with the stockholders, interacting with the employees, and presenting a positive front to the marketplace. These directors are smart enough to understand that capital is necessary, investment is necessary, to progress with better quality goods for the marketplace and, therefore, for the people that live in that marketplace – whether it's farmers growing the food that we eat or people on the West Coast generating software that makes our lives easier at the end of the day.

But I can't tell you that I know enough to single out one corporation and say they're doing a good job. My favorite corporation happens to be UPS, but that's probably because I'm invested in it and I've always liked the thought that they have a heavy stockholder base among their own employees.

I look to a company that employees are investing in to suggest to me that that's a happy workplace, that things are going well there, and people are delighted with their jobs (or most of them are). That's the kind of thing I look for, but I don't have enough information to suggest to you that I know of a board that's doing such a good job that they should be singled out.

Deborah Midanek: When the board is doing a good job, it doesn't look like it's the board per se doing a good job. The board is instead integrated well with the culture and the ethical structure and the system that's driving the company. It's not something that is distinct to the board, which is very interesting.

The power of the board is the function of the group, in that no individual director has any power at all unless specifically mandated by the board. And in the group, it's very difficult to stake out an extreme position. You can't become an outlier because your voice is dismissed and other board members won't listen to you if you're always out on one wing or the other. You have got to stay in the middle and figure out a way to move the whole group in one direction or another.

Myron Steele: I know exactly what you're talking about. A good board analogy is provided by my years on the Delaware Supreme Court. I was fortunate enough to have people from whom I could learn and people who would also listen to me even when they thought I was wrong. Over that 13 years, we [the court] had a very good relationship with the common conviction that what we did was very important even when we got it wrong. We all believed that whether people thought we got it right or wrong, we needed to explain what we did and why we did it. We also, to the extent we could without compromising principles, agreed to promote and produce a common front.

If you follow Delaware lore at all, there's a joke that there's one corporate case every decade with a dissent in Delaware. While that's not exactly correct, it's very close because of the importance of predictability and consistency and clarity. The worst thing the Delaware Supreme Court can do is start charging so rapidly in a different direction that people become confused. They need confidence that they will get the direction they're looking for from the court system. The court worked hard to present to its corporate public and its other citizens a kind of clarity, consistency, and predictability that allows, I think, better decision-making by those who have to follow our law.

Deborah Midanek: What would be the crowning comment you would like to make?

Myron Steele: I can offer a summary, rather than adding any substance, if I have offered any at all so far. I hope people will pause when they advocate change in the way constituencies interact through corporate governance in the corporate and in the alternative entity world. It is important that they think about where they're going and why they're going there. Most critically, they need to assure themselves that they have facts that support the benefits expected from the changes they seek. And it's trite, but I still must repeat: Change is not automatically progress.

Deborah Midanek: I've been refraining from calling you by name because I'm not sure what the convention is. Do I still call you Chief Justice Steele?

Myron Steele: No. There's no magic in it, but I would probably like to have it on my gravestone.

Deborah Midanek: To me, you are Chief Justice Steele.

Myron Steele: Well, I appreciate that, and I appreciate anyone whoever says a kind word. Twenty-five years on the bench, you can make a lot of friends but you can also make enemies as well.

Deborah Midanek: I expect that the clarity of your thinking goes a long way toward mitigating that. Thank you so much. I appreciate the time you have invested in this conversation.

Chapter 2
Invest in respect, trust, and procedural justice

Bernard C. Bailey

Bernard C. Bailey served most recently as President of the Committee for Economic Development (CED) and as Chairman and CEO of Authentix Corporation, a private equity owned global authentication and information services company. He has served as CEO of two publicly traded companies and held a variety of executive positions during a 17-year career with IBM. A past director of eight publicly traded companies, Bernard currently serves on the board of directors of Telos Corporation.

He earned a PhD in Management from the Weatherhead School of Management at Case Western Reserve University, where his research focused on decision-making processes, strategy, and corporate governance. Bernard also holds advanced graduate degrees in engineering from the University of California – Berkeley and the University of Southern California, and an MBA from George Washington University. Upon receiving his undergraduate degree in engineering from the United States Naval Academy he served as an officer in the U.S. Navy.

He is currently Adjunct Professor in the MBA program at the Weatherhead School of Management at Case Western Reserve University; a member of the advisory board of Egis Capital Partners, a private equity firm focused on investments in the security industry; a trustee of the Naval Academy Athletic and Scholarship Foundation; and a trustee of Trout Unlimited, a coldwater conservation group.

Deborah Midanek: Thank you for making time for me. I know that you are a serious student of governance, to the point of pursuing a doctorate in the subject. How did you get interested in this whole field, Bernard? What created you?

Bernard Bailey: It started when I took over as CEO of a publicly traded company. That was my first experience of being on the board of directors, and for most CEOs that is the situation. I had attended board meetings as COO of a previous company but had never sat on the board and had that responsibility. As the CEO, I got to see what really went on in the boardroom in detail and, more importantly, what went on outside of the boardroom.

https://doi.org/10.1515/9783110670004-003

I got to see how a CEO had to function in certain areas that you just don't see in any other position – particularly in raising funds, going to Wall Street, working with the analysts, working with disparate shareholders and their different interests, then working with the board and pulling all of that together. Governance isn't just a board of directors. Governance includes the checks and balances and all the other groups that have a role in the oversight of a corporation.

I took over as CEO of a publicly traded company in 2002, just as Sarbanes-Oxley was going into effect. We were just coming out of the Dot.com meltdown and were recovering from the shock of 9/11. This was also a period when we were starting to question income inequality, the Wall Street 1% and the protesters were vocal.

I realized then that there was no greater agent for world benefit than the corporation throughout our history. It made a difference in the development of human beings and wealth creation and the standard of living when we started to see free markets and democracy and the rights of human beings fuse together and create that value. I realized that if we don't get this right, there are a whole lot of people who will not be happy with what's going on, and they're going to destroy us.

At the center of it all is the board of directors and the responsibility that boards have. For some reason, we weren't stepping up and doing our jobs. If we wanted to get capitalism back on track, boards had to perform. That's when I took a four-year hiatus from serving as a publicly traded company CEO. I said, "I'd like to study this, to understand better why our boards are not being more effective, and what needs to be done to *make* boards more effective."

Deborah Midanek: That is a rich answer, not surprisingly. To your mind, what *is* the job of the board of directors? You led me straight to that question, and to the related question that you've hinted at: How do we determine when a board is not doing its job, and conversely how do we make them better able to perform their jobs?

Bernard Bailey: Those questions prompt a whole lot of other questions. Let me take a shot at answering. I think you asked what the role of the board of directors is and what do we have to do to make them be more effective? Why are they not being effective? How do you know if they're being effective? That's a four-hour discussion right there, so I'll try to give the five or ten-minute answer.

The board plays the *agent* role that places them in the middle of the agency problem identified by Berle and Means back in the 1920s, a function of the dawning reality of the professional manager. Up until that point in time, we watched the Rockefellers, the Mellons, all the great, great builders of the American economy, who were both owners and managers of their corporations.

But beginning in the 1920s and a little earlier, we started to have the separation of ownership and management. With that came the agency problem, the concern over whether these managers will serve the interests of the owners. How do we put a mechanism in place to assure that? You can't have a situation where you have disparate ownership directing the corporation. You must let management do that. But somebody needs to sit in the middle and serve as the agent of those owners to make sure that there's oversight and that it's being done in a responsible way.

Boards are elected by the shareholders. The shareholders use them to solve their agency problem through oversight of the corporation. Their ultimate responsibility then is to assure that the corporation is run as well as it possibly can be run. If that happens, that will create value for the shareholders.

There I am, back to that terrible word, shareholder value. But at the end of the day, that gets to your question about what the shareholders own. Do they own the corporation? The reality is no. They don't own the corporation. What they own is a piece of paper that gives them the rights to the residual value of the corporation.

What's the residual value? The residual value is anything that's left over after everybody else has taken their piece of the pie. When we talk about shareholder primacy and stakeholder primacy, all we're talking about is the pie, and who gets what pieces. Management gets a piece. Employees get a piece. Customers get a piece in lower prices or higher prices, right? Suppliers get a piece in what they are paid by the corporation. The government gets a piece. The community gets a piece in terms of trying to foster a better environment for work and workers.

But after everybody takes all those pieces, if there's anything left over, that's for the shareholders. Therefore, the board is there to arbitrate the distribution of the pie. What should go to whom in a fair way and in such a way that it creates the best long-term corporation. But if there's no residual value, if there's nothing left over because it's picked off by these other interest groups, then the whole system of capitalism breaks down. Because why would anybody ever invest? There's no more fungible asset that goes into the corporation than capital.

Deborah Midanek: There is a tension in there because if shareholders think that the board is their agent, they often think that they should be able to control the board and what the board does. What do you think about that?

Bernard Bailey: One of the big movements over the past 10 years has been increasing proxy access and making it easier for shareholders to get access to the proxy and be able to, in a fairer way, put representation onto those boards. We've required independence of board directors. We have pushed more and more to have non-staggered boards so that we can elect, or fail to reelect, all the board members every year. I'm not saying any of those are easy, but that is what the shareholders can do.

Capital is fungible. It can pick itself up and leave and do the Wall Street Walk when it doesn't feel that the corporation is being run in the proper interests of the shareholders. Can it direct the board? No, it can't direct the board. It can only elect the members. It can express its interest, and that's important to understand. Shareholders hold a piece of paper that gives them certain rights. They are not owners. We don't call them share owners. We call them shareholders. In that capacity, they have various motivations. We look at the amount of day trading and short trading that goes on. We look at what various funds have and their obligations and the fiduciary duties that they have. The corporation and its board can't look at every single shareholder and say, "I need to do what's right for every one of them." That's why their ultimate obligation and responsibility is to the corporation. Its health is what they are responsible for.

Deborah Midanek: You've mentioned that you were so taken with the importance and centrality of the board of directors in the world that we live in that you took a sabbatical and pursued a degree. What kind of degree? What were you studying?

Bernard Bailey: I hold a doctorate in management from the Weatherhead School of Management at Case Western Reserve. Boards of directors are probably the single most studied subject within corporations. Most of the academic work that's been done has been done purely by looking at characteristics of the board. Board size, board diversity, independence of the board, separation of the CEO and the chair, the duality question, and so on.

You can easily run regression analyses on that publicly disclosed information, identify correlations, and try to infer causations. The reality is that there is a huge black box that exists between those board characteristics and corporate performance. What makes it difficult to study boards is that very few people will let anybody into the boardroom, and few are willing to talk about what actually happens in that boardroom.

This then leads to the need for a more rigorous study blending both the quantitative and the qualitative to look at what's really going on. That's a long-winded way of saying that what I looked at, having served on nine publicly traded company boards and knowing lots of directors, was how boards make decisions. How do you know if they make a good decision versus a bad decision? Because what makes the modern corporation fascinating, at least under the Anglo-Saxon system of governance, is that we have a hierarchical management structure in which the CEO sits at the top of the hierarchy that manages the organization. On top of that sits a body in which there is no hierarchy in terms of how decisions are made. Decisions must be reached by coming to a consensus at that level.

By corporate law, the running of the corporation rests with the board of directors. They choose to delegate what they want the CEO and his or her management team to do in running the enterprise. There are, as a result, many decisions that come to boards of directors. Their ability to make decisions and the quality of those decisions very often determine the outcome for the shareholders and the corporation in total.

Deborah Midanek: What did you conclude about your initial feeling that directors were not doing their jobs? How did the process of looking at how they make decisions on a qualitative basis help you answer your question about how to make them perform better?

Bernard Bailey: As you'll find in so much of academic research, when viewed from afar, you kind of scratch your head and say, "Honestly, you had to take four years to come to that conclusion? We all know that." But you must prove it with data. You must prove it with theory, and you have to analyze it. To answer your question in a simple way, what you end up finding is what Yale professor Jeffrey Sonnenfeld laid out clearly. Effective boards and effective decision-making start when a group has respect for each other. There must be respect within the boardroom among the board members. There must be respect between the board and the executive team.

If people respect each other, they'll start to develop trust in each other. That trust then will lead to an openness and sharing of information. When there's a sharing of information, then suddenly everybody is talking about the same set of data around the same issue. They're able to bring their experiences, their perspectives, their legacy, their history to that discussion and it becomes a very rich discussion. That is what we mean, of course, by bringing diversity and the inclusion of different views to decision making. When you have that, the odds of getting to a good decision are dramatically higher than if you don't have respect, trust, and subsequently openness.

When you make those decisions in that way, everybody feels that they are respected. Everybody feels that they can be candid and open in their discussions. Out of that, the chances of getting a better decision are much higher. When you make better decisions, they result in better outcomes. That tends to reinforce the whole mechanism of more respect, more trust, more candor, more openness, better dialogues, better decision making, and better outcomes.

Deborah Midanek: But this starts with the respect issue. I could not agree with you more that respect is the antecedent to trust, and trust is the currency of being effective in a boardroom with shareholders, with management, with customers, with employees. That trust factor is the critical thing.

I also have sympathy with those boards of directors that have been under fire for being "male, pale, and stale." Because it's difficult if you are from a particular demographic sector to evaluate people from other sectors. For men to evaluate women, for Anglo-Saxons to evaluate Hispanics or Indians or French people. It's very difficult to assess the people around you and then to find a common language to use as you bring these people into the boardroom. How do we get that fundamental respect instilled when we're looking for more and more diversity in the boardroom, given that the directors come together for such a short amount of time?

Bernard Bailey: As you find when you start to study these problems, it's always better to have as few variables as possible. Then you can interject additional variables. Let's just start with the board that is all white males. That isn't going to allow you to have an effective board because respect doesn't start there. When you talk about respect, it boils down to first, people want to look at what you bring to the table. Do you have a set of skills and competencies? Can I respect you for that? Do I respect the fact that you work hard? That when you come here you are prepared, that you've done your work between the board meetings, that you're talking to people and you're studying the industry and the company. Can I respect you from that standpoint?

All of us who have been on boards know board members who walk into the boardroom and haven't thought 30 seconds about that corporation in the three months since they walked out of the last board meeting. They don't read the board book. They don't read the materials. Similarly, that's seen by the staff, so no respect there. I don't care what color, what gender, what background, ethnic background or anything you have, it must start with earning respect over time. A director who comes into that boardroom and is seen as a person who asks, a person who does their homework, digs into the issues, listens and is willing to hear lots of points of view – that builds respect.

Second, my work showed that the chairperson plays a critical role in creating the dynamic in the boardroom that allows that respect and that trust to be developed. This depends on the concept of *procedural justice*, developed by a psychologist at NYU, Tom Tyler. It's simple. When people feel that there's a just process, that their opinions are listened to and that their input is allowed to come to the table and be welcomed and received, then that builds respect. Because at the end of the day, they say, "Even if I didn't win the argument, people listened and heard what I had to say, and that was extremely important. That then allows me then to not be penalized and come back to the table repeatedly in the dialogue, in the discussion."

That procedural justice is an imperative in creating an environment within the boardroom where people feel that they are not just diverse but inclusive, and they're considered part of it. The importance of that is that boardrooms can often be very political environments. Politics is part of everything. The question is, are the politics in the boardroom and the procedures and the protocols that go into that decision making just and are they fair? Or are they driven by nefarious motives?

Let me give you an example. Too often we've seen the CEO start to lobby various board members before the board meeting to line up votes and secure support for what he or she is doing. There hasn't been any dialogue. There hasn't been a diverse set of opinions on this issue. There hasn't been inclusion of the other board members, yet suddenly coalition-building has started. That's not healthy to a just decision-making environment.

I don't care if they're all the same color and same gender and even the same age. You can still create the same dynamic that is unhealthy. I join a board. That board is made up of seven people. Four of them are all members of the same country club in Erie, Pennsylvania. You join that board and you live hundreds of miles away. You're not going to be the same part of that discussion as those four that live close to one another or have been on the board for 25 years together and now they're asking you to come on.

Deborah Midanek: What do you do about that? Do you simply not join the board? Or does the chairman have an obligation to find a way to level the playing field?

Bernard Bailey: Well, that's my point. The chairperson must run the board and make sure that everybody is there. That board members are on-boarded correctly. That the CEO understands that his role is only as a director on that board. That he doesn't have the authority to go out and lobby and meet with directors and do all the things they want to get to decisions that they want. It's that just process. My point is that that work is very important for the chairperson to do.

Now, what we learn is that power is a finite commodity. We don't create more of it. It doesn't dissipate out of the organization. It is finite. The question becomes, how does it get distributed? Unless you have a balanced power structure in your board, you will have dysfunction. What do I mean by that? We've seen this over and over again. This movie has played and it will play until I leave this Earth. The corporation's doing pretty good, so the board says, "Everything's going well." All of a sudden, they defer their oversight role and their responsibilities to the chief executive officer. The chief executive officer now starts garnering more and more power.

Decision making stops coming to the board. Information is not provided to the board in an open and candid way. The CEO doesn't have the same level of respect for all the board members. Trust erodes, but everything goes on fine until all of a sudden it doesn't. You don't make a quarter. You don't make three quarters. All of a sudden, or so it seems, the crisis hits. We've seen these movies over and over again, at Enron, at WorldCom. We're seeing them in not-for-profit boards. We see them today in many boards of directors, and when that happens, you have lost the effective oversight of the board long since. That power relationship is critical. The chair, who is simply first among equals in the boardroom, must set up a dynamic between the board and the CEO in such a way that there is balanced power.

At the same time, you don't want a board so strong that the CEO is a eunuch simply being directed on what to do on every matter because the board is making those decisions. That balance of power is critical in being able to create the necessary respect and trust in the boardroom.

Deborah Midanek: But let me ask the question another way. Bernard, you are talking about the principles of procedural justice. You are talking about a balance of power. You're talking about elements that, even though boards have been studied ad nauseam, are rarely discussed. The question of the group dynamics of the board itself is less considered than all the other aspects that are looked at. How do we train people in these things? How do we teach the chairman how to play that role? It's easy enough to say, "Well, if they've served on other boards, if they've been a CEO, and so on." But that is not a proxy for understanding, creating a balanced power environment, or for understanding the issues related to procedural justice.

Bernard Bailey: This is what makes it so difficult and why, in my opinion, boards have been under such criticism. Now, before I answer that question, I must go back because I didn't answer your first, second, or third question. I fell off that horse.

I'm going back because I think it's important to understand. You asked, "Well, okay, so how do you judge if a board does well? How do you know if a board is doing well?" That is a very difficult thing for outsiders to observe. The reason for that, very simply, is there is such a huge distance between the decision making and the outcome and there are so many factors that go into that that it's virtually impossible to think that correlation is related to causation of board effectiveness.

The real board effectiveness gets down to boards of directors as decision-making bodies. As decision-making bodies, what are the processes they have in place that allow decisions to get made? How are these processes done? Boards that have good decision-making processes are inclusive, bringing in the right people, asking the right questions. They're poking. They're prying in every way. Then you have to say, "That's probably a pretty good board if it's doing all of those things." Even if the outcomes are not always great, recognizing that the board doesn't have the operational control of the company, but they are performing their single most important obligation, which is to make sure that they have the right CEO in place to execute the strategic vision that they've established. These are the questions that need to be asked in the boardroom. What the board should be doing is examining the CEO and his or her staff.

What they have to be able to do is question the decision-making processes of the CEO. How did the CEO come to these decisions? Who was involved? What information did they bring in? How collaborative were they? How inclusive were they in their decision making? What were the factors they considered? When they rejected an alternative, why did they reject that alternative? What was it about that alternative? Questioning their decision making is the obligation of the board in creating a high quality process in that boardroom.

There's really only been one characteristic of boards that has consistently shot up as one that makes a difference in the outcomes of organizations. It's not independence. It's not CEO-chair duality. It's not females on the board. It's not diversity on the board. The one that makes the difference is the size of the board itself. Boards with seven to nine members have led corporations that have performed better than those that are larger or smaller.

Deborah Midanek: You think that that size group is large enough to have diverse opinions but small enough that they can know and respect and trust each other?

Bernard Bailey: What most of the organizational behavior, group dynamics work will tell you is that the best decision-making bodies are in that range of seven to nine people for exactly the reasons you're describing. I think Jeff Bezos often said that, "You should never have a meeting where you need more than one or two pizzas."

Deborah Midanek: That's wonderful because that goes back to your analogy about the pie. That the role of the board is to be dividing the pie. Thinking about board size in terms of the number of pizzas is a perfect corollary.

Bernard Bailey: Well, there you go. If you need 30 pizzas because you have 50 people in the boardroom, not a whole lot is going to get done.

Deborah Midanek: For many boards, a great deal of the value that comes out of the boardroom is the work that goes into preparing for the board meeting.

Bernard Bailey: That's right. We talked about power. We talked about the board chair and the CEO and the relationship and how that goes. But another one that's extremely important is that there has to be shared vision, a shared vision of the purpose of the corporation and what we're trying to accomplish. If people are not all working toward the same North Star and instead have disparate ideas about what should happen, that gets very difficult. I'll tell you that one of the beauties of working for a private equity company is there's not a lot of confusion about what we're trying to do. Everybody at the table knows that our objective is to create as much value as possible with the intention of selling the company at some point five to ten years down the road. We're all working to make that happen in that boardroom and with the executive team that's been hired to run the company.

When you get into some publicly traded company boards or not-for-profits, in many cases people have very different visions. What are our objectives? Is it profitability? Is it growth? Is it to be international in our scope? Are we supposed to be thinking more of our stakeholders in terms of our approach and what we're doing for employees? What's our purpose? What are we trying to accomplish? If people don't have a shared vision and have different agendas, it is difficult to get to effective decision-making in running the corporation.

I say that because I'm reading this Business Roundtable position statement. God bless them. They came up with this great thing about stakeholder instead of shareholder. They want to grind up poor Dr. Milton Friedman. What they're saying to me is, frankly, no different than what Milton Friedman wrote in his 1970 piece. What he said was, "when you do those things, you have to make sure that they are creating long-term shareholder value for the corporation."

A great piece of research to do would be to look at the compensation plans of the 182 or so signatories of the recent Business Roundtable statement. I would guess that the vast majority of their compensation is based on some type of total shareholder return. If you don't think incentives matter, you are kidding yourself.

Deborah Midanek: Well then, talk to me about incentives. Because the 1990s and the tax laws created what seemed to be an overwhelming reliance on equity-based compensation. Where do you think it should be?

Bernard Bailey: Well, that's another really interesting question. It gets to the boards of directors taking their responsibility seriously. If you think about it, there are fundamentally three ways to discipline management from the perspective of governance. One is a strong board of directors that takes responsibility and ownership for the outcomes of the corporation and takes seriously their responsibility for oversight and governance of the corporation. That's one.

A second way of doing it is alignment of incentives. If you want management's behavior to be aligned with the goals of shareholders, you set up a compensation scheme that allows them to benefit when the shareholders benefit. Therefore, equity-based compensation plans became all the rage for lots of reasons, not the least being a change in tax treatment of base salaries and bonus compensation. That's the second way.

The third way is the marketplace. When I talk about the marketplace, I'm talking about activist investors. I'm talking about acquisition of your company by other companies because another CEO sees it as an attractive asset. Why? Because, it hasn't been effectively managed, so why don't we go in there and acquire it so that we can create greater shareholder value out of it? Or activist investors who say, "You know what? This really isn't being effectively managed and, therefore, as a shareholder, I am going to go in and exercise my control of the market to drive greater performance."

Those are the three vehicles you have. You're asking now about the incentive one, which is in the middle. Certainly, incentives have to be tied to what you want to do to create long-term value. In my opinion, what happens in an incentive system is when I'm a shareholder buying into a company, I'm buying that company as part of a broad portfolio. I have the ability to diversify that risk in a portfolio. As an investor in a portfolio environment, I am expecting that company to take risk. I want them to take risk because I can mitigate that risk through a portfolio. Follow me?

Deborah Midanek: Yes.

Bernard Bailey: Now, say I'm the CEO of a corporation. As CEO, I now have a majority of my personal wealth along with that of the rest of the executive team tied up in the equity of that company. My ability to diversify my personal net worth is limited. My incentive in managing that company is not to take a lot of risk because I'm carrying the downside and can't diversify away from it. That equity arrangement in many cases creates a disconnect. That's one example. Another example is that for me as a CEO, the easiest way for me to realize value is to leave the company, exercise my options, and sell my shares. Therefore, I could do a whole lot of things that will create short-term value that are not in the interest of the long-term value of the corporation.

Deborah Midanek: For example, a share buyback.

Bernard Bailey: Well, yes, one would be a share buyback. A second one would be reducing my research and development expense. A third one would be not putting investments in place for my Horizon 2 and 3 opportunities going forward. A fourth one would be not treating my employees or my other stakeholders appropriately because I can hold that money back and let it drop to the bottom line short term. Long term I can't.

By the way, Milton Friedman never said short term. But I can do that. I can take that short-term view. I would argue that that's been the big problem; that a lot of these corporations have been run for the short term. CEOs want to blame their investors for driving them to quarterly performance, but they are incentivized to do the same thing. I'm saying that they can leave and quickly extract their personal wealth from the company, leaving behind the risk associated with the long-term consequences of the decisions they made in the short term.

My point is, like everything, it's complicated. It's not as simple as saying we all just signed a piece of paper so we're going to care about stakeholders now. Any responsible CEO always cared about stakeholders. Who in the world could say that I'm a responsible steward of a corporation but I'm not going to care about my employees and give them a fair wage and make my place to work one of the most attractive? Who in the world would say, "I'm going to have a select group of suppliers, but I'm going to treat them really badly and make sure they can't make a fair amount of money to pay their wages and attract their capital? I'm going to squeeze them really hard to do that?"

What responsible CEO would ever say, "I'm going to let this community where I live fall apart and not be a thriving community because I don't need to attract good talent into my community by having good schools and a safe environment and everything else?" Of course, any responsible CEO who's thinking long term about his corporation has to take a stakeholder view.

Deborah Midanek: We have covered a great deal of territory. What areas have we not covered, Dr. Bailey, that you feel we need to cover to get a full picture of the way the board works and should work?

Bernard Bailey: We could go on, but at the end of the day, good governance comes down to good people working together, committed to making good decisions for the long-term interests of the corporation. That's what they're responsible for doing. If at any time the environment is not allowing that to happen, then they, as the board, have to step up and take responsibility.

Deborah Midanek: How do we determine who should be on a board, who those good people are? One of my pet peeves is over-reliance on the skills matrix. I'm just warning you.

Bernard Bailey: The skills matrix starts from the standpoint of needing to have a diversified set of skills on the board. That to me is the ante to get to the table. So start there, but it isn't about that. It's almost a cliché to bring it up but everybody knows that the Enron board of directors ticked off every conceivable box for good governance. They had diversity. They had independence. They had duality of the CEO and the chair. They had all of those things, and they were a highly ineffective board. So what happened? This gets to Dr. Minsky's argument that stability creates instability. Well, it wasn't even stability, was it?

It was an illusion because the board wasn't doing its job. The only thing the board was looking at was shareholder value creation. Unless you create that environment of respect and trust and candor and procedural justice and openness in the dialogue, and seat people that are prying and questioning by nature, governance will fail. It isn't about going along to get along. It's about making sure that you're asking the right questions; that you're poking at it. That you are willing to be that dissenting voice when everything seems to be going well.

If you can create that environment where everybody feels this is a safe environment then you're going to have a better chance to get to the right outcomes. There's no skill matrix that's going to do that for you. There's no mix of gender or demographics or ethnicity that's going to get that for you. You cannot get to the same outcomes if you don't create the right behaviors in your board of directors and the right relationships and the right power structure and everybody sharing the same common vision.

Deborah Midanek: That's a beautiful concept and that is why we have boards of directors, because the device is a good one. When it's done well, it should have all of the benefits that you're describing.

Bernard Bailey: We tend to treat boards as a static body. Oh, you came onto the board at age 57. We have an age limit of 72, so you're here for 15 years. The corporation can change radically in that time. Your position can change radically. Oh, by the way, we may have made a mistake bringing you on the board. Unless you have a really effective board evaluation process, one that's as rigorous or maybe even more rigorous as it is among your executive team, you're not going to have an effective board. Evaluating each other, holding board members accountable, is essential for the effective board.

Deborah Midanek: The question of to whom the board is accountable is a difficult one. The wonderful thing you're saying is that the board is accountable to itself.

Bernard Bailey: Absolutely. Remember, it's a collective decision-making body. It's not hierarchical, so we need constantly to ask ourselves whether we have the elements we need and the right people involved to assure ourselves of the best outcome we can deliver.

Deborah Midanek: What is your preferred method of achieving an effective evaluation? There are lots of pros and cons to the different ways of doing it.

Bernard Bailey: Well, I think there has to be a 360° review process that has a degree of confidentiality to it. There has to be an obligation to talk to all the members of the board to get their input on what's working and what's not, as well as who's working and who's not. There have to be peer reviews of individual members. The attitude that, "We're all peers. We're all good, so let's just evaluate the board and fix our processes," must be avoided. In my experience, every single board I've been on has at least two board members who are not constructive to the process.

Most of the time, what the board nominates as its slate is what gets elected. Now we're back full circle to the shareholders who elect the board. But if they really don't have a choice, they don't have much to do. So who makes that choice? The Nominating and Corporate Governance Committee and the board itself are charged with making sure they put the right slate forward to oversee the company. They don't do their job in many cases.

Deborah Midanek: How can they better do their job?

Bernard Bailey: Through the processes I talked about. Open and candid and confidential evaluations of individuals, board processes, board procedures, rotation of people off committees and into where the skill set should be. It's that very difficult dynamic. I talked about trust. Trust is so important in the boardroom, but the only reason boards exist is because there is distrust.

It's combining and balancing that trust-distrust dynamic that's so incredible in the boardroom. You have to work very hard to maintain collegiality. But not so much collegiality that we end up with groupthink.

Deborah Midanek: Thank you, Bernard, for your candor in this conversation.

Chapter 3
Courage and humility combat crisis of conformity
Halla Tómasdóttir

Halla Tómasdóttir is the CEO of The B Team, a group of courageous business and civil society leaders working together to transform business for a better world. Halla started her career working for Mars and Pepsi Cola. As a member of the founding team at Reykjavík University, she established the Executive Education Department, founded and led a successful women's entrepreneurship and empowerment initiative, and was an assistant professor at the Business School. Having served as the first female CEO of the Iceland Chamber of Commerce, she later cofounded an investment firm that incorporated feminine values into finance, one of very few survivors of the economic meltdown in Iceland. In 2016, Halla ran as an independent candidate for President of Iceland where she finished second, with nearly 30% of the vote.

Halla has served on for-profit and non-profit boards in education, healthcare, finance, and consumer products. A catalyst for positive change, Halla was a founding member of the National Assembly held in Iceland in the wake of its financial collapse, where a random sample of the Icelandic nation discussed its values and vision for the future. She also founded and chaired WE 2015, a global dialogue on closing the gender gap. Her work has led her to the TED stage twice and she has delivered keynotes and participated in dialogues around purpose-driven and principled leadership for companies and conferences around the world. In 2011, *Newsweek* named her to a list of 150 women who shake the world. Following Iceland's Presidential Elections in 2016, *The New Yorker* called her A Living Emoji of Sincerity. Halla holds an MBA degree from Thunderbird School of Global Management.

Deborah Midanek: Halla, so many aspects of our lives are changing so radically, and it feels very unstable. Yet there are many good things happening at the same time as we magnify the bad things. There's a major war going on about who's in charge of our big public corporations. Are they to be controlled by the shareholders at their direction? Are they to be controlled by the directors? Are they to be controlled by regulators, or legislators? At the heart of all of that is the board. There's a

https://doi.org/10.1515/9783110670004-004

huge focus on governance; much greater attention than there has been in the entire 40 years I've been studying, it is. It is healthy, and it's confusing.

Halla Tómasdóttir: We're navigating challenging times. In my lifetime, times have never been as exciting, but also as confusing. I believe this is a transitional period, and that's more a choice than a firm belief to be honest. Change in our own lives, in our companies, or in our societies is often painful. So I feel like we might be in that phase of transformation right before we move into positive forward motion. But this period might last a while in our minds, because we consider time in relation to our own lifetime. But when you think about societal change, and that's really what we're going through, 50 years is nothing. I think we're looking at 10 really challenging but transformative years. This decade will be a constant tug-of-war between the old and the new way of doing business.

Deborah Midanek: What drives you, Halla, as you took on role of serving The B Team as its CEO? What are you trying to do in this role?

Halla Tómasdóttir: The drivers that account for why we do what we do are always complicated. My *why* has always been trying to make business a force for good. Make business a force for good, make people a force for good, make money a force for good. Everything I've done seems to come together with The B Team. I'm thrilled to be addressing many different businesses, investors, and important audiences, such as board directors, and aim to inspire them to incorporate the wellbeing of people and the planet alongside their pursuit for profit. For me, it has always been about business having a bigger role than simply serving the shareholder.

Deborah Midanek: In the world we live in now, corporations with their ability to cross borders and touch people all over the globe have a tremendous role and the potential for driving positive social change.

Halla Tómasdóttir: If you think about the times we live in, they're certainly challenging. There's a crisis of leadership. Our governments are struggling the world over and not enough of them practice good governance and successfully create societies that work for humanity. The private sector, the CEOs, and board directors, must step up and embrace the leadership we need. They can serve as critical players to address our leadership crisis. The world we live in is not working. I don't say that as a political statement.

We're facing a confluence of crisis, all of them escalating in scale and speed. The climate crisis is real and has relevance to everybody in business. We're also facing this incredible social unrest the world over, and it's very clear that the social contract is either broken or at least has serious flaws. It's not cohesive, it's not holding up. Our levels of inequality are unsustainable. Last but not least, we're in a crisis of trust. That's where I think governance is critical. I'm so passionate about it. I think that the only way we can establish trust again in a society that trusts no one anymore – doesn't trust government, doesn't trust media, doesn't trust business at large – is to actually start practicing more transparent and responsible, accountable governance.

Deborah Midanek: That leads beautifully to the question of, given where you are, sitting as the CEO of The B Team, what is the purpose of the modern public corporation? And has it changed?

Halla Tómasdóttir: Has it changed? This is a really interesting question. I actually think the purpose of the organization has always been to serve all of its stakeholders. But I would say that in the 1970s, or thereabout, it became about shareholder supremacy, at least in public companies.

To me, growing up in the Nordics, as a daughter of a father who ran his own small business, you just didn't do good business unless you took care of the people who worked for you, unless you were responsible toward the community you lived in. Yes, you needed to deliver a return in order for your business to be sustainable but we always understood that the well-being of our communities and our people is at the heart of doing business. So I would venture to say that we used to conduct business as a force for good, then we somehow lost our ways. Milton Friedman's shareholder primacy theory introduced 50 years ago made the market the most important stakeholder and over time we lost sight of the value of creating shared value. Since the financial crisis 11 years ago, we have slowly been coming to grips with how dysfunctional this has been and now we increasingly acknowledge that doing business in this way has left us with a burning planet, a broken social contract, and little to no trust. It's left us in a mess. So the purpose of the organization, and therefore the purpose of the board, is absolutely to take care of all stakeholders. Otherwise, there is no business to be done long-term, no sustainable value to be created.

Deborah Midanek: What about the question of ownership of the public corporation? Because there's a big difference between the American interpretation of that, and the European Union interpretation of that.

Halla Tómasdóttir: I would never say that the shareholders don't own the company. I will always acknowledge them as owners, but shareholders out of touch with other stakeholders cannot create value. What's also interesting, especially as we look at publicly traded companies, is that it is hard to say that those asset owners are not us. So many of them are pension funds, national sovereign funds, large indexed mutual funds. The actual asset owners are us – the people. We somehow have created this concept where we talk about institutional asset owners and asset managers and banks like they're not managing *everybody's* assets.

Deborah Midanek: It's as if they are the principals, when in fact it's their beneficiaries who are the principals.

Halla Tómasdóttir: In my view, if you're a board director, your role is to make sure that the company you serve creates value for the long run. If you do not want your company to risk death in the next decade, you better be serving the broad spectrum of stakeholders, because their expectations are that you will do right by the planet, and the people, and your communities. If you're not doing that, I don't think you can deliver return to shareholders in the era that we are now in. So, even if you prefer shareholder primacy to stakeholder governance, failing to approach your role with a stakeholder mindset is to me a potential recipe for an eventual death. It may be slow, but a company that fails to be relevant to all its stakeholders will die.

Talent won't work for you, customers don't want to do business with you, and increasingly, asset managers, particularly institutional investors, are shifting their definition of success to include ESG [Environmental, Social, and Governance] measures, embracing a more holistic definition of success in line with that of all stakeholders.

Deborah Midanek: In the middle of that mix, what do you see as being the actual role of the board?

Halla Tómasdóttir: The role of the board is to safeguard the successful and long-term value creation of that organization for all stakeholders.

Deborah Midanek: To refine it one more step, based on what you said, it sounds as if you think the board owes its fiduciary duty to the broad array of stakeholders, or does it owe its fiduciary duty directly to sustaining the corporation per se.

Halla Tómasdóttir: I would say it owes its fiduciary duty to all stakeholders. That does not mean that I don't think there's a fiduciary duty to its investors, but you just cannot uphold your fiduciary duty anymore without serving all stakeholders. Your license to operate only for shareholders has already run out – or is fast running out. So, as I often say when I speak to directors about this, you're not taking care of shareholders if you are failing to understand that the world has shifted its norms. The crisis of conformity in your boardroom is holding on to a definition of success that is no longer going to produce success.

Deborah Midanek: What a beautiful word picture: the crisis of conformity.

Halla Tómasdóttir: I think we see the crisis of conformity in lots of places, but I think it may thrive in many boardrooms. Let me just give you one example of why I say that. At the same time that we see millions of kids in the streets asking us to hold ourselves accountable for their future, in particular pushing for ambition to address climate change, we have 4 out of 10 board directors telling us that climate change does not even belong on the boardroom agenda, according to PricewaterhouseCoopers 2018 board survey numbers.

Many directors do not understand what's happening in the world around them and are therefore not adequately protecting stakeholder value. Nor are they protecting shareholder value, because this is not sustainable. Those kids don't want to work for your organization if you fail to act. Those kids don't want to do business with your organization if your brand value doesn't address their values. As a matter of fact, we already know that somewhere between 80–86%, depending on what survey you look at, of the talent that's coming into organizations expect your organization to embrace environmental and social responsibility. Societal expectations have shifted, while the boardroom hasn't.

Deborah Midanek: How do you see the role of independent directors fitting into the boardroom?

Halla Tómasdóttir: I've generally been in favor of independent directors, but I do wonder if we should broaden the way we think about independent directors. It seems that today, we mostly pick independent directors who look and feel exactly like the rest of the directors.

Deborah Midanek: Crisis of conformity continues.

Halla Tómasdóttir: We should think a lot more about how we use independent directors to confront the sameness in the boardroom. Gender is one aspect that I've long been passionate about, but I'm also increasingly thinking about the generational gap. I feel that most boardrooms are out of touch with what the future of talent, what the future of customers, what the future of investing looks like. And it is really risky to be out of touch with that.

Some of the big, highly admired, valuable companies in the world have faced different kinds of headwinds recently. The employees of Facebook wrote to Mark Zuckerberg to ask him to take responsibility for lies on his platform. Amazon employees put pressures on Jeff Bezos to raise his climate ambition. Google's employees organized walkouts because of gender issues. This is increasingly the new normal for organizations.

If the board doesn't understand how these expectations have changed, they're missing a major opportunity. Using independent directors to be more in touch with what's going on in society by having, for example, next generation representation, can be powerful.

Deborah Midanek: Those actions are all very visible. Tying that awareness into the boardroom is important, as boards can be somewhat insular. Actually, quite insular, because they generally come together somewhere between 4 and 10 times a year. Because of the value that's been placed on independence, they often lack native knowledge of the company, and they don't have deep knowledge of each other. So that comment that you made early in the conversation about trust is difficult to create within the boardroom, yet essential.

When you add in the increased pressure to bring diversity, and you get people who don't know each other, who don't have native knowledge of the company, it can seem they are not speaking the same language when they do meet because they have not established a common frame of reference for understanding each other. The system in which they're trying to function is still organized as it has been for decades if not centuries – the periodic meetings, the social dinner, and then they get on a plane and fly away again. When a new board member arrives who doesn't understand how the board operates, what are they going to do?

They're going to do what human beings do. They're going to look at what the people around them are doing and mimic that behavior so that they fit in to the group. That makes sense because they have to be trusted in order for their voices to be heard. Which can lead to the issue you have titled the crisis of conformity. The question of how to manage the modern board leads us to this question: How can we make the board more effective? How can we, in practical terms, make them work better?

Halla Tómasdóttir: The reality is that nearly every week a CEO somewhere is facing some kind of a reputational risk. This is a fairly new reality, because we suddenly live in a world where, even if companies don't practice transparency, social media and this new generation does. Things leak all the time, and it seems that many CEOs and their boards go from one crisis to the next. The model of a board that meets four times a year, or six times a year, and has a set agenda just doesn't feel very agile or fit for purpose. It doesn't feel very responsive, it doesn't feel like it reflects the world we live in today.

You know how passionate I have been about gender balance in the boardroom, I've literally invested over 20 years pushing for that and have often been the first woman in the boardrooms I was in. The reason I always pushed for gender balance, and actually changed my mind after being against gender quotas – and was for it – is because you're never going to shift boardroom culture by adding one example of "other" into the room.

The only answer I have is that we really need to shake up the boardroom to change the dynamics. Boards need to change the way they talk about things, change what gets on the agenda, change the way they work. I have found that gender balance can really help make that happen and it has been the lowest hanging fruit in the region I come from. I would venture to say that generational balance has become at least as important in our current realities. And, of course, being sure that not all of the directors have the same perspective is essential for a board to be able to reflect on and respond to the reality we currently live in. I'm not sure many boards are thinking in that way, but I do hear boards talking more about innovation, more about tech, more about intrepreneurship. I hear more conversation about these issues, and sustainability, and climate, and social issues than ever before.

A lot of people are now waking up to the reality that faced with current complexities, the board needs to be prepared to understand reality better and be more agile in responding to it. A board getting together a few days post a serious crisis to issue a press statement has already lost the opportunity to be in the driver's seat. A company now needs to be ready to respond on Twitter within minutes in order not to have a massive crisis on their hands. They may not have the answers, but they should at least express empathy. This reality has moved so much faster than boardrooms have.

I'm concerned that while the world is moving at high speed, boards are still struggling with basic questions like: "Should we get a woman on the board?" That should be a no-brainer by now, gender balance adds strength. But they should also be thinking about generational balance and about diversity of thought, so that they can understand and react in the face of this incredible speed. I'm not making little out of the fact that having been a CEO of an organization is an important background to have on a board. The understanding that comes from having dealt with all the things that come across your desk as a CEO is valuable. Often, however, those former CEOs come from the same kind of schools, are of the same age, same gender, same race, from the same region.

As long as that is considered the ideal candidate for board service, I don't think boards are going to understand these issues or be ahead of them. I think they are going to be responding to them in a crisis mode. And do we really need every board member to be a former CEO?

Deborah Midanek: There's one aspect that deserves our attention, because from the CEO's point of view, having an active diverse board full of new thoughts is a very scary prospect. It adds another element of unpredictability to his or her life. It's so often the case that very well-intentioned people, very able people, come into the boardroom and end up having no voice. Because, one, they don't get a chance to talk. But two, even if they do get a chance to talk, there are no ears to hear them. To me, the question of board leadership becomes critically important. Who is going to make sure that all these different diverse points of view and backgrounds, are organized and channeled in such a way that everyone is heard, and the CEO gets the benefit of diverse views without chaos, conflict, and confusion? We want to both embrace diversity and generate a productive result, and build relationships with management that are flowering rather than foundering.

Halla Tómasdóttir: I think this is so important, and this goes to why I was in favor of gender quotas versus making tokenistic progress. Because when you have one "other," whatever that "other" is, especially one more female, or one next generation; that addition does not create a culture where anything changes. Basically, that "other" person has two options. They can adopt the rules of the game the way it's played, i.e., walk into the crisis of conformity and try to belong. Or instead, they can be the difficult one, and I've definitely personally had some experience with that, and raise those difficult questions. And what may actually happen then, the board meeting moves to … the male bathroom, or the golf course, or …

Deborah Midanek: That is exactly what happens. I have been told I'm unprepared because I'm the person who asks the most questions.

Halla Tómasdóttir: Personally, I've always been in favor of the separation of the chairman and the CEO role, which is more the norm outside of the United States. I think of the chair role as a facilitating role, a very important role not just in the boardroom itself, but also with different stakeholder groups of relevance to the organization. It's perhaps not realistic for every stakeholder group to sit in the boardroom and I'm not saying that a board of 7, 9, or 11 can ever fully reflect the world we live in but I see it as the role of the chairman to make sure that the voices of different stakeholders get heard and considered – to make sure that the board is studying surveys about employee engagement, or changing customer insights, or shifting investor norms.

So the chair must play a stakeholder facilitator role. Equally important, however, is the strategic long-term visionary role. I'm afraid that many boardrooms, and I know everybody's trying their best, get into the habit of looking at a fairly narrow definition of what belongs on the boardroom agenda. The agenda is shaped by a fairly narrow view of the definition of success, in my opinion.

Deborah Midanek: How would you go about reshaping that agenda?

Halla Tómasdóttir: For large organizations, the use of different committees is important. Thinking about innovation, and when I say innovation, I am not using just the tech lens. I think it's really interesting that we talk quite a bit about AI, and quantum physics, and all these technology trends that are transforming the future of work. But at the end of the day, tech should serve humanity. It seems like we're too often decoupling people issues from issues around the technology transition. I'm in favor of approaching issues more holistically, just as I am in favor of ESG being approached alongside financial measures. I believe in more integrated approach all around.

Deborah Midanek: The idea of ESG being a separate focus for the board may be important as a remedial process, but ESG has to be built into the fabric of everything they do.

Halla Tómasdóttir: Absolutely, and that's not the case today. I see few boardrooms seriously embracing ESG. We had a very interesting meeting this year with 20-plus board directors present to discuss how to get ESG matters into the boardroom. What we observed was quite shocking. Very few boards actually have ESG matters on their agenda, not to mention incorporated into their mainstream strategy. There's material risk attached to ESG issues and perhaps more importantly, these are the issues that are going to shape business opportunities as we head into an uncertain future. We have evidence already that corporations that embrace what I would venture to call moral leadership see benefits to their bottom line from doing so. You can think about Bank of America on gun control, you can think about Nike on

Kaepernick. I'm not saying it's been easy for these companies to take a stand and they have also faced backlash, but it seems there are business benefits to brands who stand for values embraced by its employees and customers and perhaps it is now harder, and materially riskier, not to take a stand on such issues. I don't think a corporation, and therefore its board, has the option anymore to stay silent on things that matter to their people, their customers, the society they operate in.

Deborah Midanek: I don't know what else you gleaned from that group of 20, but the way the work of the board has been designed, and to some extent the way regulators and the SEC continue to direct it, is basically to be reactive. There's a lot to review, and evaluate, and monitor already-in-place processes and systems that seem to drive boards not only to focus on compliance, but not to focus beyond compliance. Changing the mindset of the CEO and of the chairman to use the assets of the directors in thinking about the future sounds like an obvious thing for the board to do, but it's not. Those assets have not in many cases been harnessed, yet.

Halla Tómasdóttir: Yes. as someone who lived through the most infamous financial meltdown in economic history, Iceland's financial collapse, I can tell you that that rearview mirror view of the world left my country in total ruins for a while. The country rallied remarkably well from that, but it was the rearview mirror that investors are most often in, looking at past performance, instead of looking through the front window, that caused us serious harm. I would almost say that we're at a similar time in history now. I'm not necessarily forecasting another economic crisis or financial collapse, but I'm not ruling it out either.

But the ongoing transformation, whether we call it the fourth industrial revolution, or the social transformation, this transformation that's happening is so dramatic on so many fronts that a board that is rearview mirror-facing is going to miss massive risks and opportunities. Boards need to practice *thinking the unthinkable* today. Even if you're a doubter about climate change, you're going to face it, everybody is already facing extreme weather events. If you are a global business, there is no safe haven. In fact, we're heading fast to an uninsurable world, and all companies have assets that need to be protected.

Even if you think you're doing right by your people, expectations are changing so fast that it is hard to keep up with. None of us would've imagined the #MeToo revolution, and the hundreds of executives who have lost jobs or whose integrity has been questioned on the back of that. A backward-facing board isn't going to understand the best way to address such challenges nor are they likely to make space for it if such issues are of little relevance of the board directors themselves. One practical suggestion I've always advocated for when I sit in a boardroom is to make time for unscheduled, non-agenda-driven conversation among board members. It sounds so simple, but most boards don't do it.

Deborah Midanek: No, and because of that sort of that Kabuki dance, the board meeting is highly ritualized.

Halla Tómasdóttir: And what we seem to have learned from the financial crisis is that we must now drown our board directors in paper. The fact of the matter is that most boards, particularly in financial services and more highly regulated industries, are buried in so much paper that there's no human capacity to digest all of it. There is, therefore, no space for innovative thinking, the forward thinking and concerns that people may carry around but aren't scheduled on the agenda because the board has to get through all the paper. Such practices of the boardroom are not going to enable the kind of strategic, forward-thinking, agile leadership that I believe organizations now need.

Deborah Midanek: Let's talk about how to use the executive session after, and many times before, the board meeting. I believe it is necessary to hold it after every board meeting. The leader needs to be sure that every person in the room speaks about what went right, what went wrong, what they're thinking about, and what they really want to see at the next meeting. The leader of the meeting collects those opinions and anonymizes them and takes the results immediately back to the CEO. The result can be a practical method of being sure that views are heard, and that agendas reflect the thinking of the directors. That's too slow for you, but it is a step in the right direction.

Halla Tómasdóttir: I actually like that, and it's a very pragmatic method. I have suggested that, at the minimum, you make sure that directors see each member of the senior leadership team once a year. You can schedule time into each board meeting for the various leaders to present, and you must give directors time to ask questions. Something else I learned early in my career before I was on any board, is to make time to walk the floor. Increasingly, board directors need to make visits and "walk the floor" of the companies, meet people unexpectedly in order to really get a feel for what's going on. The boardroom risks being a bubble, and the senior leadership team of a company is often a bubble as well.

Deborah Midanek: I call it the X factor. I'm amazed at the number of companies I have gone into as a turnaround manager, only to find out that the executive suite and the operating level of the company are completely separate, and there are only one or two people who cross the border. Only one or two people communicate both up and down, across the center of the X, which always strikes me as odd.

Halla Tómasdóttir: This, to me, would make the case for some kind of worker representation. Not necessarily the German or European model, but you could think, "If we heard the voice of workers, or people who actually experience what's going on in the organization firsthand, would there be value in that?" I know a lot of board directors get really nervous around this issue, but that does not mean the idea lacks merit.

Deborah Midanek: I recently joined the board of a family company as one of their first independent directors. Almost the first thing we did was arrange to listen to the employees. We spent two weeks and we talked to 10% of the workforce or, more importantly, they talked to us. When I've told others about doing that, heads swivel. Many envied us the chance.

Halla Tómasdóttir: I admire that dedication, and I think you're probably right, that part of the issue is that most people are just busy. It's already a lot to prepare for meetings, so people won't make time for it. That's why I see some kind of worker representation as a possible solution; whether you invite a representative of the workers regularly and ask them to report, or use another creative method. Not everything has to be executed in a structured way. I just know that employees offer a stakeholder voice that boards are really silly to ignore.

Deborah Midanek: In another, we hold the board meetings at the different company locations. Every time the board goes somewhere for a meeting, we have a cookout as an opportunity just to talk with people, and listen to people in an unstructured way.

Halla Tómasdóttir: I like that idea a lot. We spoke about trust earlier, and you probably know that Edelman does annual trust surveys. Recent results show that trust is low and still waning, among all institutions in society. The highest trust remains between employees and their employer. But with that trust comes this expectation that this employer of yours will do the right thing when it comes to environmental and social issues. So that trust is actually baked in on the back of your expectation that your employer will do right, will act right. If you break that, I think the backlash could be devastating.

One of the most shocking numbers in business is about employee engagement. About 85% of people worldwide, according to Gallup and others, say employees are either not engaged or actively disengaged at work. Who would be happy about that kind of return on their capital investment? I don't know of anybody who would build a factory and say, "I'm happy to be at 15 to 30% capacity." Nobody would. People are the largest investment for most businesses, if not all, so why in the world would you not try to increase employee engagement? To me, the lowest hanging fruit in your company may very well be to unleash employee engagement. Yet, for decades, we have rarely picked people to join the boardroom who are accomplished in organizational, cultural, and people practices. We rarely invite those people into the boardroom. Perhaps a bit more in the last few years as we've tackled many challenges on that front, but we really don't prioritize this. So anything we do to increase engagement and trust between leadership and employees is going to be important and create value.

Deborah Midanek: How do we define the qualities that we need to have represented in the boardroom? Because diversity is really important. I caught people's attention at a panel I was on recently where I said, "Look, diversity is nature's risk management tool." Boards tend to default to use of the skills matrix, which is an important input into the selection of board members to ensure that we have a broad array of relevant skills represented. But it can also balkanize the boardroom. I've actually served on a board where the chairman of the audit committee, who was an accounting professor and quite able, refused to express his views on the selection of the president. He believed his only role was to look over the accounting.

To me, wisdom, good judgment, and strong character may be the most important requirements.

Halla Tómasdóttir: This is so interesting to me because I started asking this question: What did a good board director look like two decades ago when I was grappling with the fact that all board directors looked the same? I find it interesting that we ask, "Have you been a CEO? Have you had a profit and loss responsibility? Are you an auditor, or have you chaired an audit committee?" It's very much about competencies, and while I won't say that those competencies don't matter, I have found through my own experience and to some extent through research, that the best board directors have personal characteristics that are incredibly important. And there are two personal characteristics one needs to really think about in leadership today, in senior leadership, and the boardroom alike. And that is, you have to embrace both courage and humility.

Courage and humility are, in my opinion, absolute necessities for successful leadership today. Courage because thinking inside of the box is just not going to get you looking through the front window. Without courage, you're not going to raise the ambition of the organization to take on some of these great big challenges that your employees, your customers, and society at large want and need you to embrace. So you need more courage now than ever before. But you also need humility. I'm afraid we may be struggling with that and that may explain why it sometimes feels as if we race rapidly downhill. Because we have a crisis of hubris also. We don't just have a crisis of conformity, but also a crisis of hubris.

It's a lethal combination, when you think you know it all, you don't ask questions. When you think that it takes exactly your experience to offer value in the boardroom, you're never going to hear from the stakeholders who have different experiences or viewpoints. And so hubris creates so many blind spots and humility is its antidote. I've been of this opinion for a long time, but I've become increasingly passionate about it in the last few years. I've been preoccupied by the need for more humility in leadership, and the current lack thereof, and how big egos get both companies and countries into trouble.

Deborah Midanek: Another way to say that is to borrow the words of economist Hyman Minsky, who said "stability breeds instability." Complacency or hubris in the face of success is extremely dangerous.

Halla Tómasdóttir: I feel there is a lot of resting on your past successes in most boardrooms. These rituals have been there for a long time, shared by people who look and feel the same as you and have the same experiences in life. This makes it all too easy to say, "What's wrong with these kids? What are they doing in the street? Is this coming from Europe? What's going on?" Or to say, "What is wrong with these millennials? They think they can have it all." Instead of listening, and learning, and really examining the evidence that is clearly all around, we default to, "We know best." We create arrogant knower cultures instead of learning cultures. I think the boardroom needs to establish a learning culture. That takes both courage and humility.

Deborah Midanek: The learning culture is so important. Some years ago, I registered a domain name and I've never done anything with it, but it was leadwithyourears.com.

Halla Tómasdóttir: It is about listening, and about learning. It is about curiosity, it is about courage, it is about humility. These are not skills that show up on a skills matrix. These are not necessarily skills you have just because you've been a CEO, although I would venture to say that great CEOs often have these characteristics. But the definition of what a good CEO looks like, or a good board director, that we find by looking in the rearview mirror, may not be what we need now. I would definitely put courage and humility at the top of my list of desired characteristics for the boardroom today.

One of the principles we defined as critical in my investment company was straight talking. I really believe in the power of straight talk. To me it encompasses honesty, integrity, transparency, and simplicity, all important ingredients to a healthy culture. I would say straight talking is an essential board practice, while courage and humility are necessary characteristics embedded in the people you choose to put in the room. I would add that I look for people with a moral compass.

What does a moral compass mean to me? It means a person knows their own purpose, embraces a purpose in their own life, and have decided to exercise principled leadership. One has to choose deliberately the principles guiding behavior at work and in life. To me a moral compass is essential. Consider Facebook as an example, or Uber and many others, who embraced a compelling social purpose when they were founded. It seems however that they are now failing at exercising principled leadership and because of that they risk losing the trust of their employees, customers, and society at large.

Deborah Midanek: You are saying that those principles that go beyond the pursuit of profit are critically important to the ability to generate that profit.

Halla Tómasdóttir: Marc Benioff shares in every interview that he leads with values and creates value with values. He says, "The number one asset of any company today is trust." I so agree with him, and what Facebook in particular is failing at right now is to earn our trust. We don't trust Facebook anymore. We may be hooked on it. We may be addicted and need to use it to stay connected, and it indeed gives us a lot of benefits, but we don't trust them and we increasingly question their impact on our lives. Is that sustainable?

Deborah Midanek: Actually, that's a very interesting point, and it comes back to your point about the composition of the board. In looking sympathetically at the question of why boards are still largely male, pale, and stale, even though that's changing rapidly, I believe it's because it's easier for people to evaluate people who are similar to themselves. It's very hard to evaluate someone who is not similar to you. As a woman, I have often been misunderstood in the hiring process. So people are surprised about what they get when I actually show up, which has generally been to my advantage because I've been underestimated. But the thing about trust is that it is easier to trust people who are like ourselves because we recognize them.

So how do we build trust across these different types, and ages, and genders, and ethnicities, and backgrounds, that is effective enough that the group can benefit from all the points of view? That's the essential challenge of the boardroom today, I think.

The first piece of that is that you don't often trust people when you first meet them, but what you look for instead is respect. If you can respect them, and respect the differences long enough to learn about them, then you can get into the arena of trust.

Halla Tómasdóttir: I agree with you that it probably starts with respect, and respect is such an important value to establish because respect means you listen to people who are different from you. The interesting thing to me is that in the boardroom, we've never considered aspects that we typically think about on other teams. We never really think about the board as a team. Because anybody who's led a team anywhere knows that trust is the foundational part of the pyramid of a high-performing team. I have not seen many boards deliberately invest in building trust among its members.

And when the board finds itself in a crisis of some sort, like the CEO lied on his CV, or was caught in a #MeToo scandal, all of a sudden, you need to scramble fast behind closed doors to figure out the right thing to do. It's almost like you find yourself running a river rapid that is rated a 10, and you have had no chance to practice your team skills in a less challenging situation, say a 4 or a 5. It's massively challenging to navigate a crisis of that magnitude without having established trust. You need to be counting on each other, but no one has really learned enough about each other to know how best to guide the raft safely through, using the team's collective strength.

Deborah Midanek: There is relatively little focus on the board as a group; as a group dynamics exercise, as a team that needs to be built as a team. And your team management background probably makes you think that way instantly.

Halla Tómasdóttir: I'm not intimately familiar with all the research. It's been a while since I've been a governance geek, but I know there's limited research in general about boards. One thing we do know from gender research is that one of the biggest benefits of the gender balanced boards in the Nordics is that it changed the boardroom dynamics.

Changing just that one variable changed the dynamics and that was welcomed by both female and male directors. All parties appreciated how team dynamics changed for the better. In Iceland we conducted surveys before we introduced the gender quota, and were using voluntary targets, and again just a few years into gender quota laws. In the first round, a third of male directors were for gender quotas, and two-thirds against it, while two-thirds of female directors were for it, and one-third against it. Only a few years after the quota became law, the survey showed that two-thirds of male directors and 90% of female directors thought that gender balance had made a positive impact. When asked why, most respondents, male and female, cited the improved dynamics and dialogue in the boardroom.

There's one more issue I really want to raise. We work on responsible tax principles at The B Team, which is pretty bold because many business leaders do not want to take this challenging issue on. It's not been easy, but you and I have been speaking so much about trust, and about ESG, and about changing expectations from society that I feel we should talk specifically about tax and how paying fair taxes is the ultimate accountability a great company interested in earning the trust of society should embrace. I am pleased to say that we are seeing growing interest from global companies in discussing responsible tax behavior. Companies are realizing that tax optimization, where finding the lowest possible effective tax rate used to be a badge of honor, may no longer reflect positively upon them. If a board responsible for a company's future isn't asking itself how it would be perceived if its tax practices, even if legal, were transparent, that board may find itself facing a similar dilemma as Amazon did in New York. Corporate tax behavior can represent a material reputational risk that any company would be wise not to ignore.

Deborah Midanek: While serving on my first board in 1990 I remember being struck by the fact that the board was constantly focusing on what was legal versus what was right. It was a controversial company, and we moved the board quite a long distance to focusing on what was right, as opposed to merely legal.

Halla Tómasdóttir: The breakdown we're having in public service and leadership in general is, no matter what our politics are, very serious. I think we can all agree that a company has a responsibility to the communities in which it operates. It uses the infrastructure of their communities, its employees send kids to school in those communities. Without good schools and access to strong infrastructure, how can your company and your people succeed? Taxes need to be paid to allow for such investments. Taxes are the base of the pyramid when it comes to corporate social responsibility. I'm not saying that companies should not conduct tax planning, but I think there's more than a legal side to taxes, and now the moral side matters to your stakeholders. Perception of the company as a good corporate citizen is an important asset, and boards need to safeguard that asset mindfully. The cost of tax practices that could not stand the light of day could become very high. I believe transparency in general may very well be the best way to protect your company from reputational risk issues and also what may help it become an attractive place of work, a business that earns the loyal following of its customers and partners, as well as a desired investment. As a board director, pushing for greater transparency on all fronts is going to help build and maintain trust in a world that increasingly sees that as a company's most valuable asset.

Deborah Midanek: Thank you so very, very much, Halla, this discussion has been such a pleasure.

Chapter 4
Independent workers and the tinker toy corporation

Carl T. Camden

Dr. Carl T. Camden is currently the founder and President of iPSE-U.S., dedicated to serving the growing independent workforce by helping them to develop their voice, secure needed benefits, and foster innovative ways of working together. While iPSE is recently formed, Carl has dedicated more than 25 years to advocating for the independent workforce. As President and CEO of Kelly Services, a Fortune 500 workforce solutions firm, he spent his career creating opportunities and seeking justice for independent workers; challenging government, business leaders, and educators to adapt to the future of work; and serving on boards for the Federal Reserve, the Committee for Economic Development, The Conference Board, multiple universities, and numerous think tanks.

In 2017 he assembled industry leaders, House members from both parties, and association leaders for an exclusive D.C. event, "Advancing the Social Contract for Gig Economy Workers," that became the genesis for iPSE-U.S. Before joining the corporate world, Dr. Camden was a tenured college professor, and started and sold his own marketing research firm.

Deborah Midanek: Dr. Carl T. Camden has one of the most beautiful minds I have ever encountered, but that's about all I know about him. Give us, Carl, a little bit of who Carl T. Camden is.

Carl T. Camden: I started my career as a college professor with a PhD in psycholinguistics from Ohio State University and went on to be a tenured professor and department chair at Cleveland State University. While there, I started with others a small company to use psycholinguistics to do better marketing and advertising. The small company grew into an okay-sized company and we sold it to an ad agency. I took

https://doi.org/10.1515/9783110670004-005

a year leave of absence and then took over leadership of the ad agency. From there, I was recruited to KeyCorp to become head of marketing.

Kelly Services then called and over I went. I didn't have the global experience I wanted. Kelly at that time was in five other countries, enough to count. I thought I would stay two or three years and stayed over 20, working my way through head of sales and marketing to COO and then ultimately to CEO.

I retired two years ago or so I thought, but now I'm actively engaged in a startup, which has big investors, and is a whole different thing to learn to manage. We are building a political structure as well as a benefit and protection structure for independent workers, which are now 40% of the American workforce. So that's the past background.

Deborah Midanek: It's interesting that you rose through psycholinguistics, sales, and marketing into operating positions and ultimately to CEO and now leader of a startup. Where did you first trip over corporate governance as a focus?

Carl T. Camden: When I went to Kelly, I was very focused on Kelly's outward facing image. I became very aware that staffing firms in general were engaged in a practice that I found to be disreputable. It was called SUTA (State Unemployment Tax Act) dumping. A corporation's unemployment claims experience would set the level of SUTA taxes required. Whenever you form a new corporation in the U.S., SUTA taxes would get reset to the lowest rate. Companies would, therefore, set up shell companies, transfer assets, and every two to three years would get a new tax ID and go back to the lowest possible tax rate. This was especially an issue for companies like a staffing firm that would have a fair amount of turnover and unemployment compensation claims. I thought that was cheating. I thought that was damaging the unemployment support system in the country.

So I went through a period of time of working with the Kelly board. It wasn't my board then; I was just becoming the COO, but I wanted to convince them that we didn't want to be tied to that practice. I also knew it would put us at a competitive disadvantage if we were the only company to stop doing that. For me, working with the board, convincing them to take this risk with me, convincing them to do the right thing at a social level even though it might be the wrong thing on a near-term profit basis, and going to war with the industry in terms of passing new legislation, was a cram course in corporate governance. I had to learn how to talk to boards about long-term gain versus short-term profits; to talk about doing the right thing even when we did not necessarily know it would lead to a good financial outcome. For me, it was an intense education on dealing with complex boards, complex financial issues, and social issues all at once. It was a big introduction to governance for me.

Deborah Midanek: What a fantastic story. One thing that is interesting about what you're saying is that fairly early on in the period of recent debates over governance, you were animating what is now called ESG [Environmental, Social, and Governance], right? You were pushing for the long-term value proposition as the better outcome for the company to espouse and I'm sure that ultimately it did turn into commercial advantage. Did it?

Carl T. Camden: Yes, at the end of the day, the *Wall Street Journal* did a story about the one person crusade to do this, backed by his company. It was a very nice story, which I use at my startup company to remind them all of what we are still all about. It led to things like joining CED [Committee for Economic Development] and the Business Roundtable. While memories were fresh, it opened up true doors to what became my biggest customers at Kelly, who shared that same value system. These great companies, all of whom I believed were highly ethical companies who practiced doing the right thing, became the foundation of Kelly.

Deborah Midanek: Did you find unexpected barriers or grace moments in dealing with the board?

Carl T. Camden: It was a good board. The Kelly board always had within it a couple of people who were not CEOs or COOs. There was a college professor from University of Michigan in the business school who quickly jumped into support. Having some people who are societally based and not just corporate officer representatives on the board helps a lot when you're making the type of an argument that this is the right thing to do.

The other CEOs ultimately all got there, but you do get that first reaction of, well, the stockholders are expecting this much per share and if you wipe out that advantage, it's not going to be there. But you know what? At the end of the day, I also got more business, won more accounts.

Deborah Midanek: It's easy in retrospect to say that it was the doing of the right thing that was driving you and knowing you just a little bit, I believe fundamentally that was true. But given your training and outlook, you were probably also reasonably confident that ultimately you would have a good business case.

Carl T. Camden: Yes, I believed. I was trained as a minister, although I don't practice. I was trained as a college professor and those are unusual backgrounds to bring into corporate leadership and into a board seat, but I believed.

Deborah Midanek: Oh, that's gorgeous. I am the grandchild of Presbyterian missionaries. I feel like I have spent my whole life as a missionary in the world of corporate activity. That being said, do you have a sense of what you would consider the purpose of the public corporation today? And then, of course, has it changed?

Carl T. Camden: It's in transition now, but I would say that, around the world, it was always a place to collectivize money, to put it to, we hope, better and more productive uses and to allow companies to achieve scale and to achieve impact in marketplaces. That's the textbook answer; I get all of that and it's true. Given I'm now in a startup, I am wondering if the modern corporation is about to undergo a far more rapid pace of change than they know, in terms of purpose and their reasons why.

But with all the public companies that I was involved with in different ways, their answers would have pretty much been the same, at least from the financial and CEO side of the company. You had to get deeper into the company before you talked about the ability to affect change or the ability to do good or the ability to make an impact in the world. Those conversations I still found to be relatively rare at the CEO level. But anyway, that's a quick summary. It's a textbook answer.

Deborah Midanek: I am intrigued at your comment that you think that the corporation is about to go through some radical changes, which may be surprising. What's driving that?

Carl T. Camden: Part of what has driven what we regard as the modern corporation has been the need to sustain effort for long periods of time. This required accumulation of capital and the preservation of talent pools and so on inside the company. It required longevity. Now, and there has to be a better name for this, I keep talking to a handful of professors about the emergence of a "tinker toy" enterprise that is assembled and disassembled rapidly.

Product life cycles have declined dramatically, so the expected life of a given product and its success in the market is now down to about three years and declining. Products change fast, and the pace of technological change is incredible. Job life cycles, as I learn working with labor unions and so on, are dramatically shorter than in the past. So the question is, is a corporate model that's based on longevity and stability and a slower pace of change going to survive and thrive? What I see is as an increasingly large number of people who are very adept at coming together quickly, forming a new enterprise, completing the task at hand, and then disassembling quickly.

I'm working with more companies that are interested in how I can help them do that and how the core of what they do themselves on a sustained basis becomes smaller and smaller. Access to capital doesn't have to be permanent; it can be increasingly based on the projects at hand. I don't know that this is going to happen, but I'm living in a world in which those conversations are very common now with corporate leadership.

Deborah Midanek: I see more and more talented senior people who have a long, useful life ahead of them having left the corporate structure. It's not just the rank and file people or the technology gurus that are expanding and contracting and coming together for projects. As I look at what my peers are doing. I'm amazed at how many are really busy doing really interesting things and would never dream of going back into a corporation.

Carl T. Camden: In the United States, we have a bifurcated workforce, in which what I call independent workers, those who are not tied to corporate structure, is primarily comprised of those under 30 and those over 55.

It's not like that in the rest of the world. It's like that in the U.S. because we tie social benefits, healthcare benefits, and so on to employment in a traditional corporate structure. People aren't willing to take the risk and are looking for more stability while they're in the childbearing years. Everybody thinks of this new group of people as the under 30s, but the over 55s now actually outnumber the under 30s, in terms of their participation in this new way of working.

Deborah Midanek: That reflects my experience. But it also seems to me, Carl, that in order for this to work, the ability to communicate across many different cultures, technical requirements, and experience bases becomes the most important element guiding success.

Carl T. Camden: Absolutely. I'm watching the whole language of work change. I've been out now speaking to the Harvard Business School and business schools around the country, about this coming change and the language of work. I'll just give you two fast examples. I was at the Harvard Business School and asked the MBA students, "How many of you have had a course about employee engagement?" Most of them raised their hand, I said, "How many of you know the metrics and what you deal with to get to talent engagement?" Nobody raises their hand.

I said, "Do you understand you're going to be asked to run companies in which more than half of the talent aren't your employees?" And I said, "Most business schools aren't teaching you what it takes to attract those workers to you, most of them don't understand … " I said, "I can tell you that making them park in the farthest away parking spots and not eat in the company cafeteria strike me as really bad moves." I encouraged them not to focus on how many people are employed, but instead to think in terms of how many workers have to be deployed to achieve their goals.

Though the business schools aren't there yet, there is a new language of work emerging, a new way of thinking about everything from employees to how work is done to what a corporation is. It's going to be an exciting time for the people who are in our disciplines who come after us. They're going to live through very interesting times.

Deborah Midanek: In this emerging corporate model, what would be the role of the board of directors? Which, to date, is still a legal requirement for the formation of a corporation.

Carl T. Camden: The boards were set up, obviously, to represent the interests of the investors. And to some degree, that's still critical, but I think that that's always the simplistic and easy answer and it leads to bringing certain types of people onto boards.

I've increasingly been challenging boards to define their job as to ensure that there is a culture that we can live with, that we can trust, that we respect. That we're not just the guardians of the money, but we're also guardians of the company's reputation. We're also guardians of the company's place in society. For that, we have to have an impact on helping the management team shape the culture to ensure that we don't, in our drive toward profit, which remains very important, damage the company's push to develop a long lasting culture. As I see the new model of the corporation emerging, people are going to be increasingly attracted to the cultural elements. Is this a company they want to have on their resume? Are they going to want the experience of having worked at a company that's effective at changing society for the better, as well as representing the shareholders?

I think that if boards want their companies to survive, they're going to have to help management teams address both making money and helping to shape a culture that's going to be enduring. At the end of the day, if corporations continue to evolve the way I think they will, it'll be the culture and the beliefs that are critical to the long-term survival along with their business processes that make them unique. But it's going to be the board's job to guarantee that the management team doesn't forget about the culture in a fast-changing business world.

Deborah Midanek: That's a wonderful answer and it leads into the next question, which is, to whom does the board owe its fiduciary duty?

Carl T. Camden: Sure, and it's murky for a good reason, which is society and the government allowed these corporations to arise that have that particular focus, but also with a clear expectation that they would serve society at large. That they would participate in creating a better and more just society. That was always the expectation, it wasn't that we would rape, pillage, and plunder, and leave behind devastation. It was that we were being given special powers, special authority, some degree of freedom from some levels of oversight, with the notion that we would return that trust. Not only by making the economy richer and wealthier and people and the investors happy, but that society at the end of the day would be better off.

Deborah Midanek: To me, board members are similar to the parents of the corporation, charged with keeping it safe. To make sure that it doesn't run out in traffic, that it doesn't take drugs, that it doesn't do bad stuff, that it learns to develop its own judgment, and to contribute to the world. Where are you on where the value of independent directors lies? You mentioned earlier that the greater social view was of value on the Kelly Services board. What do you think about it?

Carl T. Camden: I often think of the board as being the guardians of the corporation. While corporate management is doing its thing, maximizing goals, doing the best they can, the board has to play the guardian role to make certain that the company's behaving well, has good values, is growing up well, and so on. I think that you get to a better perspective with outside views coming in.

As CEO, I've had to answer questions when the board was challenging things, that I never would've thought of as being a question. I've enjoyed having a college professor or two on the board. And they don't even have to be from the business school, they could be from sociology or cultural psychology, all would be fine.

I may be an outlier, but I've been happy to have outside, and I mean really outside, directors as well as some people who are comfortable with the industry, combined with a small number of key investors and a key officer or two of the company. My experience has been that the more diversity on the board, and not just diversity in terms of women, ethnic background, and so on, but diversity in backgrounds, matters a lot to keeping a holistic view in front of the leadership teams.

Deborah Midanek: I agree with that. Nature teaches us that diversity provides protection against risk. Diversity of thought and background and opinions is very valuable to a company. Having it on the board offers a very important protection to that company. I stay away from the whole question about women on the board because it's always struck me that it was backwards to say that we need to have more women on boards because women are left out. That's the wrong end of the periscope, it's got to be that we need to have more variety on boards because companies have a variety of customers and we need perspective to make sure we are not going over the cliff.

Carl T. Camden: I used to raise some controversy early on when I was speaking to business schools, saying diversity does me no good if I turn off all the lights in the room and everybody is saying the same things and talking the same way and has the same set of experiences. That diversity only works on the company's behalf if they're bringing into the room with them a real diversity of thought patterns or real diversity of life experiences or real diversity in community experience. I said apparent diversity isn't going to win the day. It's going to be real diversity that wins the day.

Deborah Midanek: Well, it sounds like you have contributed a great deal to the quality of board thinking. I have experience in maybe 20 different boards, serving as a director. I have found, more often than not, a highly ritualized kind of behavior where certain directors speak, others don't. Certain rituals are observed about how information is communicated, so the opportunity to get that diversity into the room, in terms of building the conversation, of hearing from every individual member, can be a difficult thing to achieve. Do you have any thoughts about how you have managed to do that? To get the real benefit of diversity reflected in the board's decision making?

Carl T. Camden: It's difficult because of the way boards operate and the way CEOs react to boards. It's difficult because, in reality, the period of time surrounding the board meetings on publicly traded companies is generally a Kabuki dance.

Deborah Midanek: Exactly. Highly ritualized.

Carl T. Camden: Right, highly ritualized. The committee meetings all happen in the right order, and everybody is cautioned both on the board side and on the management side, not to say things that are going to invite long conversations. Often not because the conversations would be unwelcome, but because they are on an hour schedule here, they have to get this done there.

The people on the Kelly board who I thought were playing their governance role well made it a point to call up and say, "Hey, Carl, you might be having a tough time, you might be having a good time, I don't know which it is. You want to go out to lunch?" And we'd go out to lunch and in that type of unofficial atmosphere, I had somebody I could talk to. The CEO's not going to talk with folks inside the company, maybe not even to the COO. So having a board member that you can trust that way is very important.

One particular director would give advice over lunch, but there was no harm, no foul if I didn't follow the advice. I've had board members who offered advice and if I didn't take it, I realized it wasn't advice, it was an order. And then I had to deal with that. That type of unofficial mentoring from board members, that trusting relationship is worth way more than their attendance at the meeting.

Deborah Midanek: I realize that the main issue that the CEO is worried about is the risk of board members rocking the boat. I understand why it has become so ritualized. But I've also thought that a lot of the value of the board meeting comes from the work of preparing for the board meeting. The process of having to stand back and think about the reports you're going to share with the board members is a healthy process.

Carl T. Camden: I think when it's functioning well, the prep is good, and you're dealing with committee chairs at that point who have specialties in the zones that you're prepping for. When I was thinking about personnel issues, personnel policies, the compensation committee chairman was awesome. I think you're right. It's in the prep for the meetings, the prep with the committee chairs, that real governance happens. Then again, I go back to what you and I were talking about earlier, that most board meetings are just Kabuki dances. You're just following the ritualized steps you're required by law and custom to follow.

Deborah Midanek: There are various kinds of bullying that can go on in the boardroom because there's a strong, perfectly understandable desire to conform. It is risky to be an outlier on the board because your voice will very likely be dismissed.

Carl T. Camden: You can be an outlier once they've gotten to know you, once you've delivered, but your first year or two on a board, most are quiet, trying to absorb what is going on, what the culture is, and how much room there is to maneuver. Ultimately many on the boards I've been on do ultimately find their voice.

Deborah Midanek: What can we do to move corporate governance forward? As I listen to you talk about the emerging corporation, I am compelled to ask how do we do better?

Carl T. Camden: I don't have answers yet, but I can tell you things that I've fretted about for a few years. When I was in charge of Kelly and I was operating in 30-some countries, I had a responsibility to 30-some countries. I had a responsibility, I felt, for how they dealt with labor, for their social safety net. I had a responsibility to help them with competitiveness, even when some of those countries were trying to kick the U.S. butts on competitiveness and my U.S. side was trying to kick the other side.

I was also on the board for several years of a Japanese publicly traded company, as the only non-Japanese person on that board. And I can tell you that the coordination between what the government was trying to achieve in Japan and what the company was trying to achieve was intense and frequent. It was one of the largest labor-oriented companies in Japan. If, for example, there was a concern that wages weren't keeping up with inflation rates, there was always a conversation with the companies as to what could the government do that would help and not hurt?

But when you're housed in a country or in multiple countries and you're of size, you do have a responsibility to that country. You are a core part of the infrastructure. You can exist only because that country created a macro environment that enabled you to exist and succeed. It's a great question you're asking, what is the role? I don't know this number anymore, but the percentage of U.S. GDP created by the 500 largest companies in the U.S. is huge. It accounts for a significant part of the tax base, and thus the support for the government.

In the U.S., however, more so than in Asia and in parts of Europe, we keep a distance between the large corporations and their boards and the government sector. What contacts there are tend to be more unofficial or by appointing you to boards of X or Y rather than actively trying to figure out how we work together to make things better. Here in the U.S., we're scared over corporate influence from large companies.

Deborah Midanek: But that fear has also been around since our inception. It's embedded in the way we were formed, which is quite distinct from Japan, for example, which carries a radically different heritage forward and a radically different ethos about what is good. What I find to be the overarching question, which is what you're focusing on, is what does it mean to be a citizen? I think that that is such an important question today. In the midst of the news cycle, in the midst of the quality of candidates our government seems to be able to attract, in the face of fear over climate change.

Carl T. Camden: It's a trust and mistrust issue. I have come to trust most of the large corporations I'm involved with, but again, maybe because I'm involved with companies that focus attention on public policy. They care; they care about sustainability. Sustainability isn't an extra little add-on to them.

Deborah Midanek: That would translate into taking the long-term view in the boardroom.

Carl T. Camden: Now that you've said that, I realize that most of my favorite customers at Kelly Services had existed for 50 to 100 years, and had a long-term vision of what it meant to be present in the world, and were able to make decisions that would have a 10 or 15-year as opposed to a 10 or 15-week perspective.

Deborah Midanek: I find it such an interesting irony that our short-term focus can be argued to have come from the need of our institutional investors to demonstrate competitive performance every quarter, or risk losing the money they manage or not being able to fund obligations to their pensioners. Now, and perhaps healthily, I'm not yet sure, the pressure to be thinking about ESG, until recently marginal considerations for investors, is coming from the institutional investors. I'm thinking what a fabulous possibility that represents. It may be that these same people can find a way to relieve the pressure that results in what we call rampant short termism. I'm far from a believer, but it's possible.

Carl T. Camden: In our startup, we've actually been able to talk to some companies about fulfilling corporate social responsibility roles, especially with European-centered companies. There is always openness to that as a discussion. Not as much yet in the U.S., but even some of the U.S. companies, especially the ones who are operating on a global scale, are now talking about their social responsibility. I think it's good.

I do think that the U.S. is now ready for a broader perspective on governance. The board members I talk to are drifting away from the mercantilist perspective, and are concerned about social good. They are concerned particularly with the focus on sustainability.

Chapter 5
Taking a stand in the community

Catherine A. Allen

For more than 30 years, **Catherine A. Allen** has been a thought leader in business innovation, technology strategy, and financial services. Currently, Catherine is Chairman and CEO of The Santa Fe Group, a strategic advisory services company that provides briefings to C-level executives and boards of directors at financial institutions and other critical infrastructure companies in the areas of cybersecurity, emerging technologies, and risk management.

Her current board commitments include Risk Sense, Belief Agency, and Pocket PatientMD. She formerly served on the boards of Synovus Financial Corporation, El Paso Electric Company, and Analytics Pros. Recognized in 2018 by the National Association of Corporate Directors as one of the 100 most influential U.S. corporate directors, she serves on the advisory board of Women Corporate Directors and the Executive Women's Forum. Catherine is the former Chair of the Board of Trustees and member of the National Foundation for Credit Counseling and formerly chaired New Mexico Appleseed. She is a member of the Museum of New Mexico Foundation and International Folk Art Alliance boards.

Among many other awards, *Cyber Defense Magazine* in 2019 named her among the Top 25 Women in Cybersecurity; and she received the US Banker Magazine Lifetime Achievement Award for her outstanding contributions to financial services and technology. She received an honorary doctorate from the University of Missouri in 2015 and holds a B.S. from the same university, an M.S. from the University of Maryland, and is ABD from George Washington University.

Deborah Midanek: Who is Cathy Allen and how did she come to be? I know that you grew up in a small town and your father was a banker. What has been the passion that has driven you along in your life?

Catherine Allen: I'd say the driving factors in my life have been three things. I always wanted to work in business and went into retailing early on because it was the only way I saw for women to be in business and move up, be CEOs. My father showed me

https://doi.org/10.1515/9783110670004-006

that businesses can be ethical and do the right thing and be good citizens. He used the bank he led as a platform to do good in the community and assist with economic development. So I wanted to have a business, to be involved with businesses whose mission I felt was to do good, to create opportunity, and to hire people and treat them well.

Another passion was for public policy. Again, this came from my dad and my mother, who were both behind the scenes very involved in shaping public policy and showed me the interface between the two. Their example showed me that you really can't say, "Oh, I don't like politics, I'm not going to be involved in it" if you're in the community, because many of the important moral and value issues that we grapple with are shaped by the political environment.

The third thing that's driven me is the promotion of women: women's rights, more women on corporate boards, more women in the C-suite, more women politicians, in order for women to have a voice. I learned that very early, in that I saw women not having much of a voice in a small town in Missouri, except for a few. I saw women not getting promoted.

When I saw what wasn't happening, it drove me to make things happen for women. Those three things have carried through in everything I have done in my past as well as the future. I'm trying to choose wisely, where I put my time around those three areas, making businesses ethical, shaping public policy and promoting women.

Deborah Midanek: That's a beautiful summary, Cathy. How did you get interested in corporate governance per se, which provides a good combination of all three of your interests?

Catherine Allen: Corporate governance drives access and opportunities. It drives the ethical behavior of organizations and the mission and values of an organization. And it also is something that I saw my father do. He was on the school board because he wanted to make sure that all the money didn't go to the football team and that, in fact, the French program had some money. I saw how he used being on that board and the Board of Public Health for the state. He was finance chair for many senators and governors, and I saw how important it was. In fact, Dad used to say, "It's more important to be behind the scenes in governance than it is to actually be the person out there running for office, or even being the CEO in some cases."

He gave me the idea that it was important to be on a board, and to shape governance. When serving on boards, I've always gotten on the nominating and governance committee, because I felt that was a way to shape the composition of the board, and the ethical behavior of the corporation.

Deborah Midanek: Your focus on public policy, on values and principles, suggest that you do believe that the purpose of the corporation is bigger than making a profit. Can you describe what you think the purpose of the modern public corporation is?

Catherine Allen: I can, but first, the Business Roundtable said recently, "Well, we're going to start focusing on the stakeholders rather than just the shareholders." Let's make sure that they actually do that as opposed to just saying the words, but I wanted to say, "Well, duh." This is what research shows what women think about on boards more than men. We tend to look at stakeholders versus shareholders. We understand the organization's impact on our employees, our customers, our vendors, our regulators. We look at corporate goals in a more holistic way, not just shareholder return.

And women tend to look at risk in a more holistic way. As it is turning out, it's women that are bringing up things like climate change, or geo-political risks, or reputational risk way before the men on boards get there. I think what is driving this renewed emphasis on mission and values of an organization, this larger perspective, is the reality of Gen Z, and even Gen Xs, who are much more attuned to the values and mission of an organization. They focus on the mission and values expressed by the corporation. For example, "I'm going to buy from Nike, because I like the stand that they took on Colin Kaepernick," or "I don't go to Chick-Fil-A because they're anti lesbian-gay rights."

The younger generation, and I think the boomers are following their influence, are demanding that an organization define what their mission and values are – and then live up to it. And if they don't, social media will take them down in a very short period of time. I'm on the board of a creative agency called Belief Agency in Seattle, and they have big clients, marquee clients, that they first work with to identify their beliefs and values; then they look at how they're communicating that through various media, and how their products and services aligned to that, and how their behavior aligns to that. They and their ads have won all kinds of awards.

They're onto something, and that is that corporations today have to identify in a larger sense where they are in the community. And this is not new. If we look back to the turn of the 20th century, some major corporations felt it was important to give money, to change the community, to provide jobs, but we lost that, especially in the 70s, 80s, 90s, 2000s, where the goal became focused on shareholder value only.

Deborah Midanek: That shareholder primacy started to rise in the 70s for a whole host of reasons. And it's interesting to see it swinging around.

Catherine Allen: I have two examples from a public company board I serve to share. I was the one that wanted to know our vulnerability, or our liability, due to climate change because we have coastal exposure in Georgia and Florida. My fellow board members were rolling their eyes, and their first answer was, "Well, on homes they have to have flood insurance." And I said, "What about what's happening in many of the communities in Miami and Fort Lauderdale where they have repetitive flooding and may actually be ruining the water system, or access to the water system or the water table? These property values are going to go down." So we investigated it. And we discovered we had a lot of potential liability. And we're at the point where we're very careful about loaning anything that's in any water area. And it's an example of, again, getting people to see broader risks that are there.

The second story arose when Trump was the candidate, before the election, and I said to the board, "If Trump wins by chance, we really need to talk about the impact, the geo-political risks." And I was told, "Oh, Cathy, that's what we have lobbyists for, and I don't think we really need this geo-political risk issue to be part of the risk committee discussion." He said, "We're not an international company, and our lobbyists handle this." I said, "Well, I think you're going to see that this administration if he wins will be quite different." The next board meeting was held on the exact day that Trump was tweeting about Boeing, and the stock price of Boeing went down. The risk committee chairman came over to me and said, "Cathy, maybe you're onto something." So we added it to the risk framework.

We were a US-based company, coming to the reality that we're all geographically and globally connected, and what happens does impact us. The reality of what's going on in the world makes every board have to take a more holistic, bolder, and more community-focused approach to whatever they are doing.

Of course, the recent focus on ESG is encouraging. This is a shout-out to BlackRock and ISS, and many of the other investor groups. They're the ones that are taking the lead on diversity and inclusion, on climate change and cyber security issues, forcing corporations to talk about what they are doing around these matters in their proxy statements.

Deborah Midanek: Yes, it is interesting to see the world shift to passive investment, to ETFs, and in such a huge proportion. These large investment intermediaries bring us a wonderful irony: those who brought us short-termism in the first place are now pushing for long-term thinking.

Catherine Allen: I totally agree, I agree. If they're on both sides, they want you to meet the sustainability requirements and, by the way, how did you do last quarter?

Deborah Midanek: They have to compete based on their returns, with their peer group, to keep the money that they manage. It's a never-ending circle. But one question, though, is that often investors assert that they own the company by virtue of owning shares in the company, and that is a much murkier area than it appears to be. Do you have an opinion about that?

Catherine Allen: The short answer is, I don't know, because I'm not a legal expert, but my opinion on it is that you're a shareholder, you own a portion of the business, but so do the employees and so does the community. Ownership is not just dollars, it's the legacy, it's the reputation in the community, it's what you provide, it is employment in the community. I tend to call them more stakeholders than I would owners, but I think that just because you own stock, doesn't mean that you can dictate everything that they do, if, for example, it includes polluting the environment, or discriminating against employees.

Deborah Midanek: The European Union has addressed this by stating that the shareholders of a public company do not own the company, that what they own is a piece of its residual income. And their ownership of that income comes with certain rights, like the ability to elect the board, but it does not constitute ownership of the enterprise, which is interesting. We have not moved toward that clarity here. And I don't know if we need to, but it is an interesting comparison.

To me the role of the board is a very simple and clear one, but that's not true to many of the people I've spoken to. Do you have a strong view as to what the actual responsibility of the board is?

Catherine Allen: The actual role of the board is traditionally to focus on strategy, CEO succession, and fiduciary responsibility – and all of those are important. I think the role of the board also has to be to provide ethical and moral guidance and the vision setting, which is part of the strategy. It must also be able to articulate and guard the values of the organization. And I think we're going to see more and more members of the board or certainly the lead director or chairman of the board speaking out, just as a CEO speaks out about the values of the organization. They're going to be required to do it in some ways, but I think that's more and more its role.

Let me take this apart. Fiduciary responsibility is implicit, things like not committing fraud or money laundering, or making sure that you're paying people correctly. Regarding CEO succession, I think that compensation committees are morphing into being talent management committees, and it's not just a CEO succession, but also the practices in place regarding the CEO's direct reports, and maybe even one level down. We learned from Wells Fargo that your sales compensation can drive people to do the wrong thing. That is much broader than just CEO succession, and strategy includes vision, values, mission, and being flexible enough to pivot when you need to; it's your strategic alliances, and it's also your reputation and public perception.

Deborah Midanek: You mentioned fiduciary responsibility. Do you have a sense of to whom the board owes its fiduciary duty?

Catherine Allen: Okay. I would say to multiple people, including first, of course, to the shareholders. Because you are elected by the shareholders, you are there representing them, but you also have a fiduciary responsibility to your customers, to your employees to keep them employed, to your vendors to be able to pay the bills, to not go bankrupt. And then, I'd say, to the community and to your regulators as well. I have been in banking for a long time, and part of the role of the Fed and the OCC has been to make sure that there's stability, and that you don't fail. It's not just your shareholders. I think it is owed to every other stakeholder that you have.

Deborah Midanek: Another trend that has accompanied the shareholders becoming so dominant is the rise of independent directors, pretty rare before the 1970s. And now roughly 90% of the directors of all public companies are independent. If you believe they are important, why do you think so?

Catherine Allen: Yes, I do think they are important. Part of that is because independent directors can argue the issues without fear of goring sacred cows or treading in rival territory. Sometimes, however, independent board members serve so long that they're not truly independent, because they have become creatures of the CEO. And that's not a good thing. The truly independent board of directors is necessary because it gives another voice, and the ability to advise and mentor on management practices or give insight into strategy that the current management might not have, or may be too insular to see.

I see independent directors as bringing different skill sets and ideas and connections. I see them helping to resolve management issues where there needs need to be a change, whether it's of the CEO, or other members of the board. I see those are all positive. The negatives are, if the independent directors are too close to the CEO, or they've been there too long, you might as well consider them management. I'm not sure how effective they are. And sometimes you get people that just don't devote the time that they need to understand the business or the issues. I was interviewed a couple of months ago by *Agenda* magazine. They were saying that more and more directors are saying that it's so much work, they're having to have more meetings and spend more time reading and getting up to speed. I said, "Then too bad, they shouldn't be directors." The difference between today and even 10 years ago is that the velocity of change and the complexity of the issues require board members to meet more, especially the committees. A board director not working to do that, to stay on top of the issues, issues that often change in six months, then they're not really an effective director.

Deborah Midanek: Conceptually, it makes sense that independent directors offer an array of people with different experiences and diverse backgrounds and genders and ethnicities bringing their perspectives to bear. For that group to be effective, however, there needs to be a leadership system that recognizes that it's important to make sure everybody's voices are heard. The leader must ensure that the work of the board is done with active engagement as opposed to a passive after-the-fact rubber stamp. How do we build the leaders, Cathy? How do we make sure leaders know how to do this?

Catherine Allen: I totally agree, because I think diversity is very important, but if you don't have a way for all voices to be heard, or if there are cliques, then that diversity is mitigated. And managing diversity of opinion is a lot harder than having people that all think the same way. I think in the past, often, you just had cookie cutter groups that all got along, all played golf together, and didn't want to cross each other. Because of that, they could miss many important issues or perspectives, so that is a negative. That said, when you have diversity on a board, it's critically important for the lead director or the chairman to get to know each of them individually, to make sure each of their opinions is heard, and maybe to coach or mentor them on how to have their opinions heard, or be more accepted. I'm a big fan of committees as a way to educate directors on unfamiliar issues. The use of committees can also help members to develop their points of view, following broad discussion at the committee meeting.

The more you get to know people, the easier it is to understand their perspectives, and find ways to work together. Providing casual settings, whether board dinners or off-site meetings or something else, allows board directors to hear different opinions, acknowledge them, and then mitigate the differences, or let those differences stand but not in an acrimonious way.

On one of my boards, there were too many egos. And this one guy, the chairman of the board, was the wrong person for the role because he was the only one who talked – according to him, he was the smartest person in the room. The rest of us were dull, he didn't want to listen, he would interrupt people, he was rude. Thus, we had a board revolt and kicked him off the board because he just didn't get it about listening, and he had a personality that didn't work in a board.

Deborah Midanek: That is tricky, but the good thing is that your board found a way to take action. I would put that down to a board doing a good job. And can you think of an example of a board that's not doing a good job?

Catherine Allen: When I first went on to a particular board, even though they had independent directors, one of them was the dean of a college to which the CEO had given significant money, and though it was a public company, family members, one quite aged, held stock and remained on the board. There were only three truly independent directors, and it was tough to move them along. We had a management team who were just not doing right things. The board had to take action, and so we eventually got the two CEOs to agree to resign, and the son of one of them to be the new CEO. He was very good, but his father, who didn't want to leave being a co-CEO, continued to undermine him on many of the decisions. Outside investors started buying more stock, including young hotshots from New York who wanted to prove something. They forced one person onto the board. I could see where this was going and volunteered to be the one to roll off the board, because the remaining board members didn't like conflict.

They didn't want to take on this investor that came onto the board who then brought another investor, and then another investor on. They tried to sell the company and wanted a quick turnaround on it. Their prospective buyer was the company's arch enemy, a company with a bad reputation for ethics. The conflict-averse incumbent board, however, did not have the guts to fight. It was demoralizing for everybody in the company, because it felt like selling out to the devil. And in the end, regulators stopped it, and the company is still on its own, and has rebuilt itself. It has, however, lost its credibility in the community because it was going to merge with the devil.

It's an example of a board that was too focused on conforming and was not willing to fight when they needed to fight against these investor groups. And it ended up ruining the company's reputation as well as its financial situation. They're still around, but it's going to take them a long time to recoup.

Deborah Midanek: To be effective on a board, the individual ego needs to be set aside. When the board is working well, it's the *group* that is succeeding, and not an individual. It sounds like there were various people in that situation who were not putting their egos aside. They were arguing over slices of the pizza, rather than worrying about the whole pizza. And that's a really interesting dynamic, particularly when it gets to shareholder activists. They are looking for a return in their own portfolio, not so much for an overall benefit for the corporation and all of its shareholders. Very interesting. How about the CEO? How do we hold the CEO accountable?

Catherine Allen: I'm seeing a trend in compensation committees, shifting to become talent management committees. Boards are looking beyond just one person, the CEO, to the team that the CEO has put together. They are holding the CEO accountable for broader succession planning, for their team building and their team succession planning. If they can go down, two, three, or four levels, and see the people there, they can form an idea of the CEO's ability to attract, keep, and grow talent for the company. Another way to hold the CEO accountable is to be specific in the evaluations of the CEO as to what you want them to do, and to articulate what measures are being used in compensating them. Specify how meeting sustainability goals, or meeting diversity and inclusion goals, are to be measured. Aligning the strategy and the ethics of the business to the compensation and the development plan for the CEO and the entire team is essential.

The development of the muscle fiber of the company is indeed an important part of what the CEO needs to do. How do we make sure that is happening?

Here is a story that's a great example of really understanding the team approach and what motivates people. I would say all people want to be recognized, want to have the opportunity for development, want to grow, and, if they are smart, our companies are realizing that. My example comes from a university development team, basically a sales team raising dollars for the university. They give individual bonuses if they meet whatever their goals are. On top of that, they have stretch goals, wherein everybody in the organization from the secretary to the data analyst gets 8% if they reach that stretch goal. Finally, they have a blow it out of the ballpark goal of 15%, and every single person shares in that if they reach it.

When it's just individual goals, sometimes people knew there was money to come in, but they would hold it to the next year if it exceeded their individual target. But with every member of the team helping each other, not just the guys that were out there raising the money, they would celebrate it as a team, too. The first year, they made the 8% goal, and they couldn't believe it, and from then on, they've made the 15% goal. These were not easy goals. That 15% goal was 30% over what they raised the year before.

Deborah Midanek: Here's the overarching question. Do you think our corporate governance system is working?

Catherine Allen: I would say I'm on the cautiously optimistic side of it, because I think there are forces on the other side that revert back to being just about the money. External forces, however, are causing board members to be more concerned about reputational risks, concerned about their stakeholders as well as shareholders, concerned about geopolitical risks, understanding the importance of the corporate director role, that it's not just a rubber stamp or even a let's go golf and have a good time. I think it's going to shake out those board directors that are more conscientious than the ones that aren't, because the work is more.

Younger generations are very different. They're different in the workforce, they're different as investors, they're different as consumers. These demographics alone are changing the shape of organizations, and if they're not flexible enough to meet those needs, then they're going to die. I think boards are realizing that, I think they realize it's very different than it was even two years ago. Where that's happening, I think those companies will survive and the board members will be more conscientious. Where I am less optimistic is in industries, and there are fewer of those now, that do not have a lot of outside pressure right now, or that lack competition and haven't had to change for a while.

I'm optimistic longer term. In the short term, I'm concerned about the dollar pressures that will push people to not do the right thing. And I'll give you an example on AI and machine learning. We all know that that's going to take over many jobs, and going to create new jobs, too. Companies have a choice, they can either implement AI and machine learning and fire people, or they can implement and retrain and find new roles for their employees. If you just want to make short-term money, you're going to fire the people. If you have a longer perspective, you will retrain.

One financial services company I have been involved with really went downhill for quite a while. People were mad because they lost their savings and people were laid off and so forth. When we started machine learning in the loan process and mortgage area, we retrained employees and put them in better jobs, and we worked very closely with the communications people to place stories in the local newspaper about how Joan had been retrained to do X, and no longer has to do Y. We offered vignettes, so that instead of it getting out that we were bringing in machines that might take away jobs, we said right from the beginning that we're doing it, and we're retraining employees. I'm glad to see the route the boards are taking today. I mean, it's more in line with my value system, where I started this whole conversation, so it makes me feel better about businesses.

Deborah Midanek: Corporations, especially those that cross borders, and cross many borders, have the opportunity to transform the globe, to hold the universe together in a way that governments have a much more difficult time doing today. What else can we do that could improve corporate governance in a time when corporate leadership is so important to the globe?

Catherine Allen: I will always say that the tone at the top is critically important, as is nurturing an ethical corporate culture. I think boards and CEOs need to focus on that, and on really being able to articulate their value systems. I go back to Chick-Fil-A. They do a good job of adhering to their values. As a consumer and investor and employee, you may choose not to like their values, but they're aligning their behavior to their values and living that out.

Having robust discussions about articulating our values, and then questioning whether we are living those values is essential today. If we say we value diversity and inclusion, what are our numbers? And what are we doing to achieve them? If we say we value giving the best customer service that we can to customers, what are we doing to live that? That's aligning strategy with values in execution.

I was once part of a round table looking at how technology was going to change e-commerce and change the financial sector. A former regulator later told me: "I remember that you had such a sense of authenticity, and integrity, and you respected the regulators, and you worked with us." She said, "As opposed to the person who headed the roundtable at that time, who was just awful and my nemesis there."

Finding ways to work more closely together as partners in an emerging world has never been more important. There's so much research on the value of having diversity of backgrounds, experiences, ethnicity is so important to innovation and creativity and being able to be flexible. We are going to continue to grapple with high velocity change and increasing complexity and interconnectedness of issues. We've got to be very flexible and agile in the future. Having that diversity will help us, not to be compliant but because it will help the company stay flexible and agile.

Deborah Midanek: Absolutely, it's nature's risk management system. As I hear you talk about these things, Cathy, I'm taking back to your beginnings, growing up in a small town. When you grow up in a small town, you know you live in a goldfish bowl, and you have to treat everybody with respect, because you never know how they're going to feature in your life in the future.

Catherine Allen: That's right. You may not like them very much, but you look for the best and then you find a way to get along. It was great training for my corporate life.

Deborah Midanek: Is there anything else you want to be sure that we get a chance to discuss?

Catherine Allen: Really think about models that create employee engagement. And today, I think your employees are your greatest asset that you have, so think about how to keep them engaged. Work to keep them continuously learning, having opportunities to grow or move up. Finding ways to keep your employee engaged, is really important.

Chapter 6
You cannot govern what you do not understand

Bob Zukis

Bob Zukis is a leader in corporate governance and a pioneer in digital risk oversight. Bob teaches at the USC Marshall School of Business and is the founder of Digital Directors Network, where he's working with leading firms to advance their boardroom ability to understand and govern systemic risk in complex digital systems. He has over 30 years of applied business strategy, operations, and technology experience as a retired PwC Advisory Partner where he worked and lived on four continents and 20 countries. He is an author and keynote speaker, and holds an MBA from the University of Chicago and a BBA from Texas Tech.

Deborah Midanek: Would you tell us a little bit about yourself as background for the reader? Who are you, Mr. Zukis? I believe you spent quite a number of years with PWC before developing your teaching career and digitaldirector.com.

Bob Zukis: My career has been spent in new frontiers at the intersection between business and technology. I worked for almost 30 years at PwC as an advisory partner, which took me around the globe: nine years in Tokyo, two in Hong Kong, two in London, a bit of time in the Middle East, always focused on new markets, new products, new services, new boundaries for business.

Now I'm in academia as a professor at the USC Marshal School of Business, and also an entrepreneur where I'm the founder and CEO of Digital Directors Network.

Deborah Midanek: What are you teaching at USC?

Bob Zukis: We've pioneered the only executive education program in North America for digital and cybersecurity risk oversight for corporate directors and CEOs. There are two programs in Europe, but we're the first one in North America to help leadership shape and secure the digital future. I also teach corporate governance for MBAs, strategic management, global business issues, and structured problem solving.

https://doi.org/10.1515/9783110670004-007

Deborah Midanek: It does seem as if it's a deficiency in many curricula that they don't look at this issue of corporate governance and decision making in a complex world. Corporate leaders have to be good at that.

Bob Zukis: Technology has simplified our lives in many ways, but at the same time the world has become very complex because of these same developments. We're helping executives understand their complex digital systems for the first time and the intersection of that complexity with their efforts to shape and secure their digital futures. How do you begin to understand risk across those complex digital systems? We're helping them understand the systemic risks in this complex world and are creating new approaches, new methodologies, new frameworks that help leaders understand the inherent risk in the digital world that we've created.

Deborah Midanek: The degree to which everything is interconnected. Is that what you're talking about?

Bob Zukis: Yes, and that's the big difference between systemic risk and non-systemic risk. It's about how things relate and interact. Some people refer to this as the "Butterfly Effect." A butterfly flaps its wings in Cleveland, and that creates a tornado in New Zealand, that's the analogy. It's about how we understand the interdependencies between component elements and how the system works. We saw the concept of systemic risk emerge globally subsequent to the financial services melt down of 2008 that ended up creating a contagion effect, a systemic eruption that started to domino across different firms, across different issues and individual parts of the complex financial system. Some of the regulators began to talk about systemic risk post-2008 in new ways. We're also seeing it in other domains – planetary health, for example, is a systemic risk challenge. So we're bringing this thinking to the digital environments that companies rely upon and that their businesses increasingly rely upon. We are taking that next step forward in risk management to help them begin to frame and understand, anticipate, and mitigate the risks of those contagion effects. Most people think of risk in a negative context, but it's also about the upside or the opportunity risk of using these technologies to create and shape a much better world. The issues apply to both positive and negative perspectives, they are two sides of the same coin.

Deborah Midanek: I saw a movie the other day that hasn't been released yet, but it was called Fantastic Fungi, and it's about the role that fungus plays in the world. This movie was fascinating about the mycelium, a huge underground fungus network that breaks down, basically, discarded matter, whether oil spills, corpses, or whatever, and regenerates them into something else.

It makes me think about the natural world and the degree to which it is an interconnected system at the same time as we're talking about the digital world being an interconnected system. The World Economic Forum has done some really nice writing about interconnected systemic risk. You must have followed that or maybe even created it.

Bob Zukis: I didn't create it. I am aware of it. WEF came out with some great data around the digital future, estimating that by 2022, 60% of global GDP will be run through digital. That's pretty amazing when you think about it. So when our world is becoming this connected, this interdependent, this fast, we had better start to understand and recognize the implications of that.

Deborah Midanek: A world in which such a huge majority of "value" is ascribed to the intangible as it is today, about 85% or more, is very different from the world that we grew up in.

Bob Zukis: That is what that number is: 85%. Fully 85% of the value of the S&P 500 is attributable to intangible assets. If, therefore, you don't understand the digital world that we live in and that is our future, then you're at a distinct disadvantage. Board members and directors in general don't understand it as well as they need to. We need new ways to conceptualize it and understand it.

Deborah Midanek: Is that what brought you to your interest in corporate governance? As you say, despite many advances and changes, it's still the case that many boards of directors live in a silo. They live in an ivory tower in which they're highly protected.

Bob Zukis: That's exactly what brought me to the issue. I retired from PwC six years ago, and started to get involved with our boardroom liaison practice. We've got a group of executives that build relationships and understand governance issues within the firm's clients, and a lot of our clients' board members were starting to ask questions about social media. Facebook was about to do its IPO then. They really didn't have any understanding of social media beyond the hype. I was running our IT strategy and ops business, so I got called to talk to them about the issues and I frankly expected to see more people like me in the boardroom, i.e., technology executives, but they weren't there. I found that rather curious because I spent a career understanding technology, how it creates and shapes value, and certainly how it brings new risks to the organization.

The types of people and technology skills I expected to see in the boardroom were not there, so I couldn't let that go. I stayed focused on that over the last six years, and kept beating that drum for digital diversity in the boardroom trying to figure out the problem. Why aren't there more people like me that understand these issues serving on boards? Their absence to me was pretty scary, because boards can't govern what they don't understand. Given how important these issues are to the future of business and the world that we're creating around ourselves, I felt I needed to create a rallying cry for digitally informed representation in the boardroom. I am now working on that, including helping the corporate directors that are already in the boardroom understand these issues.

Deborah Midanek: Boards in general have been very conservative about change. In that six years, have you made progress in improving digital awareness and sophistication in the boardroom?

Bob Zukis: Yes, but not as quickly as you'd hope. The burning platform of cybersecurity risk has woken boards up and driven the conversation. Six years ago, I was a lonely voice out there. The headlines, the massive data breaches, and the fines have woken directors up to the issues. They are at least having the conversation now. Some progressive firms are taking steps in the direction that they need to take, and regulators have certainly woken to the public interest issue of data and privacy risk. Next steps are what do they do about it, that's where we are stepping in and all companies need to have an approach to these issues because they are so foundational to their futures.

So securing the digital future allows me to begin what is a much broader conversation.

Deborah Midanek: It is a huge subject that can stop conversation. What is the approach that you recommend to building the requisite ability to govern what we don't understand? How do we learn it? How do we transform our boards into effective instruments to do it?

Bob Zukis: I think there are three legs to the stool. First, it's getting qualified technology experts into the boardroom and then onto boards as corporate directors. Boards can't govern what they don't understand. We saw this 17 years ago with Sarbanes-Oxley when for the first time regulators forced corporate boards to have financial experts in the boardroom. We're at a similar point for technology expertise. In hindsight, it is amazing to think that it was less than 20 years ago when it was a novel concept to have somebody in the boardroom who understood a financial statement. It will seem absurd 20 years from now that we didn't have boards that had qualified technology expertise on them.

Technical and digitally savvy people understand business more broadly than they're given credit for by the existing governance community. There is a highly qualified cadre of people out there who want to help. I know they're very ready, willing, and able. They are starting to get pulled into the boardroom, and they are also starting to wake up to the fact that they can add a lot of value to the board. So the first step is to get the skills onto the board.

The second step is the board's approach to these issues. Committee structures have a huge role to play in the governance agenda. I'm a big believer in the use of a technology and cybersecurity committee for every public company. And those two things go hand in hand. You can't have cybersecurity risk bolted onto an audit committee as an afterthought. Any innovation, any forward looking technology decision you make, you have to concurrently consider the cybersecurity risk profile that you're inheriting with those very same technologies.

So it's the skills and then it's the structure. You have seen some companies put technology committees in place, but right now it's a very small minority – less than 12% of US public companies. The third leg is the approach and agenda to understand systemic risk in complex digital systems. A new approach to risk management is needed, and it has to focus on systemic risk, which is the contagion effect across a system. With these three things we'll actually have created the practice and profession of digital and cybersecurity risk oversight. Those are the three legs of the stool, the skills, the board structure, and the scope of the risk oversight approach that boards need to take to understand these issues.

Deborah Midanek: I agree that digital sophistication is mission critical. But as I sit as a director thinking about how to be sure that the company I'm working with has it, the question of defining it is difficult. There are many ways of looking at bringing on a technology-savvy director. It is easy to see the possibility of bringing on knowledge of technology that may not be related to what the company actually has to do. I can see the following happening: You find a technology expert, you put them on the board, and something good is supposed to happen. Well, we need to be better and clearer about defining what technology means. What kind of skills and aptitudes we're looking for, and whether in fact the entire board should have a certain threshold knowledge. It is risky to allow boards to think they are covered because they have a technology guy.

Bob Zukis: I think the entire board needs to have a level of knowledge in these issues, and you're absolutely right: What is technology expertise? What's digital expertise? Board members that don't come from a technology background think that those are the same thing.

We're helping with that too. We've identified eight critical domains that comprise the core of any digital system with our core framework, called DiRECTOR™. These domains individually are complex specialities, and together they work to power most companies' digital value propositions, which is increasingly becoming just the company's value proposition. These domains cover data, information architecture, risk communications, emerging technology, cybersecurity, third parties, the operation of IT, and regulation. Those eight domains comprise the overall systemic risk framework that we've created. Instead of looking at technology as a black box, we have put some structure around it, and made the issues understandable so that directors can begin to get comfortable with them. This framework can create a common language to use to understand digital risk.

We're also educating and certifying CIOs, CISOs, and corporate directors to this body of knowledge to business school standards.

Deborah Midanek: That's what's needed, a common language. When we think about boardrooms, the easiest thing to do is bring on someone who looks just like yourself because you can evaluate that person. It's much harder to evaluate people with diverse backgrounds and ethnicities, and genders, and ages, and so on. Then once they're on the board, to develop the common language – first of respect, and then ultimately of the trust required – is really difficult.

So now we'll be adding this other dimension, familiarity with the eight aspects of the framework for effective digital risk oversight. How do we do that? Where does it start? Do we invite Mr. Zukis and the Digital Director Network to make presentations to boards of directors about how to do this? Do we send people to school? Do we recruit a particular type of person to the board? Is the answer all three of those things?

Bob Zukis: All three of the above, and that is exactly what we're doing at DDN, in conjunction with USC Marshall. The first steps to empowerment are awareness and then education. We created the first executive education program in America focused on digital and cybersecurity risk for directors at USC Marshall because we wanted academic prowess brought to the issues. This stuff is hard, it needs to be taught to the highest standards. DDN and others have the ability to offer boardroom briefings on these issues, but there needs to be more structure than what's been taking place so far. That's why we've created these frameworks and methodologies to begin to get people to talk from a common perspective.

DDN is also curating a group of technology executives that understand these issues, that want to use that common language and propagate that language into their networks and communities. Many of them are looking to join corporate boards as directors. We are over 400 executives, directors, CIOs, CISOs, and growing. It's a grassroots movement to begin to put that common language in place, and to help their own boards as well as to add value to other companies through directorship.

Deborah Midanek: Do you see more companies inviting the CIO or CISO, or CTO; do you see them inviting the chief officer in that subject matter into the boardroom as they do the CFO?

Bob Zukis: All the time. We've created a training class to help them. The Qualified Technology Expert, the QTE, is the label that we've put on those CIOs and CISOs. We've got a one day training class that makes them boardroom ready and boardroom confident. It teaches the foundations of corporate governance as well as the foundations of these frameworks. It also teaches how to communicate a message that a director will understand from a value and risk oversight perspective. What's been happening in most cases now is the CIOs and the CISOs speak one language and the boards don't understand that language because they speak another.

So we're helping them as the Rosetta Stone around digital and cybersecurity risk. We're the universal translator to connect the governance community and governance professionals with the technology executive who can contribute to long-term corporate value creation and protection.

Deborah Midanek: In many companies, the technology function has the ability to hold a company hostage because nobody understands what they're doing, and there are plenty of technology executives who like having that sort of power and having the budgetary control that goes with that. Are you finding that these walls are hard to break down, or are you finding that the risk climate has changed enough that everybody sees that the walls have to break down?

Bob Zukis: The walls are breaking down because the consumers and the users of technology have basically circumvented the walls. Fragmentation is taking place outside of the traditional IT silo. We have seen marketing take over a lot of the technology spend, and we have seen the rise of data privacy officers, something that the FTC forced Facebook to put into place. The organizing model for technology is playing catch up to the phenomenal socialization of technology across the organization that's been driven by the end user for the first time.

Think about that. We as consumers are a lot more sophisticated in our computing lives today than we ever have been. We used to get exposed to the latest and greatest technology through our companies, and they would spoon feed and roll out different innovations and technologies to us, but that's all changed. Now we get things much faster, and we digest them, and we go up the learning curve outside of the organization. That is putting pressure on organizations to keep up. So the organizing model is lagging significantly behind where we are as consumers and employees.

Deborah Midanek: You're absolutely right about that. I have a PC, I have an iPad, I have the MacBook Air, I have an Apple watch. I'm a user of all these systems, and I realize that I speak a different language to myself about all this stuff than I did just a few years ago.

I can't imagine my grandmother in her 60s, as I am, learning to navigate this world in which we need to be our own digital problem solver because there's just nobody to ask but Siri and Alexa.

Bob Zukis: Change management used to be common for large-scale enterprise technology projects. The biggest hurdle used to be getting the end users up to speed and confident and getting them trained to use the technologies.

Now that's flipped. Companies can't keep up. Companies can't step into that latent capability that's out there ready, willing, and able to hit enter. The consumer and employees have been educated; we know what works and what doesn't work. We see it every day and we particularly see what doesn't work within our own organizations. We've got the power to work around our organizations. Imagine the phenomenal loss of control within the enterprise around its technology footprint. You see fragmentation of the organizational model with different executives owning pieces of the technology future, pieces of the digital future. The board is nowhere in the conversation yet.

That's the problem. There's no leadership. We have a digital leadership crisis in companies globally, and without that leadership, you're going to continue to see technology underperform, and create risk all over the place, as it's doing right now.

Deborah Midanek: So fascinating. Think about the board function, and we can look all the way back to the way the Dutch East India Company borrowed the structure of the guilds in which the owners of the ships had all been members, so they could pull them all together and have some legitimacy and credibility because everybody was represented. So it was not about the optimal way to run an operating company, but it became the common device throughout the world that every corporation is required to be supervised by a board of directors.

But almost by definition for much of that period, the board has been in a passive role, dealing with events that have already happened. Reviewing financial statements, reviewing progress, reviewing this, reviewing that, but always reacting to rather than leading, or trying to define the future. Now, increasingly, the board is expected to play a role in strategy and to exercise not just leadership, but imagination. The board has to first recognize that there is a leadership issue in order to begin to think about how to fill it.

Bob Zukis: Think about the opportunity there. Management teams that understand this and see their board as a value-creating part of the whole equation should be screaming the loudest. They need their boards to understand these issues and for the board to be digitally diverse and digitally competent. If the board doesn't have their back on these issues, then the target is squarely on management's back professionally. They've got an enormous vested interest to make this happen. I'm not sure they've realized that yet, but we've seen corporate leaders get fired over these issues.

Just think about that phenomenal opportunity for the companies that do see this differently, that do understand the role that the board can play in strategic value creation with the new tools and technologies that we have to work with. That recognition is an immensely powerful tool for the company and for the shareholders. Institutional investors and other stakeholders in corporate value creation also aren't beating the drum as loudly as they should be around this issue, and we've seen research from MIT that clearly identifies that digitally diverse boards can be an enormous value driver.

Deborah Midanek: Moving toward another dimension, I've been thinking about the whole human resources function lately and the fact that it has also gone horizontal. So the junction between technology and talent development is an important dimension to think about as well. If we can organize technology to reduce the mindless parts of the job so that there's plenty of time to think, just imagine the value that could be unlocked from that.

Bob Zukis: Yes. That and other aspects of digital dexterity drive the company's ability to claim the next revenue dollar, to claim more than their fair share of market and achieve competitive advantage. That is a boardroom issue. People don't talk about it in those terms, but the race to digital transformation, the inevitability of digital disruption increasingly are the drivers of competitive advantage. In addition, everyone's feet are getting singed by cybersecurity breaches. We cannot allow those, however, to distract us from competitive risk or opportunity risk and what we can achieve off the back of these technologies.

Deborah Midanek: Yet, that also depends on believing that the team at the table has defined the opportunity set in such a way that we can see the path. Do you have any good stories, Bob, without naming names, that describe transformation of a board that moves from not really understanding digital thinking at all into adopting your framework and how it has worked? Obviously, nobody ever finishes this process, but I'd love to have an object lesson about how you got a board's attention, and the first thing we did was this; then it developed into that; and now it's heading toward the other ...

Bob Zukis: We received a call from a DDN member serving on a publicly traded company board. The board was looking for gender diversity, and they wanted somebody that understood the risk issues around technology and had a background in their particular market sector. We had several DDN members who were good fits, and one in particular who was an executive chief risk officer for a large public company who understood the value that she could bring to the boardroom. As chief risk officer, cybersecurity reported to her, and her digital background was strong.

That board started with the recognition that they needed someone in the room that was digitally literate to work shoulder to shoulder with them. They identified a candidate and brought her onto the board, and we were delighted to help. So that first leg of the stool starts with getting somebody onto the board that understands these issues. The next step is to organize the board more effectively, and then the third step is to develop the digital agenda and approach that the board is going to put in place to support management to drive long-term value creation and preservation.

Deborah Midanek: What about the obstacles to developing digital literacy on the board? It has been difficult on many fronts to bring change into the boardroom. While disappointing, it's also understandable that the board has typically been a conservative vehicle. What obstacles do you run into in trying to get people to open their minds?

Bob Zukis: There are a lot of obstacles and challenges related to board reform and board transformation. In this domain, I think it's understanding the answers to the questions. It is very difficult to govern what you don't understand, but some boards have awakened to the challenge. They do not yet understand the next steps they should take. There's a lack of precedent and a lack of practice to tell them next steps on these issues.

Some companies one would think would adopt progressive governance practices have yet to do so. Uber, when they IPO'd, adopted some leading practices in corporate governance, especially for Silicon Valley, such as separation of the chair and the CEO role. Then, inexplicably for a technology-enabled company, they slammed cybersecurity risk oversight into the audit committee.

I think they did that just because that is what everybody's always done, and didn't think through the possibilities. At DDN, we're trying to craft the vision of the digital governance future: Here's what you can do, here's why it works, and here are the others that are starting to head down that path. We are documenting and identifying the leading practices in the digital arena to give people some comfort that there are standards evolving for board approaches on this issue. We're creating some standards ourselves to lead them onto a more effective path as well. I think that probably the biggest barrier to achieving true boardroom transformation in this space is the lack of understanding of where to go, and what to do next.

DDN was formed because we are all walking into the unknown. We need to develop the path just as the Dutch East India Trading Company did. We're the ship leaving the port trying to lead these companies into a different world, the digital world. We don't know what it holds, but we know it's out there and we need skilled navigators who can help get us there safely.

Deborah Midanek: You mentioned that institutional investors are not as sensitive to this issue as they might be. It is interesting to see them moving more and more toward the "ESG" space. One would think that digital development might fall into G, or maybe it needs to become "ESTG." Where do we start in getting investors up to speed on this? They certainly deal with it themselves because these are huge organizations that are very technology-dependent.

Bob Zukis: I think it goes back to helping them understand the significance of the value creation opportunity. You would have thought they would have been a lot more active on the value preservation side because the cost of technology breaches is up, and is only going to keep increasing. And it's the shareholders that bear the ultimate cost of these significant fines. The downside risk of market value degradation is real. As to longer-term value creation, we are heading into the unknown and they don't know what they don't know. We're back to square one regarding educating them on what's possible and how they can help drive that kind of transformational change and, most importantly, what's at stake.

Deborah Midanek: I have had more than one person suggest that technology now makes it possible for the end user, as you called it a bit ago, to vote their own beneficial interests and not have to be constrained by the votes that are taken by those that are serving as their fiduciaries, the investment managers. I'm not sure that that is a workable thing from the point of view of human attention, but it certainly is from the point of technology. That approach would cut out the institution in the institutional investor.

Bob Zukis: There has been an enormous shift from retail investors owning the majority of corporate America in a broadly distributed ownership pattern to three asset managers, BlackRock, Vanguard, and State Street, having beneficial ownership of corporate America. You would hope that these investment managers are the smart money and will start to understand these issues and exert a little more pressure and influence. They do that quietly behind the scenes. Whether they are pushing the right levers on these issues is still to be seen. As to the private equity firms, I've had conversations with two private equity firms who are scoring their investment hypotheses solely around the degree of understanding the company exhibits regarding digital transformation and disruption. That's their investment hypothesis and they see the upside in leaders who understand and can harness digital transformation.

Deborah Midanek: The concentration of ownership in those three financial intermediary firms has frightening aspects, but one of the potential benefits of it is that they're in a position to drive the transformation of companies toward a more informed or intentional use of technology to create value.

Bob Zukis: Yes. Private equity, on the other hand, is a little bit different because they want to take a much more active role in their portfolio companies. But again, are they really taking an operating partner mindset in their portfolio companies on these issues, I'm not seeing it. I haven't seen anybody really step up to that level yet, but the opportunity is certainly there. One would think that the private equity managers will probably understand and act on the opportunities first as opposed to the institutional investors, but look out for activist investors as well. When they see under-realized value, they move quickly and can stir the pot effectively.

Deborah Midanek: That makes sense, but it may take a while for them to develop the imagination needed to recognize that. Many have gone through business schools that do not offer the enlightened approach of the USC Marshall School regarding bringing broader influences into the MBA classroom. Many have been trained to think that the answer is in the spreadsheet. I have spent my life as a corporate turn-around person, going into disasters and figuring out what went wrong and how we can fix it. So often we find that there was a failure of imagination and leadership, and that smart people just did not recognize the next step.

Bob Zukis: One of the things we purposely do not do in these classes at USC and DDN is talk about the shiny new technology object, because there's always a new tool. We go to the root level to understand what economic or social driver that the technology is exploiting. A lot of the tools and technologies created over the last decade are exploiting massive improvements in transaction costs. They have significantly lowered transaction costs so that people can use data and information and technology to connect in new ways and transact with their markets much more efficiently. Lowering transaction costs creates a more efficient marketplace, and capital flows to the most efficient market.

Amazon's secret sauce is their ability to create exceptionally efficient markets. They are much more efficient than the companies and industries that they displace. It's nothing more scientific than an economic advantage being exploited through technology in new ways. They understand these tools and how they can use them better than most.

Boards don't have that kind of a conversation. They talk about the shiny object, the tool. They don't talk about the economic impacts and the facts.

Deborah Midanek: In my experience, there is a lot of structure to the conversation in the boardroom. The opportunity for thoughtful conversations about alternate futures, alternative scenarios, possibilities, are difficult to build in board processes. Is that your experience?

Bob Zukis: Exactly; that's why you need a tech and cybersecurity committee, that can spend more time and be more focused on these issues, and to have some of those abstract conversations. Bring in the experts as directors, spend more time with management teams, and think more about the realm of the possible than you can at the full board meeting.

Your point is also interesting because the average board size is 10.8 directors, and the average director spends 240 hours in their role. That translates to fewer than two full-time equivalent professionals performing as steward and overseer of $100 billion or even $1 trillion companies. That is not a lot of time to do the very, very big and very, very difficult job of overseeing value creation and preservation, not to mention understanding transformative issues and the risks they bring.

Deborah Midanek: Yet many people in the company are counting on that lack of time as a way to keep the board from rocking the boat. On the other hand, some of the most confident CEOs I have known have looked to their board as a trusted sounding board. Some board meetings are organized more like seminars. They shrink the required compliance-oriented agenda to a small part of the meeting and use as much of the time as they can for exploring themes and what ifs; to define the obstacles, and think about how to overcome them. There are few boards that operate like that, but their number is growing.

Bob Zukis: It takes a unique CEO to want to step into that. But that's what's needed. Digital success starts at the top. So does digital failure.

Deborah Midanek: It really does. The thing the CEO wants is to know that the board has his or her back. The easiest way to have the board have his back is to have the board not be terribly well informed about what's really going on. That way he or she can count on solid support rather than a thought-provoking question. It's a very human thing. Is there a better way to organize the board? Given your focus on the realm of the possible and on looking at what it takes to move a new way of thinking into the board, you must also have given thought to how you think boards really should be designed.

Bob Zukis: There was a recent book about outsourcing the board to professional board services companies.

Deborah Midanek: I am familiar with that idea.

Bob Zukis: Such professionals could be held accountable to a much higher standard, and bring specialist skills to the board as needed. In theory, you could see where a board could add a lot more value with that model and be a lot more adaptive to rapidly changing market conditions. The model doesn't fly on its face, but if you take it to the level of looking at the current board structure and what can be done within the current constraints, you can begin to envision an environment where you have a lot more frequent board refreshment than we currently have. Board diversity should be a much bigger issue, not just identity or gender type of issues, but cognitive diversity to really understand the world that the company has to exist within, and react to, in order to survive and thrive into the future.

That would bring a lot more dynamic evolution and change to the board than you currently see. That's all possible right now, but it's not happening.

Deborah Midanek: Yes, indeed. Yet, if you look at the average age of the board and the fact that the age range is very tight, I imagine that it's not likely that these aging directors are not going to be replacing themselves with people of a similar age, though that certainly could happen. I think that we're going to have a lot of change very suddenly as the boards that are now in their late 60s or early 70s finally have to give up their positions. So I'm hopeful about this.

Regarding outsourcing the board, perhaps we could move toward something smaller such as outsourcing the chairman. As discussed earlier, our corporations in general need seasoned and intentional leadership dedicated to getting the highest value and performance out of the people in the boardroom. The chairman needs to know how to ensure that every voice is heard, to be sure that there is broad diversity and its value is captured, to be sure that imagining the possible is incorporated into board proceedings, to be sure that we're focusing on the active application of wisdom and judgment and not strictly on rubber stamping.

I could imagine a professional cadre of chairs that can be developed in the same way you are describing the qualified technology executive, and we have the qualified financial executive. It may be that having to have a qualified governance executive could be helpful. That could be credentialed through a central organization.

Bob Zukis: I think the professionalization of directors is a logical next step, too. It could involve specified credentials or certification, or establishing a standard for continuing professional education. It also anticipates directors who are professional directors, not part-time directors, not sitting CEOs who are running full-time public companies.

That would involve a significant change to all aspects of boardroom service from compensation to the time commitment required, but is it really good enough to have so few technologically qualified experts tasked with overseeing risk upside and downside for billion dollar companies? Seems like we could and should do better.

Deborah Midanek: The current models available are driven by a variety of people and motives, and are often quite self-interested.

Bob Zukis: Regulators have made board reform happen before in the United States, that was a big part of Sarbanes-Oxley. A federal charter has recently been proposed.

Regulators have clearly shown that they're going to throw the book at those experiencing digital lapses, as they have done with Facebook. When the private sector does something bad enough long enough, the regulators step in and the do what they did with Sarbanes-Oxley to protect public interest and capital markets.

Deborah Midanek: Last year, the Equifax debacle was stunning, absolutely stunning. Management did not even tell their board for three weeks. Your comment raises another question, Bob, which is that if boards are behind the eight ball with respect to digital sophistication, regulators certainly are too. How do regulators deal with the learning curve?

Bob Zukis: Well, fortunately or unfortunately, they react and overreact to a crisis situation. SEC Chairman Clayton in October 2019 made the comment that he doesn't think there are 4000 cyber experts available and prepared to step onto corporate boards – referring this back to Sarbanes-Oxley and that requirement to add qualified financial experts onto boards.

Well I think they *are* 4,000, and even more who can help on the broader digital agenda. That's squarely in line with what we're trying to address at DDN. I've reached out to Clayton to make him aware that we're working to fix this. Regulators are in exactly the same boat as the private sector regarding their need to understand these issues, and their learning tends to lag the private sector.

In this arena, however, they clearly understand that data security and integrity is critical to the public interest, much like financial reporting integrity was in the public interest when Enron, WorldCom, and other financial reporting failures led to Sarbanes-Oxley. They will throw the book at this in a similar way to what they did with Facebook, which was a Sarbanes-Oxley-style response. They'll hold executives accountable for data protection, civilly and criminally, and make them sign off on it. They'll hold companies accountable by making them take a more structured management approach, and they'll hold boards and directors accountable for their approach to these issues.

Deborah Midanek: What have we not covered that you would like to be sure we discuss?

Bob Zukis: Let's go back to the systemic risk framework and those eight domains that I described: data, information architecture, risk communications, emerging technology, cybersecurity, third parties, operation of IT, and regulation. Through them we have identified the causes of systemic risk from the perspective of complex digital systems. The severity of systemic risk is driven by the replaceability of a component part. A simple example to illustrate what I mean is the automobile. The automobile is a complex system comprised of a collection of combustion systems, electronic systems, cooling systems, suspension systems. But when the complex system in the automobile has a flat tire, the whole system fails, so that's what systemic risk is about.

So what is replaceability in this context? In the automobile example, the risk to the whole system of failure of the tire component was reduced by putting a spare tire in the car, with the requisite tools to replace it. Within most digital environments, companies don't understand where their potential flat tires are, so planning replaceability of the right component parts remains difficult. If a needed replacement is not available, systemic risk and its costs increase.

Beyond replaceability, we next look to the interconnectedness of the system. The risk factors spell out R-I-S-C-X: the size of the system, its complexity, its heterogeneity, its cross jurisdictional nature. We have identified those causes of complex digital systems risk, and we're teaching boards and companies how to look at their worlds through that lens.

Deborah Midanek: I am familiar with a company in which the sales department had their own heritage system. Its creator died a few years back and the system was not fully documented and its native operating system is old. They had to reverse engineer it and figure out the system backwards in order to make repairs to it and enhance it. The company is beginning to realize that it's not a good idea to build systems that depend on one person's knowledge to manage them. They would be in a less risky position if we could get components of existing systems we could buy off the shelf, and perhaps customize them. In that method, they can have a whole community of people who can help with their systems.

Bob Zukis: Yes, and nobody's had that conversation in the digital context yet, so we're starting that conversation. Taken together, the DiRECTOR™ framework is designed to help board members understand these issues in a context they can understand.

Deborah Midanek: Smart is as smart does. I think we're coming to the end of our time together. Thank you for your time and insight. You're undertaking a massive and necessary effort, but it should become contagious at a certain point. You'll hit a tipping point and then you won't be able to keep up with the demand.

Bob Zukis: Yes, I think that's exactly what's going to happen, and I think we are going to scale up dramatically. For every corporate board, the time for discussion is over. They need to start taking steps to solve these problems, and we're here to help.

Chapter 7
How is it we have earned that return?

Anne Sheehan

Anne Sheehan is currently Chair of the SEC's Investor Advisory Committee, a board member at L Brands, and a senior adviser to PJT Camberview. Previously she served for 10 years as the Director of Corporate Governance for the California State Teachers' Retirement System (CalSTRS), the largest educator-only public pension fund in the world, where she was responsible for overseeing all corporate governance activities for the fund including proxy voting, company engagements, and managing over $4 billion placed with activists and ESG managers.

Prior to CalSTRS, she served as Chief Deputy Director for Policy at the California Department of Finance. During her tenure at Finance, Ms. Sheehan served on both the CalSTRS and CalPERS boards as well as serving as the Executive Director of the Governor's Post-Employment Benefits Commission. Ms. Sheehan served as the Chair of the Council of Institutional Investors for two years, and served two terms on the NASDAQ Listing Council. A member of the Advisory Board of the Weinberg Center for Corporate Governance at the University of Delaware, and of the Board of Directors of the 30 Percent Coalition, Ms. Sheehan has been named one of the 100 most influential people on corporate governance by *Directorship* Magazine for the past eight years.

Deborah Midanek: You have had a really interesting career including a significant period of time at the apex of institutional investor influence over corporate governance, given your role at CalSTRS. How did you get there? Why was it interesting?

Anne Sheehan: My background is in public policy and politics. One of my degrees was in political science as well as history. I started out after college in Washington, D.C., on Capitol Hill, and spent a lot of time in the public policy arena; then worked in the Reagan administration; and then moved to California working in the same issues, public policy on the public sector, working for Governor Schwarzenegger, which is what got me to the governance issue.

I was the Chief Deputy Director of the California Department of Finance, so I sat on all the boards that the department was involved with: the treasurer's office, and

https://doi.org/10.1515/9783110670004-008

various policymaking boards here in California, which included CalSTRS. Separately, I had been appointed to the personnel board, and through that, I also sat on the CalPERS board.

While I was working on CalSTRS, the governance issues really caught my fancy. That is how I came to develop a love and a passion for governance and corporate governance. Because when you look at an investment pension fund, as institutional investors they are asking companies in their portfolio about their governance, and I've always felt that we should be able to hold a mirror up to our own activities and demonstrate good governance ourselves.

As a board member, I looked at our governance, our transparency, and our processes. Being on a board like CalSTRS, which is a public pension fund that's created statutorily, there are limits in terms of who can serve. We have constitutional officers on our board, publicly elected officials on our board, representatives of the employees who are the beneficiaries: the teachers and the community college teachers. Notwithstanding the fact that our board was created statutorily in the public sector, there were still good governance practices that we ourselves could entertain.

One of the things I looked at was the *Clapman Report* that talked about U.S. governance practices for a pension fund, by Peter Clapman, who used to run corporate governance for TIAA-CREF a number of years ago, and is extremely knowledgeable in the governance area. That was one of the first things I was interested in. The second was that I got the board to adopt a campaign contribution policy to restrict contributions from our investment managers. I felt that accepting such contributions could unduly influence the selection of investment managers and did not think that was a good idea. That's one of the reasons I got to know Arthur Levitt, because he had done the same thing at the Municipal Securities Rulemaking Board when he was Chair of the Securities and Exchange Commission, because many investment managers were making campaign contributions to these locally elected officials, who then made the decision on who got to manage money for that municipality or that county.

So it was my concern that we had a similar potential for a conflict there with people who made campaign contributions to the elected officials on our board, given the role these elected officials had in selecting and overseeing investment managers.

Deborah Midanek: I've always thought that taking pension plan board members or trustees on trips to Japan all-expenses-paid and so on was a sticky wicket.

Anne Sheehan: It's a tough one because you do want to train the trustees in terms of what their role is, and what it should be. It is important to explore your fiduciary role as a pension fund trustee and what you are supposed to do in that role. These are tough jobs and I do think training and understanding your role is extremely important, but having it sponsored by people who then seek to do business with the fund for which those trustees are responsible makes for a bit of a conflict. The Rotman

Center at the University of Toronto is very good in doing trustee training in an academic setting, as are others, and the cost of trustee participation should be borne by the pension plan.

I served as a board member for four years on the CalSTRS board, and for a year and a half on the CalPERS board, which is where my passion for governance really came from. It was interesting because CalSTRS adopted the campaign contribution reform, while CalPERS did not. Subsequently, when the whole placement agent controversy at CalPERS emerged and revealed that board members were being bought off, their CEO ended up in prison, and the SEC and the state stepped in with regulations. Our effort at CalSTRS in terms of the limitations on contributions predated that. I saw firsthand the influence that contributions had in manager selection because, as you can appreciate, there's a lot of money that needs to be managed. In choosing investment managers at a big fund, you want to make sure that from the beneficiaries' perspective you're choosing based on their skills and who's the best one to manage the money, and not on who makes the biggest campaign contribution to one of the board members.

Deborah Midanek: What's really interesting about what you're saying though is that, as someone who is focused on governance of the fund, you in turn will have a very real appreciation of the dilemmas faced by the directors of companies. The opportunity to compare and contrast gives you insight that is not generally recognized as part of the pension fund community's toolkit.

Anne Sheehan: Having been on those boards and seen the parallels, I think you're exactly right. From the perspective of a pension fund trustee, what is the right role for the trustee? It is very similar to examining the right role for the board member. Not managing the day-to-day, but taking a step back and considering to whom you are responsible. Who are you representing there as either a board member, as trustee, or whatever the role is you're playing, and are you able to balance that so that you can properly play the role of overseer? That is what a board does: it makes sure that the various parties, the stakeholders, the shareholders, the beneficiaries in the case of a pension fund, all benefit. How does the board represent those constituencies? What is their fiduciary obligation in that regard?

It has been helpful as I've made the transition to serving in a corporate oversight role to bring some of those pension fund governance skills to the table. We really talk about the governance of the institution, how it operates, what the rules of engagement are. We make sure we oversee management, determine where we draw the line. We consider board issues such as: How do we make decisions? How do we keep people informed? Who are the financial experts on the board? Who brings some other expertise to the board, and what kind? The experience with the funds in balancing the myriad issues has been very helpful as I've gone into serving the board of L Brands, Les Wexner's company, which includes Victoria's Secret and Bath & Body Works.

It's been a fascinating time as a governance person on that board to participate in some of the changes and structures they've agreed to, including a proposal to declassify the board going forward. We are working hard to improve performance of the company so the shareholders benefit.

The whole field of corporate governance fascinates me, especially as I started at CalSTRS on the staff in that newly created position of director of corporate governance the Monday morning after Lehman Brothers went over a cliff. That was my first day. It was, to say the least, an opportune time to begin my new responsibilities. We sat around the trade desk daily and watched the portfolio sink and sink and sink until we finally stabilized in March of that year and began the slow crawl back.

I think it begged the question of where were the boards of these companies? Where were the boards of Lehman Brothers and Bear Stearns? Did they have no idea what was going on, and the risk that was building up, and the bets that were being taken? Where were the people asking, "Isn't this a bit much?" So the corporate governance of those firms, which then spilled over to the broader, general economy, drove the engagement that shareholders had. I think much of the change that came as a result of Dodd-Frank and heightened focus on corporate governance since the financial crisis has come from looking at the culpability of those boards of directors and the shareholder value that was just completely destroyed during those years.

What did they try to do to help prevent it? Because if they did a little digging into some of those financial products and looked at their risk profile, I think they would've recognized the need to dial back a bit on this.

Someone who had been at Lehman said, "If the music's playing, everybody's dancing, so you gotta get up and play in the game." So that really drove some of the policy changes, some of the more active engagement by shareholders, not just at financial services companies, but all companies.

Shareholders are trying to strengthen the tools they have to hold directors accountable for their performance and their behavior. So the move to majority vote, to getting rid of classified boards, to the whole "say on pay" issue [the ability to regulate board pay levels], reflect that effort. We as shareholders are asked to vote for the directors, including the members of the compensation committee. If, for example, we didn't have say on pay, we could vote against the election of the compensation committee members. I think that say on pay is an early warning sign for companies that they've got a problem and that the directors could be held accountable for it. You know as well as I do that the one thing a director sitting in the boardroom does not want is to be the one who gets the lowest positive votes of all the directors. Everybody wonders, "What's wrong with you?" when the other directors get 99% and you get 70% positive votes. I think individual directors are paying more attention to their responsibility.

Deborah Midanek: Let's return to the basic question of what in your mind is the purpose of the modern public corporation?

Anne Sheehan: If we fast-forward over the last 10 years, there is greater focus on the responsible corporation. Some of that is definitely coming from shareholders, asking how you are making money and whether you are doing it in a sustainable and responsible way. I also think corporations in this day and age are being tasked with trying to address and solve public policy problems, because our traditional public policy mechanism is not working as it was intended to.

Deborah Midanek: Corporations have a good deal more freedom than do governments at this point.

Anne Sheehan: Society gives a corporation a license to operate. So the issue is what other responsibilities and obligations go along with that license to operate as a corporation? We often hear Milton Friedman quoted as saying that the sole purpose of the corporation is to make money for the shareholders.

Deborah Midanek: At the time that was written, in 1970, that was regarded as absolute heresy.

Anne Sheehan: Correct. Now we've come a long way since those years but people still will say to me, "That's really the goal." But if you're making money for shareholders by burning up half the Gulf of Mexico, is that really a sustainable way for a business to reward its shareholders? I do think directors are much more attuned to that and I think shareholders are as well. At CalSTRS we were pretty active about how we voted. One of the things I implemented at CalSTRS was that we put our votes out there publicly when we cast them. We didn't wait for the forms to be filed at the SEC.

Deborah Midanek: That amplified the votes' impact.

Anne Sheehan: Right. We said, "This is our view." Everybody knew how we voted and what was going on. From a governance perspective, we were transparent about both our policies and how we voted. Other funds followed suit. You'll see, it's usually us, Florida, Ontario, and others, including CalPERS now, that post their top 500 holdings.

It's those kinds of steps that we're happy to be open and transparent about, such as what we think about certain directors, what we think about a shareholder proposal, whatever it is. When you ask me about how the purpose of the corporation has changed over time, I do think there is much more focus on their social license to operate. As you know, we did a big engagement with Apple on the impact of phones on children, and children's development, to determine if there are enough mechanisms to make sure children are not being exposed to everything that is out there on the internet? To explore the safety mechanisms and identify how can parents make sure they're tracking what their children are doing.

I think from the company perspective, that is a responsibility for them because they've created this product and the impact of that can be huge on a certain sector of the population, and so it is important to know what they are doing to respond to needs of the parent. It's a business imperative, but it also can be seen as a social imperative to make sure that the handling of that product is correct in the hands of those young children.

Look at Facebook in terms of privacy issues and all of the things they have gone through. I think there is much more of a focus on the social roles that corporations play in society. Now I do think in Silicon Valley, the very nature of the workforce they have there creates interesting tension. At Google, for example, a large share of their shareholder proposals came from their own employees this year.

Deborah Midanek: I thought that was really fascinating.

Anne Sheehan: Yes, that's a very new trend for companies. Will it spread to others? I don't think we know yet, but I think if other companies are smart and are watching what's coming across the horizon and the issues that they hear about from their employees, they'll have to make sure that there's a mechanism to respond. If you're an old line company, you don't want your employees to have to use the proxy to get their point across. I think you're smart to attune yourself to the issues that some of your people are complaining about.

As you know, some of that came up as a result of the #MeToo movement. That's one of those areas where we're not quite sure where it's going to go, but it's worth watching.

Deborah Midanek: The very first corporation granted limited liability by the government that was chartering them was chartered to achieve a joint private public purpose, and that method of chartering continued for over 300 years. The first one of record was the Dutch East India Company. Now it's sort of granted as a commodity without any sort of quid pro quo, but awareness of the fact that governments do in fact *allow* the companies to exist is important to keep in mind.

Anne Sheehan: I have talked to some corporate types who at times forget that. As you say, when you go back to the history of corporate governance, it's important to remind directors of the companies that they can operate because they have a social license to operate and therefore they have obligations as citizens. Now, most good management teams and boards recognize that and it's built into their DNA and how they manage, because it also translates into good business.

I recognize that some pension funds and some of the Socially Responsible Investment (SRI) funds or others are accused of having a political agenda. At the end of the day, our political agenda was paying the benefits of the teachers in the state of California. To make sure that we have sustainable investments that we can rely on to pay those teachers' pensions for the next 50–100 years. Period, the end. That is what the agenda is.

Deborah Midanek: One of the fascinating dilemmas we face is that part of the reason that private equity and hedge funds have grown so significantly over the last few decades is due to the needs of public pension funds in particular, as well as the corporates, to fund their obligations to those pensioners. Many, therefore, have been tempted to go for absolute-return type strategies that are alleged to be uncorrelated with the broad market. I rarely run into people who recognize that whole chain. They think that the hedge funds and the private equity guys sort of exist as a world unto themselves. They really are creatures of our pension fund structure, and to an extent our university and foundation endowments.

If we could address our pension fund shortfalls – that I hope CalSTRS does not experience – and try to figure out a rational solution to that, we might be able to convert the pressures for short-term results into something perhaps more manageable. I know it's not possible, but there are connections there that are often forgotten.

Anne Sheehan: Yes, because the returns that a private equity investment, or venture fund, or some of the old alternative investments can provide over the long term can help us meet our financial obligations. Plus, they also provide for diversification of the portfolio as a risk management tool – to avoid having all your eggs in one basket. In the old days, only fixed income investments were allowed, but if you're getting only two or three percent return, it's very hard to meet the obligations. So if you can get a little more of the equity risk premium from some of these other asset classes, you can provide, over the long run, a better return. You do need very good people who can select the managers that you want to manage that money, or develop, as the Canadians have done, your own skilled expertise in-house to make those investments, but it definitely pays off in the long run. Building the skill set in house can save money by avoiding paying management fees of 2% of the assets and 20% of the upside.

Deborah Midanek: We blew past one question. It's very easy in the post-Milton Friedman world to fall into recent trends of thinking that the directors are directly accountable to the shareholders, and that the goal is to maximize shareholder value. From where I'm sitting, that language is very appealing, but if you actually sit and think about it, it's really hard to figure out what that means in terms of behavior. So, I grew up across the street from Adolf Berle, hearing that the corporation is a person, and that the director's job is to embody that corporation, and protect it as it would a child. In protecting the viability and the sustainability of the corporation, the director is serving the interests of the shareholders by generating sustainable residual income.

That's not a terribly popular view in a world in which shareholder primacy prevails. How on earth do you maximize shareholder value? You need a timeframe, you need a standard, you need a definition of shareholder, but that's a phrase that stops everybody cold.

Anne Sheehan: Well, certainly there is no doubt that the directors have an obligation to the shareholders.

Deborah Midanek: Absolutely.

Anne Sheehan: It's their capital that they have put in to get a return for the investments they've made. For a fund like CalSTRS, we were heavily indexed. Our public equities portfolio was over half of the entire portfolio and two-thirds to three-quarters of that was indexed. So we were in these companies for the long term. We used to tell companies, "As long as there are teachers in the state of California, we're going to be invested in your company. So we have to figure out a way for you to do your job and to make sure that we develop a relationship so that we can help you further. What we need from you is good returns, produced in a way that takes into account the views of the other stakeholders." I think this is where, at the end of the day, it is all about the returns.

I think what has happened is the development of a more nuanced approach regarding how you take into account the other stakeholders as you are seeking that return for your shareholders. The company has employees, it has the community it operates in, and there are other stakeholders that I think directors have an obligation to consider while carrying out their fiduciary obligations. What are we doing? How is it we have earned that return? What can we do better? What can we do more transparently? Yes, it can be a matter of using the capital in the most efficient manner, but it can be tempting to take shortcuts that hurt your long-term performance. Striking that balance is very difficult. As you said before, trying to communicate to your shareholders who want a short-term return and don't want to look over the long run, it's a huge challenge.

Turning a big company in a new direction, where you need to be strategic about the future of your business, or going into new lines or new markets, you've really got to be ahead of those things in terms of what is happening in the marketplace. That's the difficult balance where I think the directors really have to help management see and navigate those challenges. I have always felt the role of the board is to provide strategic oversight; to help to develop a long-term strategy and make sure it is being executed, and then hiring and firing, not just CEO, but the management team you are putting in place to carry out that strategy.

They are there to support management, and also to challenge management and to make sure management is doing the right thing on behalf of all shareholders. That's what they need to remember. They do need to make a return for their shareholders, but so much goes into that equation nowadays, and so much more pressure is on directors and companies to explain and articulate how they are doing their business.

The board owes its fiduciary duty to the shareholders and in some regard to other stakeholders, to employees, to the community. I guess under strict fiduciary law for CalSTRS we owed a fiduciary duty to beneficiaries because you the steward of their money.

Deborah Midanek: For a long time corporate law had it that the directors owed their fiduciary duty to the company, and through that, to its beneficial owners. That their job is to protect the sustainable future of the company and that is the way it gets to the shareholders. That's the strict interpretation that has shifted a bit in the last 50 years.

Anne Sheehan: That's exactly right, and that company is there because of the shareholders, but it goes beyond, as you say, that shareholder primacy role that some people felt. As a shareholder, I did not want to substitute my judgment for that of the directors inside that boardroom – that's not my role. I don't have the information.

We did not end up voting for some of the executive compensation proposals that told the company how to structure their pay. We were happy to vote against their pay, and when they'd come to talk to us, we'd go through the shortcomings we saw, but it wasn't our job to design their pay package, that's their job. That's why we paid them. Now we can give them our input and they get the messages loud and clear, because usually if CalSTRS had an issue, we weren't the only shareholder that had concerns over the structure of the pay, or the metric, or whatever the issue was, but ultimately it's up to the board to interpret that. They are going to get a lot of input from a lot of players, but as I've told them, they are going to see a theme emerge, and then they need to balance what the corporation needs to carry out their responsibilities with the input from shareholders and other stakeholders.

Deborah Midanek: Over the time that you did this, did you see a shift in terms of the people who were talking to you and how they were talking to you? In other words, it's not the CEO and the CFO alone anymore. It's also the independent directors, and there's a direct communication channel.

Anne Sheehan: I do think it is beneficial to have an independent director and I think we're sort of there already, but it is also extremely beneficial to have directors who have industry knowledge. I don't want a board where nobody has any experience in the business line.

Deborah Midanek: Sure, it's a challenge not to have native knowledge of the company or industry.

Anne Sheehan: Putting the board together is like a creating mosaic, finding the pieces that you need to operate most effectively, and then finding those who can organize the group to operate well. It is important to create an environment in which people can be open and honest, and contrarian on some issues. When a consensus is reached, however, everybody needs to able go along with it, as the decision the board ultimately makes is unilateral. That's a lot of governance process issues and underlines the importance of how you operate inside the boardroom. Does everybody have the ability to communicate their views? You don't want a small subsection of the board and the chair or CEO moving the decision along while everybody else is told, "This is what we're going to do." That is a dysfunctional board. Everyone needs to provide input into the process. Now, as a new board member, it takes you a while to get up to speed, but I think you have an obligation to ask questions, to learn, to understand what the process is, to understand what the history is, so that you can figure out what your role is as a director, and how to be the most effective director that you can be.

A lot of people feel that the independent side has gone too far, but I think you can get input from management any time you want, so do you need to put other management folks on the board? I don't think that is necessary. The CEO needs to be there, and perhaps the COO or others, but you can always get the input of those people, and they ultimately work for the CEO, so there may be awkwardness related to that. Certainly, industry or market knowledge is very beneficial. Each person needs to bring something valuable to the table.

Deborah Midanek: So where are you on board leadership?

Anne Sheehan: On board leadership, my preference would be an independent chair, and not a combined chair/CEO. I think fundamentally there is a conflict in the roles. The board is there to oversee management. If the chair of the board is also the manager that you are overseeing, there's an inherent conflict there.

Deborah Midanek: It's a design flaw.

Anne Sheehan: It *IS* a design flaw. I get the idea of the lead director, but at the end of the day, as you say, it's a design flaw. You can empower an independent director, but do they lead, do they run all the board meetings? They're not the chair. It has become an ego thing for these guys, and it is mainly guys, to have both titles.

I think slowly that is changing. Even Warren Buffett said when he goes, they'll separate the positions. Shareholders have said, "We don't expect you to strip that title from say, Jamie Dimon, immediately, but when he ultimately retires, think about separating them." I think separating the roles is gaining in support, and as you may know, when I was at CalSTRS, we had a big to-do with the Bank of America when they recombined the positions for Brian Monaghan.

Our point to them was not only do we like the roles to be separate, but it was your shareholders who voted to separate them. Be respectful enough to ask your shareholders if they will now support combining them. I said, "If you had put it up as a proposal, you would've gotten 80% support." Instead, they spent a year trying to defend this. They had to call a special meeting to take a vote of the shareholders to recombine it, which they did win.

As a result, shareholder money was wasted when they should have asked the shareholders at the beginning. I didn't agree with the result of the vote, but I live and die by shareholder democracy. If the shareholders vote for it, that's good.

It's unheard of that shareholders voted to separate the positions in the first place as they did at BofA. So knowing what an exceptional action that was and then to dismissively take this position that, "Oh, we're going to recombine it because we think it's the right thing to do," is disrespectful. It's insulting. All the guys sitting in that room may have thought it made sense as they carried both titles. They all had the title.

Deborah Midanek: And that is the reason we want more different perspectives in the boardroom. Right.

Anne Sheehan: Right, to a fault. They finally got there, and people said to me that I just did not like Brian Monaghan. I think he's a perfectly fine person, and they were missing the point. This was poor governance process and was not at all about the people involved. I am happy to live by the rules of corporate governance, and if the shareholders vote for it, fine, but give them the courtesy of asking them to vote on the matter as they did before. Don't be so arrogant and presumptuous to presume that you know better than they do what the structure should be.

Deborah Midanek: In addition to the design flaw, to do the job properly, the work of the chair is quite significant. Among other things, the chair needs to understand the dynamics of dealing with the shareholders, the board members, and management, and be sure that those courtesies are observed. It's a big job. I find it difficult to see how, regardless of the obvious inherent conflict, how one person can develop and manage the board and perform the CEO's job at the same time.

Anne Sheehan: In this day and age, the point that you make about working with the shareholders is important. The CEO may have one view in meeting with shareholders, and an independent chair should have a similar view, but could also bring some different perspectives to that discussion.

So if the combination chair/CEO is meeting with the shareholders, they're going to filter what they hear through their own lens. We're all human. But if you have an independent chair meeting with those people, they'll filter it through the position of that independent chair, not the day-to-day CEO manager of the company. It goes to that design flaw issue that you talked about.

You asked about defining success for a board and how it can be evaluated. It's almost like the Supreme Court's definition of pornography: if it goes bad, you'll see it through the results.

You can't always say exactly what is good, but there are many good boards and companies operating under the radar that do a good job, and that get out there and talk to their shareholders. I think the lion's share are doing that. It's these awful ones like Tesla where I don't even know where to start.

Deborah Midanek: A simple way to think about building a board is to say it should be comprised of people who have the experience and the courage to tell the CEO when the CEO is wrong. That's what Tesla needs.

Anne Sheehan: That's exactly right, but they won't get on the board and stay on the board if they do that. But if they manage to get there, it is also important that they can walk away and not need the money they give you for being on the board if you can't live with your conscience about what you're doing on behalf of shareholders.

Deborah Midanek: It is not easy though to be that voice. You do have to be willing to walk away because it's very easy to make yourself an outlier and to get yourself marginalized. If you want to stay, you need to move gently from the center of the group in order to be effective as a director. You need to keep communication lines to all the other directors alive.

Anne Sheehan: Right. You need to help educate them. You don't want to sort of say, "Who could approve this, this is stupid." But instead say something like, "This is how this is going to be seen. This is what we need to think about. Let me tell you why I don't think we should do this. This would be the perception." And bring them along. That's why the different skill sets that people bring to the boardroom are important.

Deborah Midanek: It takes a lot of work to keep that level tone, and be balanced, and work the corridors, and so on. When I was younger, on that Drexel board, for example, I had recruited the independent directors, but they were men that were twice my age. I walked around saying, "Hey! What do you think about this issue? Do you think that was the right way to look about it? Could you look at it this way?" Slowly I managed to get my ideas presented, using their voices.

Anne Sheehan: That is the tactful way to proceed. You don't want to insult them and ask, "How the heck could you make that decision?" But instead use phrases such as, "Tell me what you're thinking," or "Here's another perspective." There is a real art to the way you bring up issues and slowly get them into a safe place to consider or reconsider the decisions they've made. We've all seen people come into boards like a bull in a china shop, and after everybody raises their eyebrows at them, they talk, the group moves along. Since nobody pays attention to them, they're ineffective in that regard. So the matter of how you work within the system to convince people we need to make some changes is very important.

There are so many flaws with some compensation programs. The way the shareholders look at this, the biggest problem is when the share price has been declining and executive compensation continues to rise. Alignment is what shareholders are looking for. They know you need to incentivize these people, but there's got to be some alignment so that the pay is for performance. You don't want to pay for failure, and that's what drives shareholders crazy.

In structuring that, boards are getting better. It used to be easy to tell when compensation committee chairs didn't understand the pay structure, as they'd want to give you the head of HR or their comp consultant, who are not going to do anything but defend the program. I want to talk to a board member I can raise issues with and be sure they understand how the comp structure works.

Deborah Midanek: Right. I find it interesting that we're finally getting to the point where there's recognition that using the same compensation consulting firm that management uses makes no sense. It's the same issue as with the audit committee. A separation is required so that you don't have management telling the consultant what they're supposed to tell the board.

Anne Sheehan: Dodd-Frank requires that the comp committee should have an independent comp consultant advising them.

Deborah Midanek: It's taken a very long time for that to be recognized as necessary. It's why independent directors exist. I see all these studies that conclude that independent directors don't improve the performance of the company at all. To my mind, that was not the question they were there to address. While it would be nice if they could improve corporate performance, the issue is that management cannot monitor and oversee itself. So there needs to be an independent director group that is charged with that monitoring, or the design does not make sense.

Anne Sheehan: Yes, that's exactly right. Moving to your other questions, should shareholders give direction to the board? I think shareholders can provide input to the board, and every shareholder may have a view about compensation issues, or board refreshment, or whatever the issue is. I think it's very important for board members to hear from shareholders not just on analyst calls, but also when they meet with some of the governance proxy voting people. A lot of directors don't understand that some of the folks on the quarterly calls are not the ones that vote the proxy. Some are, some coordinate, so make sure you know who your voting shareholders are. Get out and listen to them, especially if you've had a bad vote, or if you've had a bad year and you're retooling. You've got to get out and communicate with your investors, and it can be done in person and by calls, but it must be done.

Deborah Midanek: Management resistance to that is going down, but management resistance to that has always been the major obstacle, as far as I could see.

Anne Sheehan: You're so right about that. When I was at CalSTRS, I would pick up the phone and call a director, and my friends at the company would be so mad. My view was that talking to them would not give me the unfettered truth that I could get if I called a director. And I wanted the director to hear my views directly.

Deborah Midanek: You bet, and if the director isn't smart enough to be able to make the distinction between the kinds of things that can be discussed with shareholders and the kinds of things that cannot be shared with shareholders because they're too sensitive, or you're discriminating among shareholders, or whatever, the director certainly shouldn't be a director of the company.

Anne Sheehan: No, that's exactly right, if you're not smart enough to figure out that distinction. Now one of your questions that I did want to touch on was the board's role in establishing the tone at the top and the ethical corporate culture. I think that has become an even bigger issue for boards over the #MeToo movement, and some of these other ethical lapses. When I was at CalSTRS I would meet with directors and ask, "Okay, if you had a cancer in your organization, how would you know? What is the board doing? What is the mechanism?" As one of my other responsibilities, I'm on the Wells Fargo Stakeholder Advisory Council, created after their fiasco. From talking with people inside the company, it seems that a lot of folks knew that they had this issue. What remains a mystery is why the noise did not get to the board level.

Was management stifling some of the complaints that were coming in? Were they not looking at exit interviews? Were they not looking at whistleblower reports? Corporate culture is so important because if you have a bad corporate culture, it can completely destroy a good strategy. Doesn't matter if you have a great strategy if your culture's wrong.

Deborah Midanek: As Peter Drucker famously said, culture eats strategy for breakfast.

Anne Sheehan: I think boards need to pay more attention to this and get inside the corporation to get a sense of the culture. Go into branch operations, go talk to people down on the line, don't only do it when you're being escorted by one of the senior people and people are afraid to talk. You need to get a sense of what is going on inside the corporation. It's not easy to do, but the problem is that, if there's a blow up, the board's going to be held responsible. That's what board members have to remember. If it blows up, where was the board? To me, good news or bad news, we're all in this together, so always give me the bad news.

The bad news is more important than the good news. If you're having a big exodus, if you have a problem, if you have a sexual harassment complaint, I don't care what it is, let us know. Tell us what you're doing and how we can help support you in getting through this. So I do think the whole issue of culture and the ethical corporation is becoming much more of an issue. I think shareholders are asking companies what they're doing on these matters.

Deborah Midanek: Is the corporate governance model for stewardship working?

Anne Sheehan: I think many more shareholders and companies are looking at their jobs as stewards, which I think is a good word to use. We used to have a saying at CalSTRS that poor capital allocation is the worst corporate governance offense there is. Capital allocation is key to the success of a company, and overseeing that is so important. If you're not using the capital correctly in terms of your investments, whether it's long-term R&D, whether it's share buyback, you are in for trouble. So any company has to resist the short-term pressures. Everybody watches the

24/7 news cycle and the market goes up, and down. The key is to have a good solid capital allocation plan, and then communicate that to your shareholders. Tell them this is what we're doing to invest in the long term, and this is when we believe it will pay off.

You've got to communicate that. That goes back to the importance of having that relationship with your long-term shareholders. They're going to be with you through thick and thin and you've got to be able to say, "All right, this is going to be a tough quarter, this is what's going on, this is the plan we have to move on from this, and please stick with us."

They'll be patient, but at a certain point, you've got to deliver on those promises, or they will go. So it is a *trust but verify* kind of thing.

Deborah Midanek: You're leaving me feeling very optimistic about the future of corporate governance, which is wonderful.

Anne Sheehan: I mean at heart I'm an optimist on governance. There are always exceptions. For example, some of Silicon Valley companies have some of the worst governance, with their two classes of shares that say, "thanks for your capital but you only get limited input into the process."

Shareholders have demonstrated that they don't like that and they want it sunsetted. If you feel that as you emerge from being a private company, you need to have training wheels for a little while, go ahead, but at a certain point take off the training wheels. You're now a grown-up company operating in a capital system and you need to survive on your own. Google does not need the control that they have. If they perform as they have and do well, their shareholders are going to support them. They don't need the belts and suspenders of the dual class structure.

Deborah Midanek: It's fascinating. I can't believe that I can still talk about this stuff with such excitement and engagement when I've been talking about it now for a long time.

Anne Sheehan: I love it; it's fascinating to me. There is a lot of process required, and putting the systems in place to be able to respond to what comes at you. People ask, "What is corporate governance?" My response is that it is about setting up processes and procedures so that you can function through thick or thin and you know the rules of the road, and do not have to make them up as you go along.

Deborah Midanek: What we do is organize the process of making decisions as well as we can to give us a really solid foundation. That then frees us to respond to what happens around us.

Anne Sheehan: People want to make it complicated, but these are the rules of engagement and the procedures that we need to follow. That process and procedure can be your friend when you get into trouble.

Deborah Midanek: As the saying goes, process is what saves you when all else fails.

Anne Sheehan: This is what we do. So yes, I am an optimist. The pendulum can swing, and I think a lot of people felt the pendulum had swung too far to the shareholder primacy model. What we need is to balance what the board and the company need to carry out their mission, while reminding them that they have stakeholders who have a vested interest, especially the shareholders, in what they're doing. So how do you balance that? You need to communicate and get input and build the dialogue. It's not just a one-way communication, it's a two-way process that goes back and forth.

Deborah Midanek: I love that part, the way the investor relations function developed in the 1950s. GE started their own because they didn't know how to deal with the likes of Evelyn Y. Davis, who owned tiny amounts of shares but made it her business to question and sometimes chastise management at annual meetings.

Anne Sheehan: Oh, yes, everybody has a story about Evelyn.

Deborah Midanek: Eventually they figured we may not be able to trust shareholder communication to PR firms because they might break the securities' industry rules and so on, so we better do this in house. At that time, the board was regarded as an adjunct advisor to management, so connecting shareholder communication to the board seems not to have been considered, which was another design flaw. It's been an uphill battle to try to make the concerns of shareholders audible to the directors, and then to establish the ability for the directors to communicate with the shareholders.

Anne Sheehan: For a long time, Exxon would not let their directors talk to shareholders. Finally, that has changed, and those days are over. So progress has been made and I continue to be optimistic about more to come. The whole issue of the political pressure placed on the companies now, is it fair? My guess is that will ebb and flow.

They need to be aware, they need to be briefed, they need to be articulate in explaining what's going on. That's just sort of the way of the world these days because there are no secrets with the 24/7 news cycle and social media, anything can go viral immediately. That's another challenge I think board members have these days. They've got to be aware of what's trending out there.

Deborah Midanek: Thank you so much.

Chapter 8
Respect for the individual opinions of each and every one

Paula Stern

Paula Stern founded The Stern Group in 1988 and leads its practice, serving national and multi-national companies and organizations on business, political, and technology policy issues that affect their competitiveness in a global economy.

She is a former chairwoman of the United States International Trade Commission. In that role, Dr. Stern analyzed and voted on over 1,000 trade cases involving a broad range of industries and issues. At the time, she was the second-highest ranking woman in the executive branch of the U.S. Government.

Among many other roles, she served as a member of the U.S. Department of Commerce's Advisory Committee on Renewable Energy and Energy Efficiency, the Executive Committee of the Atlantic Council, The Conference Board, the Council on Foreign Relations, the Inter-American Dialogue, the Advisory Council of the Wilson Center's Women in Public Service Project (WPSP), and a legacy trustee at the Committee for Economic Development (CED) of the Conference Board. Other public service includes membership on the congressionally mandated National Academy of Sciences' Panel on the Future Design and Implementation of U.S. National Security Export Controls, the U.S. Congress' Office of Technology Assessment's Advisory Panel on Technology, Innovation, and U.S. Trade, and the U.S. State Department's Advisory Committee on International Economic Policy.

Dr. Stern is a former corporate board member of CBS, Infinity, Duracell, Harcourt General, Hasbro, Scott Paper, Walmart, Westinghouse, Avaya, SSMC, Neiman Marcus, Diversified Search, and Avon. She also serves as Senior Advisor to the National Center for Women & Information Technology (NCWIT).

She began her Washington career in the 1970s as Legislative Assistant and Senior Legislative Assistant to U.S. Senator Gaylord Nelson, and also was a guest scholar at the Brookings Institution, where she wrote a definitive book on Congressional-Executive foreign policy making, titled *Water's Edge: Domestic Politics and the Making*

https://doi.org/10.1515/9783110670004-009

of American Foreign Policy. She was also Senior International Affairs Fellow at the Council on Foreign Relations, Senior Associate at the Carnegie Endowment for International Peace, Senior Fellow at the Progressive Policy Institute, and a member of The Trilateral Commission. Dr. Stern also held the Alkire Chair in International Business at Hamline University, St. Paul, Minnesota.

Dr. Stern's writings and commentary on foreign policy, trade, competitiveness, workforce, tech, and women's issues have been widely published in scholarly and popular journals as well as *The New York Times*, *The Wall Street Journal*, *USA Today*, *The LA Times*, *The Chicago Tribune*, and other mainstream media. She is a contributing columnist for *The Hill*. She was named one of the top women influencing the American economy by *Ms.* magazine, and honored by The National Women's Economic Alliance Foundation with its Directors' Choice Award for Leadership. She is a frequent public speaker and media commentator in the U.S. and abroad.

Dr. Stern has a BA from Goucher College, an MA in Regional Studies from Harvard University, a PhD in International Affairs from Tufts University's Fletcher School of Law and Diplomacy, and honorary degrees in Law from Goucher College and Commercial Science from Babson College. She is a recipient of the Alicia Patterson Journalism Award and the Joseph Papp Award for Racial Harmony from the Foundation for Ethnic Understanding.

Deborah Midanek: I am delighted that we have a chance to speak, as throughout your career you have made a major contribution to creating the glue that will keep this world together. It is no accident that many of the people that I've spoken to in the course of this second book are not attached to an institution at the moment. Most of them are fairly free to speak and say what they want. We are blessed with a group of thoughtful people who speak plainly, as I know you will.

Paula Stern: I'm overwhelmed by your ability to write so beautifully and clearly. I was quoting from your last book at dinner tables all weekend. I learned a great deal from reading your account of the history of the Dutch East India Company. It's wonderful what you've done. I just hope I can give you something that you can work with.

Deborah Midanek: Of course you will. And the breadth of opinion is what's so interesting. We need to have the points of view of all the different parties that are part of this great stew that's brewing that we hope will turn into something really, really strong and powerful. We may as well be optimistic because the alternative isn't very exciting.

Paula Stern: Amen.

Deborah Midanek: How did you get interested in governance? Tell us about you, Paula. How did *you* happen?

Paula Stern: I suppose my interest in governance derived from my interest in government and values. How did I "happen"? According to my college political philosophy professor, I always said I wanted to work in government in a top government position. I grew up in Memphis, Tennessee, where both my mother and father were active civic leaders. While I was attending the segregated public schools, my big brother Gerald, eight years ahead of me, was a young lawyer in the Civil Rights Division of the U.S. Department of Justice assigned to bring court challenges of Jim Crow laws and practices which disenfranchised Southern black voters before the U.S. Civil Rights Act was passed.

He did a lot of dangerous things trying to register folks to vote who were labelled "Negroes" in those days, in 1963. He was assigned to live with James Meredith when they integrated Ole Miss. I was in high school at that time and looked up to his shining example. The idea of the civil rights initiatives that my brother was involved in excited me. In my eyes, being a government servant was a really big deal. That's what my ambitions were.

After grad school, my first assignment on Capitol Hill was working as a legislative assistant to U.S. Senator Gaylord Nelson (D-Wisc.), who served on the Finance Committee where the trade laws were basically shaped and made. I did anything that had the word "foreign" in it. That included policies related to trade negotiations, the Export-Import Bank, the U.S. International Trade Commission (ITC), the Treasury Department, and the Departments of Defense, State, and Veterans Affairs.

Eventually, I was appointed Trade Commissioner and Chairwoman of the U.S. International Trade Commission. I had the most wonderful experience at the ITC, which, in effect, acts as a court to deal with companies, industries, or unions representing an industry when they petition the government asking for import relief, for protection from foreign competition. Then we needed to determine under the law and in view of the various economic considerations, whether the petitioning industry was actually injured. Finally, we needed to examine whether the causes of the injury were imports or whether it was management, cost of labor, cost of transportation, or other competitive forces within the domestic marketplace that was creating the injury.

There were three or four different statutes that laid out my responsibilities for examining these industries. The microeconomic assessments were fascinating. My family came from retail. My parents started a furniture store in Memphis next to my grandfather's dry goods store, and I loved commerce as much as government. I loved being able to focus on the dynamics of an industry and the performance of individual corporations within it. After having served in the government for 16 years, and having had a spell as a journalist, and gotten my PhD and published a book – *Water's Edge: Domestic Politics and the Making of American Foreign Policy* – during that time, I was juggling different possibilities when I left the Commission.

I became a Fellow at a think tank and a consultant/public speaker. I was very lucky also to meet a woman along the way who had been serving on corporate boards. We were fellow members of the United Nations Association of the USA where we participated in exchanges with our quote "counterparts" in the USSR. This marvelous businesswoman, Claudine Malone, said, "I'd like to suggest your name for a board that I'm sitting on." She said there had been a second woman on this board, which was extraordinary in those days. Scott Paper was seeking to fill the board vacancy left by the death of her colleague, a prominent DC-based African-American attorney. Evidently, it was believed that I, as someone who had headed a government agency, could sit with CEOs and be effective.

When I left the Commission, I was soon appointed to the Scott board. From there, a law firm advising a company spun off from the Singer Sewing Machine Company approached me to join the board of what was known as SSMC. In those days, headhunters exerted little effort when it came to trying to diversify the board with various points of view. Instead, they would say, "Let's see who the women are on the bigger boards and go from there." Over the years I have been lucky enough to serve on about 14 different public boards, all U.S.-headquartered. I've also sat on an international advisory board of an overseas multinational.

Deborah Midanek: What did you find interesting about that service? Serving on such a large number has given you a lot of opportunity to compare and contrast.

Paula Stern: Feeling confident requires having some experience. I got more assertive over the years, but there were times even with Scott Paper, early in my experience on boards, where I did assert myself very strongly.

There are so many lessons to be learned. I guess one of the overarching lessons was that there are tendencies within the board to form subgroups. I don't think people have written much about that, whereas there's a lot of attention paid to the CEO vis à vis the board. In fact, within the board there are often elite groups among the board members – those who serve on either the executive committee or a special committee, for example. You often see, in my words, "second class" board members who hear about a decision last. If some directors are excluded from segments of the governance process, this is clearly a fiduciary issue.

Deborah Midanek: What were the attributes that you felt made boards most successful at using the strengths of the full board? What made that possible?

Paula Stern: I really do think it's a personality thing with the CEO. If that person really does want to be taking full advantage of all the individuals on the board, it is a matter of respect for the individual opinions of each and every one. I think that's almost a personality trait.

Deborah Midanek: I can understand why boards were for a long time, and still are to a great extent, "male, pale, and stale." It is easiest to evaluate and therefore trust people similar to yourself. I have some sympathy for that because the last thing the CEO wants to do is have boat-rocking by his or her board. On the other hand, nature's risk management system is called diversity. We need to get diversity of thought and opinion; experience, gender, ethnicity, and everything else, heard in the boardroom. But if we're going to do that how do we build that thing that you just mentioned – which is respect, the precursor for trust? Trust being the most important ingredient that makes a good board work. But in order to get there, first you have to respect everybody's opinions. Which is not easy to do in the kabuki dance of the boardroom.

Paula Stern: There are chairmen and then there are Chairmen. The ones who are great listeners make sure that there's not a second class. At Avon, I had a wonderful experience with a superb "outside" chairman, Douglas Conant, who had served as President and CEO at Campbell Soup. He was terrific in making sure that he found out every board member's point of view and represented it, even if the board member was not in the room when he conveyed the "board's views" to the CEO. He really trained himself to listen.

Deborah Midanek: Betsy Atkins did a YouTube video a couple of years ago on how to run an executive session. She had a very efficient approach. Hold the executive session after every board meeting, or before, if you can. Make sure that it's a standard practice so that nobody puts any special weight on the existence of the executive session and sees it as a normal-course event. The leader, whether the chairman, the lead director, or someone else, should go around the room and ask each individual, "What did you like about this meeting? What got your attention? What are you really worried about?"

Paula Stern: And "What didn't get said"?

Deborah Midanek: Right. What do you want to see in the future? What needs to be discussed? She said that's where, if you haven't gotten everybody's voice in the board meeting, you make double-dog sure that you get it in the executive session. Then you write up the notes quickly. Anonymize them and take them straight back to the CEO.

Paula Stern: Doug also really made it a point to schedule phone calls with each board member so that he could take a reading in advance. There was a time when we were hesitant to put down in writing some of our evaluations because the company was caught up in litigation triggered initially by the Foreign Corrupt Practices Act. As a consequence, the only ways we could be really frank was at the start and/ or end of each of the in-person board meetings in executive sessions and via individual phone calls.

Deborah Midanek: I think the point that we're making here is that the work of leading the board is a very different kind of work than the work of leading the company.

Paula Stern: Oh yes. Absolutely.

Deborah Midanek: We don't need to go all the way to the hard-and-fast rule to say the chairman and CEO must be separate. But we do have to say there has to be someone who's charged with making the board perform properly. Did you find, in that circumstance, that the board worked well because of that man's extraordinary efforts?

Paula Stern: Yes, oh yes. Though the company got a lot of bad breaks and poor legal advice, the board relationship was strong. The members really, really worked well together.

Deborah Midanek: Interestingly, I find that developing those strong bonds of trust required to work well is often associated with having no choice but to surmount challenges. Board members get the opportunity to get to know each other and to feel that their work is meaningful.

Paula Stern: You're absolutely right. If we want to get to the Al Dunlap thing, I'll tell you about that. That was before the internet, before emails, and it was all about phone calls. I feel like I really stepped in something there. Can I give you my little story? It's a cautionary tale about placing autocrats in the CEO's seat.

Deborah Midanek: Please.

Paula Stern: Scott had a special committee that was responsible for searching for a new CEO. And the night before a regularly scheduled board meeting the search committee arranged a gathering to introduce the person they had selected to the entire board, presumably to assure support from the board to approve his appointment the next day.

We had dinner and a cocktail hour beforehand, and I was introduced to Al Dunlap. They had sent me a bio in advance, and that is all I knew. In those days, I couldn't Google him, but now you can find him by typing: "Chainsaw Al." Based on the bio, I called a person whom I knew had worked with him at a previous company. He must have said something that put me on alert. I spoke briefly with Dunlap at the cocktail hour, and probably mentioned our mutual acquaintance. I don't know what else we talked about, but there was something wrong, something off with this guy.

When we got back into the van to go to the motel where most of the out-of-town board members were staying overnight, I asked the chairman of the search committee who was highly recommending Dunlap, "When you do these reviews (of your recommended candidate), do you also do a medical exam?"

Deborah Midanek: A psychological assessment.

Paula Stern: I didn't want to say mental or psychological. The search committee chairman said, "Well, what do you mean?" I said, "A medical exam, in which mental and physical health are evaluated. You want this man to become our CEO and I have a bad feeling about him. Do you have some analysis of his behavior?" Of course, they think I'm ridiculous and he gets voted in.

The next thing we hear by phone is that he has asked one of the board members to leave the board in a nasty way. Dunlap had already told another board member who was flying over from the Netherlands that, "We're not going to facilitate your flights anymore so you're going to have to leave." That was a fait accompli, but I called the first guy and said, "You can't go off the board like that."

Deborah Midanek: Well, the CEO generally doesn't have that power. He has power of personality but he doesn't have the law.

Paula Stern: He didn't have the law. But after his nasty encounter with Dunlap this particular board member still wanted to leave. While I have no idea if this was the case or not, I had the feeling that Al Dunlap was threatening somehow to blackmail this board member if he didn't leave.

I said to this board member, since "we're going to have another board meeting in a month or so, why not wait, resist Dunlap's ultimatum, tender your resignation to the full board, and let the board, not Dunlap, formally accept your resignation?" The next month before the formal board meeting, we had an executive committee pre-meeting to orchestrate the acceptance of the board member's resignation.

Next thing I know Dunlap told Claudine Malone, me, and a third board member – who was then on a ship in the middle of the ocean and couldn't communicate by phone – that we had to go. What do you do? Legally, we had a fiduciary duty. And an ethical duty. What is good governance? You can't go to the press. You can't go to anybody for fear you're going to tank the stock or you're going to do something that will hurt the company. Long story short, those who Al suspected might question his authority were all tossed off that board. And that was a public company.

Deborah Midanek: That was probably a mercy for you. It would have been very difficult to hang in there and fight with Al over all the crazy stuff he did to that company.

Paula Stern: Exactly. And then he went on to Sunbeam, and that's where they finally caught him. He never did go to prison but died before they jailed him. So, we were talking about communication, and making sure that every one's voice is heard or risk having second class board members like myself. But I did assert myself.

There have been other times when simply by asking questions, by probing, you can plant a seed, whether your view prevails on a particular issue or not. That was how I felt when I sat on the board of one of world's largest retailers – Walmart. I remember asking in a formal board meeting, "Have we ever done a study that tries to tally up what the costs are to the corporation from the turnover of our employees?" I never did get that study done, but I persisted in raising the question. I feel like there were some back benchers – some of the senior management who sat in on these board meetings, including at least one who ultimately became CEO after I was gone – and they did learn, I think, the value of training personnel and investing in a longer term relationship rather than treating employees as disposable. I also asked about exploring greener designs for our "box" to reduce energy costs.

Deborah Midanek: Well, you get people thinking. Having served these various boards, do you have a clear sense of what you believe the role of the board actually is?

Paula Stern: I do think it is to be the eyes, ears, and antennae that one person, the CEO, just cannot do alone. Many corporations have such huge impacts and are properly concerned about their brand and marketing, but management can't see or know everything. So we try to have a diverse enough board that some people are tuned in to reputational risk, branding, the law, compliance, and how will the company look at all the different regulatory agencies. Another person may have a comparative advantage in considering mergers and acquisitions and the strategy of the corporation with regard to whether you grow internally or externally. So you use your different experiences. Apart from the professional experience and work that they've come from, they also have to have a certain level of character and a certain value system that the CEO respects and may need to be reminded of every once in a while, while he or she is busy thinking about the P&L.

Deborah Midanek: Do you have any opinions about the discussion of short term versus long term and the way that the shareholder has become dominant?

Paula Stern: Well, I think the irony of the large pension funds is that their governance has to deal with their beneficiaries, whether they are teachers or unions or whatever. This may have helped them be more responsive to questions about long-term performance and not just short-term shifting based on the latest quarterly results. They have to balance the long and the short terms far more than they had been doing.

I don't know if this is a natural pendulum swing where we're just coming into some sort of an equilibrium. But it is ironic that this narrowing of the number of big owners on the stock exchange makes them have to be responsive to the people who have put their money in these pensions.

Years ago when I wrote the first articles on the women's liberation movement in 1968 for the *New Republic* and the *Atlantic* I was invited to give a speech to an audience in Manhattan sponsored by a large conglomerate. I spoke about women, of course, but also about the whole question of to whom is a corporation supposed to be most responsive? Responsibilities to shareholders, the community, the employees, and so on were in greater balance in those days. This was followed by a period where corporate focus was increasingly on the shareholder, and other constituencies were unimportant. As we refocus on the corporation and its community, I do think that, while this may be a pendulum swing, we don't want to swing back again.

Deborah Midanek: Your experience gives you some perspective on the tone at the top, and nurturing an ethical corporate culture. How does the board make that happen? That was likely not something that featured heavily in Al Dunlap's mind.

Paula Stern: I agree with you. I wasn't suggesting that Al Dunlap at the time was immoral; I just thought he was crazy, and thus the wrong person to be CEO of the company. But the majority of the board supported his selection. If "Chainsaw" Al were at the helm of a corporation today, the whistleblower legislation, the internet, and social media may have driven us toward more transparency, which may link to greater sophistication and fewer secrets regarding what's going on behind the boardroom doors. I do think there is greater concern about longer term values and not just the short term P&L on a quarterly basis.

Some of these ethical concerns, I fear, may dissipate once we're no longer in a full employment economy. In the current environment, boards and CEOs don't want to upset their employees, particularly in the information tech area. There's such a demand, particularly for technically skilled talent, that they are concerned about satisfying some of the employees' concerns. Google and Facebook employees themselves are bringing forward their issues at their employers' annual meeting and other public fora. That is not a favorable sign about their belief in their ability to be heard by their bosses. Until now, such actions by employees were almost un-heard of. Tolerance for that, and for addressing their concerns about climate change and other issues requiring long-term thinking may go away when full em-ployment recedes and top management may not need these folks as badly.

Deborah Midanek: Let's hope that some of it gets baked into the cake long enough to become part of the fabric of the boardroom.

Paula Stern: That's the question, is it baked in the cake or is it a pendulum swing?

Deborah Midanek: I don't know what we're transitioning to, but it does feel as if the rapid-fire changes in technology and communication and the horizontal world that we live in now are scary, and incredibly positive and powerful at the same time. That's our challenge, to take advantage of these communication devices in a way that is very positive and builds the future.

Many boards are islands unto themselves in that there are so many rituals about the way the meetings happen, the information goes out, the process goes on, and the ritualized kabuki dance is led. I love it when boards start using technology to communicate and to clear the consent agenda to allow more time for real discus-sion and conversation at the face-to-face meeting. That is very possible in today's world, yet many companies lag behind the curve on that.

Paula Stern: You raised something about the rituals, and you were talking about the good practices of having executive sessions either before or after the meetings just so that everybody's voice is heard with regard to the agenda being totally com-plete instead of something that was put together by the corporate secretary. But there's also, as you say, the need for time and space for the strategy discussion. You have to start at the beginning to define your strategy and address the strategy every time the board convenes. It just can't be something we do once a year or that one committee does. Everything the board does has to fit within the strategy. How you choreograph that may be different in different boards. I need to say that because I was never satisfied by the degree of board focus on strategy. The strategy needs to be the North Star, in that every decision needs to be supportive of, and consistent with, the strategy. Yet, strategy needs to be both set in place, but subject to circumstantial revision.

Deborah Midanek: Much of the material the board is looking at addresses the last quarter, the last 12 months. It may look at projections and so on, but the board is essentially in reactive mode examining things that have already happened.

Paula Stern: Exactly. A lot of it is dictated by compliance thinking.

Deborah Midanek: How do you take that mindset, and say, "Okay guys, now we're all going to think freely and creatively about the future." Especially when a great many people in the room are independent directors and therefore have no native knowledge of the company and limited knowledge of each other. I'm not saying that this is impossible by any means. I'm saying that the fact that those two things are true needs to be reflected in the way the board thinks about strategy.

Paula Stern: I completely agree. You reflect and articulate my thinking so well.

Deborah Midanek: How we can make governance better? What do you think the critical things are that we need to do to keep on improving?

Paula Stern: You talked about tone at the top. It matters so much if the CEO wants an effective board and is open to having it happen. How confident and courageous is the CEO, and how willing to hear from other voices? We haven't even talked about the issue of compensation. But I think rampant overcompensation is outrageous. The large gap between what the average employee gets and what the CEO gets is a real problem.

What are they thinking? It seems unethical. Having a huge compensation package isolates the CEO. On a day-to-day basis you become isolated from your customer, because you are in such a different stratosphere that you lose perspective.

Deborah Midanek: Inevitably you begin to think that you have a whole different entitlement in this world because you've earned it.

Paula Stern: Yes. And you haven't. I see this self-isolation of the entitled, outrageously over-compensated CEO as almost a dumbing down. They can't think about longer-term issues because they know that they're only going to be around in the short term. They're going to take care of themselves in the short term. There's some sort of a relationship there, between their longevity and their compensation and how that then works into thinking long term versus short term.

Deborah Midanek: One possibility is not just to use equity linked compensation, but to restrict the recipient's ability to sell it until five years after they have left the company.

Paula Stern: That could have an important impact; it could help make the difference between a revolution and the necessary evolution. By definition of sitting in a boardroom, you're committed to an evolution. Because if you're pushing for a revolution, it's really hard to do that from inside the board.

Deborah Midanek: Thank you very much for these interesting remarks, Paula.

Chapter 9
Driven to develop a framework about how the world works

Jane Diplock, AO

Jane Diplock, AO serves now as a professional international company director. She has chaired and been a member of many boards and committees in the public, private, and not-for-profit sectors and has been involved in standard setting at global and national levels.

Among her many contributions is her service as a founding member of the International Integrated Reporting Council, a global coalition of parties united in pursuit of adoption of integrated reporting on an international basis as a means to improve communication about value creation, advance the evolution of corporate reporting, and make a lasting contribution to financial stability and sustainable development.

She is currently Chair of the Regulatory Committee of the Abu Dhabi Global Market, a director of the Singapore Exchange, a director of Australian Financial Services Group, a member of the Public Interest Oversight Board, a member of the International Advisory Committee to the China Securities Regulatory Commission, and a member of the International Advisory Board to the Securities and Exchange Board of India.

Previously she was Chair of the Executive Committee of International Organization of Securities Commissions (IOSCO) for seven years and Chair of the New Zealand Securities Commission for nine years, following an executive career in banking and public service. She was awarded the honor of Officer of the Order of Australia in 2003.

Deborah Midanek: Jane, tell us a bit about your background and what drives you.

Jane Diplock: I started my professional career as a lawyer, having studied Law at Sydney University. Then, while I was a junior lawyer at the Deputy Crown Solicitor's Office in Canberra, I completed studies in International Law, International Economics, and International Relations at the Australian National University. I had previously received a Bachelor of Arts (Honors) and a diploma in education. Later I was a

https://doi.org/10.1515/9783110670004-010

Chevening Fellow at the London School of Economics. So I had a fairly eclectic academic career, you might say. At one stage, my father asked me if there were a university faculty I hadn't tried.

Deborah Midanek: Wonderful perspective.

Jane Diplock: Curiously, one of the first jobs that I had was to prosecute companies who failed to produce their company returns. So my interest in corporate law and corporations started right from the beginning of my professional career. But after that, I came back to Sydney, my home base, and began a job in government, in policy. I became head of the Cabinet Office of the New South Wales Government. I negotiated a contract for a new casino in Sydney, and Westpac, the bank, was on the other side of the table. They asked me, after those negotiations, to join their merchant banking team.

I said to them, "I have what you would call a rapidly amortizing asset. Everyone in government will answer my phone call today, but in 18 months, no one will. So teach me about financial structuring," which was one of the elements that I felt I lacked in my quiver of capacity arrows. They sent me to the New York School of Investment Banking and I ended up being a director of their merchant banking company.

Following about four years doing merchant banking transactions for them, the New South Wales Government asked me to return to head up a government department, which I did for the next four or five years before deciding that I wanted to do some work in the federal government.

At that stage, a friend of mine was chairman of ASIC, the Australian Securities and Investments Commission, trying to pull together all of the state Corporate Affairs Commissions around Australia. He asked me to come in, and help him and I was named Regional Commissioner for New South Wales. I'd only just got into that job when I was headhunted to be the Chairman of the New Zealand Securities Commission. I said to the headhunter, "I know nothing about regulation really." He said, "You'll be perfect." So I went to New Zealand to head up that Commission. It was great experience and soon after that I was elected Chair of the Executive Committee, the governing board of the International Organization of Securities Commissions (IOSCO). A role I undertook at the same time as Chair of the New Zealand Commission for seven years.

On the governance side of things, I had actually been on boards since my time as a young lawyer, when I was appointed to the Snowy Mountains Engineering Corporation board, the engineering company owned by the Commonwealth Government that had built the Snowy Mountains hydro electric scheme.

Throughout my whole career, I have been on not-for-profit boards, private company boards, or boards within government, in parallel to my executive career. So really, my whole career has had a governance theme right from the early days. I've been a director at the Australian Financial Services Group for perhaps 23 years.

I chaired the YWCA in Sydney, the Women's College Council at the University of Sydney, was on the board of the National Heart Foundation. I've been involved in this space for as long as I can remember. The boards that I'm now on, which are really global boards in one way or the other, feel like a natural progression from this history of being involved in governance, really, since probably my late 20s.

Deborah Midanek: So you've seen not only a wide variety of organizations and participated in their governance, but you've also seen governance at many levels: country, region, and global. Also, in crisis, with the IOSCO experience.

Jane Diplock: Absolutely.

Deborah Midanek: You didn't stick, for example, with merchant banking. You've continued in the oversight, and policy role, shaping organizations. So what would you say it is that drives you?

Jane Diplock: I think it's the intellectual fascination; the complexity that requires a framework of thinking that is broad and requires a combination of skills. It also uses my interest in the human, social, and environmental, as well as the financial capital. I am endlessly intrigued by the questions of how these elements fit together in the world. So at every level, the challenges are not dissimilar, but changing in scope and scale. The policy area in particular I think is a totally fascinating one, because it intersects with geopolitical forces and the way in which the global economy works, and that's the area that I'm finding most stimulating, and always have.

What's really driven me is to develop a conceptual framework about how things work, and how the world works. That's the thing that fascinated me when I went to my first law lecture, because it was explaining the interactions that actually make commerce and human interactions work around the world. It gives you a framework of thinking.

Deborah Midanek: With that perspective, we get to the question of this book: What in your view is the purpose of the modern public corporation? It was easy enough to see it in 1602, but what is the purpose today? Has it changed?

Jane Diplock: I think it definitely has changed. Whether it's changed or whether the perspective on it has changed is a moot point. From the early development of the corporation, perspectives on how it should be run, who should control it, and who should own it have changed over time, because the society around it has changed. The behaviors of the Dutch East India Company would not be tolerated today.

So the changes that have occurred in the global transformations over time have been reflected in the nature of the corporation, and understandings about what the corporation can and should do in society. I believe the law is lagging in some jurisdictions about this because short of the Industrial Revolution, I don't believe any time in modern history has seen such a transformation as we're seeing today with the intersection of the technological revolution and the climate change revolution.

As they come together, we are seeing the role of the corporation challenged. That challenge is being reflected in different regulatory frameworks around the world, in a lag effect I would argue. Some jurisdictions are far behind and some jurisdictions are trying to catch up with the reality of the role of the corporation today.

Deborah Midanek: Do you dare venture into discussion of which jurisdictions seem to be moving in the right direction? Which frameworks have adjusted and which are lagging?

Jane Diplock: Let's start with the concept of the corporation itself. I think that Adam Smith, and the 19th and early 20th century philosophers who talked about the corporation, had a very limited view. They considered that the current shareholders of the corporation as owners were the only important stakeholders and no other stakeholders had any real interest in the corporation. Any obligations of participants in the corporation were purely for their benefit.

As these two revolutions have been developing, the climate change revolution and the technological revolution, these ideas have changed as have corporate balance sheets. In 1975, about 85% of a company's assets were in its tangible assets. Auditors went around and measured containers, and counted boxes, and looked at and counted shelves of inventory. They could tell you what the value of the company was by its tangible assets. Sometimes 10%, sometimes 15%, were in the amorphous goodwill, intellectual property categories.

Move forward to 2005, and 85%, of the value of a company lies in those intangible assets, and perhaps 15% are in the tangible assets – if that. Let's put that down partly to the technological revolution. I also think it's got something to do with the climate change revolution, but we'll get to that. Investors are now saying, "I want to know about the majority of the value of the company. I'm not so interested in the tangible assets, useful though they are." So when you look at IFRS (Integrated Financial Reporting Standards), or when you look at FASB (Financial Accounting Standards Board), the actual calculations for the intangibles are difficult, not easily understood, and quite complex. Those who are currently engaged in setting international standards for non-financial (or pre-financial metrics) are a number of bodies, GRI, SASB, The Capital Coalitions, among others. As yet there is no globally agreed to set of standards.

So, that's one issue that is important. But if you're looking at the value of the corporation itself, you now have to look at the complexity of supply lines, the complexity of distribution lines, the size of corporations, and the size of the employee framework that's within them, as well as the nature of the interaction between the corporation and its physical environment – the environment, meaning pollution, meaning issues of waste, and so on. The questions of their valuation are interlinked with the company's response to climate change issues. All of these issues mean that the corporation, as it always has been, but whether recognized or not, is embedded in its community and in society, in a very obvious way.

How these issues now affect the valuation of the company has been well publicized. Ask BP about oil leaks, ask Volkswagen about pollution restrictions in its car manufacture, and see what happened to their share prices as a result of those issues. This means that the community and the corporation are now in lockstep and unable to be disentwined one from the other in relation to the valuation for that company.

My view is that the directors of the company have an obligation to the company to maintain the sustainable viability of that company over time. The current shareholders have a right to a reasonable dividend out of the profits that are able to be made in an efficient and effective way by the work of the directors and the company itself for the period of time they own the shares.

The directors also have an obligation to the future shareholders, an obligation to the people who assist them in producing this profit, and to the community in which the activity is based. All these obligations lead to the requirement to protect the viable productivity of the company and its sustainability in the short, medium, and long term. That's what integrated thinking asks the directors to do, "Think about your business model, and how it is sustainable over the short, medium, and long term, and tell your shareholders and other stakeholders how you're going about that." The goal is to avoid the company facing a Kodak moment and instead to actually survive and thrive, assisting the community and the society it works within.

Deborah Midanek: You touched on the ownership of the corporation. In the US, the idea seems still to be entrenched that the shareholders own the company and that the duty of the directors is to serve as the fiduciary for the shareholders. To me, the directors are fiduciaries for the company and need to care for it as they would a child, a person.

Jane Diplock: That's right. The Stewardship Code of the UK makes this very clear. The word stewardship is, I think, very useful. Directors are stewards of the company for the time of their directorship. Your objective, as the director, should be to ensure that the company is sustainable.

Deborah Midanek: Yes, indeed. So now, where do independent directors fit into this? Because you can argue that management cannot supervise itself, as a construct of the law. But you can also argue that independent directors have a difficulty being effective, because they have no native knowledge of the company and they often do not have much knowledge of each other. So their ability to function as a group, may be less than desirable. What is your thought about independent directors?

Jane Diplock: To my mind, that is too pessimistic a view. In my experience, the executive director or CEO is perhaps the most motivated by short-term-ism, because their remuneration is almost always linked to a short timeframe. They are usually remunerated contractually on an annual basis. There may be relatively longer term vesting of stocks, say over a three or four year period, but that is still relatively short term in the life of the corporation. Independent directors, have a duty to take a truly independent view. They also have a duty to learn about the company's operations and processes, to fully understand the business. I think there is always a learning curve about a company, when newly appointed as an independent director, and it's important that an independent director take that very seriously and actually gain sufficient information and knowledge to be able to make a sensible contribution. There's no doubt about that.

Independent directors should be seeing their situation as an opportunity to contribute to the company. I think it's nonsense to think that many directors are so highly motivated by their directors' fees that they would throw their ethics out the window and continue to just play along with management.

I think it's rather arrogant to suggest that highly intelligent people, who've been performing complex executive roles, cannot then apply themselves to a slightly different industry and be able to actively participate. Certainly, around the board tables that I'm sitting on, I see people making significant contributions, technically, strategically, and in a policy sense, without necessarily having been the CEO of a company in the same industry.

Deborah Midanek: I am a strong proponent of the value of independent directors. It's easy to look at Enron, however – with all of those really strong, well qualified directors who really didn't have a clue as to what was going on – or Parmalat, and point to director failure.

Jane Diplock: I would argue that the discussion of those companies revolves around fraud. I think fraudulent activity is in a completely different category. Where directors are confronted with completely baldface lies by management, and numbers are actually fraudulently produced, then that's a very different situation. It requires a very different governance response. That's an argument of the extreme, which shouldn't be used to argue what good corporate governance is about in general.

Deborah Midanek: I agree with you. Do you have a measure for what you think is a successful board?

Jane Diplock: I believe it depends on the industry, it depends on the nature of the business model, and it depends on the actual objectives, in a sense. I think it's quite different, to look at a charitable trust, and ask who would be a useful board member and what the board composition of that should be, as distinct from an engineering company, which is seeking contracts and doing actual digging in the ground. I would argue that it requires quite a complex skill set and good judgment to develop the theory of the appropriate makeup of a board, to assemble the talent, personal qualities, and experience you need and put those constructively together. That is the true talent of the nominations and governance committee of the board.

Deborah Midanek: Beautifully said. In the right hands, the skills matrix is very valuable, but it tends often to be taken as gospel and without regard to the fact that what you need is judgment and wisdom above all else, as well as people who can work together playing a multiplicity of roles as the job shifts and as different challenges emerge.

Jane Diplock: Absolutely. One challenge will need a technician, another challenge might actually need someone who's very competent at weighing ethical dilemmas. Another challenge will require someone who can read people very well. In the choice of the CEO, it's critical to understand what the strengths and weaknesses of that person are likely to be. So there's no tick box arrangement.

Deborah Midanek: Have you seen nominating and corporate governance committees do a good job assembling a strong mix of people on the board?

Jane Diplock: I have; and I've actually seen them change. On one board I was on, I replaced the one woman on that board. My foray into trying to change this was to suggest that every slate for new directors should have at least three women on it. This resulted over time in there being three women on that board, because when the requirement to have at least three women on the slate was agreed to, they found three talented competent women to include on each slate. The requirement merely enabled a wider comparison of talents, skills, and the mix that was needed for that particular appointment across a broader group of candidates.

Deborah Midanek: What do you think of the California legislature's mandated requirement that a certain percentage of directors on boards have to be women?

Jane Diplock: I've changed my view on that, actually. I had been opposed to quotas fearing that the quota might be filled in a tick box way and people less able appointed rather than somebody with real talent and experience. I've spoken to some of my friends and colleagues in Europe, where these mandatory quotas have been in effect for some time. What they've found is that when there is a quota, then the committee that is looking for candidates actively goes out and finds a group of talented women. They claimed that they had not seen any token appointments just because they're women.

It actually meant that really talented women were found and that the boards were enhanced. Both men and women were telling me this. I listen to the perspective of people I know and respect. It well might be that the quota system can be abolished once you've seated a number of very talented women and the talent pool is well recognized.

I think the headhunting industry's got something to do with this as well. They pick the easy candidates that everyone else knows and likes because they are not eager to take risks. It is easier to propose a known quantity.

Deborah Midanek: That's the right way to put it. But back to government-mandated quotas. Are we saying that the boardroom has lagged so badly that government must intervene?

Jane Diplock: I think that's a very good question. And I think the answer is yes, to be honest. That's the conclusion reached by the Scandinavian countries, and others in Europe. They decided that they had waited 20 years for men dominating boards to understand that it's not just the right thing to do, but the bright thing to do, otherwise there is a ridiculous myopia because you're neglecting 50% of the talent pool.

Deborah Midanek: Well, you also get, I believe, risk reduction by bringing multiple points of view to the boardroom. It's the argument that is obvious in nature. Diversity brings better health, lower risk, and because you get multiple points of view, you have a more robust result. But it's very hard in many board situations for the kind of candid discussion to occur that would bring out those diverse sets of opinions.

There is a tendency, I believe, in many boards, at least in the US, not to want to rock the boat by speaking one's mind. And if you do speak your mind, and it's not what the rest of the group is thinking, you risk isolating yourself, and becoming an outlier, and losing any influence you have with the group.

Jane Diplock: Most highly professional boards are not run as autocratic fiefdoms. They do really want to gain a consensus. A good chairman wants that, and is open to and welcomes a contrary view. Certainly, in the boards that I'm on, the chairs are willing to say, "Well, actually, that's a different way of looking at it. Perhaps we should consider that." There is a real effort to get a consensus.

That's how really excellent decisions are made. The resignation of a director is a highly controversial matter in a publicly listed company. Your major shareholders would be asking, "Why did that director resign?" So it's difficult to oust a director for a contrary view. Now, if the person is a complete rat bag, and by mistake you happen to have appointed them, then that's something that has to be worked around by the chair.

Deborah Midanek: Can shareholders give direction to the board? Because shareholders today may have no choice but to be invested in the company, given the size of their holdings, they may be looking for the sustainable long-term view, and are much more focused on the ESG components and the intangibles than has been true in the past. In what way should boards and shareholders communicate, if at all?

Jane Diplock: There are a number of ways that shareholders communicate and some are more effective than others. For example, let me take the one end of the spectrum. You have a non-executive director who only turns up to a third of the board meetings, doesn't appear to be pulling his or her weight, and the attendance is, of course, publicized, so everybody knows it.

A group of institutional investors who own a large proportion of the shares come and privately say to the chairman, "We can't support the continuation of this director. It appears that this person is not participating in the board as they should and we will not support their re-election." That's one way of doing it and it does happen.

Second, there are now a number of proxy organizations that ask shareholders to give them the proxy for their shares. And they can be influential, because if they are opposed to some major strategy, then there is a challenge to the board about that, if they can gather enough votes.

Often it is an element about the effect on the community of some aspect of the company's business model, perhaps a pollution issue, perhaps some other element such as closure of bank branches in small communities, or whatever. And these can have a reputational effect on the share price and on the company itself. So that's another way this can happen.

Third, individual shareholders who stand up at an AGM can be quite effective in addressing reputational issues for the company. So shareholders can advise the company, but unless they have a majority or a large holding which is influential in the voting process, they can't direct.

Deborah Midanek: Those were beautifully parsed situations that you just laid out. Now, in what circumstances can board members talk to the investors?

Jane Diplock: Well, at the AGM, an investor can ask the board member a question. It's up to the chairman to decide whether he considers it an appropriate matter to be answered by that board member or by the CEO. Apart from that, shareholders do sometimes approach board members individually. It is really a matter of very fine judgment, and sometimes policy of the company, as to whether that's a matter that is properly to be discussed with that shareholder, whether it's a matter to be handled in confidence with the board, or whether it's a matter that should go to the communications officer in the company.

Deborah Midanek: There is a growing expectation in the US on the part of institutional investors that board members speaking with them will be a regular part of company communications.

Jane Diplock: I think it's a matter for the board itself to decide.

Deborah Midanek: This leads to another interesting question. There is a lot of focus on establishing and maintaining the "ethical tone at the top." There is debate as to whether the board can, in fact, have an impact on the ethical culture of the company. What are your views on that?

Jane Diplock: I actually think it's vital that the board demonstrates a totally ethical position in relation to every aspect of the company business. It doesn't mean, necessarily, that everybody in management will act completely ethically, but there should be zero tolerance demonstrated by the board for any unethical behavior. For example, if ethical malfeasance by some staff member is revealed – by the compliance committee, through the internal audit committee, or is reported by the CEO to the board – it should be very clear that the board has a zero tolerance for this. The board sets the corporate culture.

Deborah Midanek: This leads to a couple of wrap up questions, Jane, in that your experience with boards seems to have been significantly better than mine. Do you feel that the current corporate governance model for stewardship is working?

Jane Diplock: Which model is the question, because I do believe that the integrated reporting and integrated thinking model is the 21st century model. That model, where adopted, will work. But if one relies on the 19th century Industrial Revolution model of the corporation, I think a lot of corporations run the risk of a Kodak moment and going out of business.

Deborah Midanek: So where can we learn more about integrated reporting and integrated thinking in action?

Jane Diplock: Have a look at IntegratedReporting.org. There are a number of companies, including companies in the US – GE, for example, and European companies like Unilever – that are engaged in this way of looking at their businesses. Those companies are looking over the short, medium, and long term, and looking at their sustainability, and reporting that to their shareholders, and other stakeholders. That's the model that is going to work for this century.

Deborah Midanek: That is heartening. What else can we do that improves corporate governance, when corporate leadership, given the scale of many of our companies, is so critical to global sustainability? Forget about individual corporations, the globe needs help from corporations to sustain itself. How do we help?

Jane Diplock: I'd like to segue slightly and illustrate what we *could* be doing. I talked at the beginning about the intersection between the climate change revolution and the technological revolution. Where I think those intersect in a hopeful and optimistic way is with the *United Nations Sustainable Development Goals*. These goals have been adopted by every country in the world. I believe they're our hope for the future.

They are comprehensive and cover climate change, life below water, life in cities. They are asking us to look at the way in which the elements of climate change can be somewhat resolved by the technological revolution. Business and corporations have an absolutely vital role to play because many developments they are looking at in their research and development will be focusing on matters that are reacting to climate change risks.

The Financial Stability Board under Mark Carney has required that financial institutions identify climate change risks as a financial stability issue for the entire globe. All corporations should be seriously looking at this. Investors certainly are. There is a task force on climate change disclosures that's been set up by the Financial Stability Board. So at a global level there's a real concern that all corporations should be actually identifying and articulating their climate change risks, and articulate about how to address and mitigate those risks. R&D is one of the solutions to that.

That is where the United Nations Sustainable Development Goals can help. The issues that have arisen there can only be addressed with the assistance of business and corporations. It won't happen through governments alone. It will only happen if there are passionate approaches by corporations to this.

My own project has been to start a stock exchange matching funders of research with academic researchers to find the best solutions to the United Nations Sustainable Development Goal challenges. Corporations could fund their R&D research to find the best research outcomes. That's what I envisage.

Deborah Midanek: What a wonderful place to conclude this fascinating conversation. Thank you, Jane.

Chapter 10
The job of the company is to make the world a better place

Roger Martin

Professor Roger Martin is a writer, strategy advisor, and currently #1 ranked management thinker in the world. He is also former Dean and Institute Director of the Martin Prosperity Institute at the Rotman School of Management at the University of Toronto in Canada. Prior to his time at Rotman, he spent 13 years as Director of Monitor Company, a global strategy consulting firm he cofounded, based in Cambridge, Massachusetts.

Roger is a trusted strategy advisor to the CEOs of companies worldwide including Procter & Gamble, LEGO, and Ford; and serves as Chair of The Good Jobs Institute and the I-Think Initiative, and on the Board of The Nine Dots Prize.

His research focuses on integrative thinking, design of business, strategy, incentives and governance, democratic capitalism, and social innovation. He has published 11 books, the most recent of which are *Creating Great Choices*, written with Jennifer Riel (Harvard Business Review Press, 2017) *Getting Beyond Better*, written with Sally Osberg (HBRP, 2015) and *Playing to Win*, written with A.G. Lafley (HBRP, 2013), which won the award for Best Book of 2012–13 by the Thinkers50. He has written 26 Harvard Business Review articles.

A Canadian from Wallenstein, Ontario, Roger received his BA from Harvard College, with a concentration in Economics, in 1979, and his MBA from the Harvard Business School in 1981. in 2018, he was awarded a Doctor of Laws (honoris causa) by the Royal Military College of Canada.

Deborah Midanek: Roger, who are you and how did you develop this passionate interest in thought processes and the corporate behavior that expresses those thought processes?

Roger Martin: I would have to blame my late mother. She would never answer my questions. She would always encourage me to think it through myself, in a nice way, but it was frustrating at times. If I lost my little toy truck, she wouldn't say,

https://doi.org/10.1515/9783110670004-011

"Oh, you should check the toy basket." She would say, "Well, Roger, why don't you start with where you can remember vividly last having it in your hand, and then think of all the places you've been since then, because it'll be in one of those places." So I'd have to think it through myself. That, I think, inculcated in me an innate view that I could figure stuff out. I think that stuck with me for the rest of my life.

Deborah Midanek: What an incredible gift that she gave you and that, through doing that, she gave to the world. Your expression in your writings and in your speech is amazingly clear. To my mind, you approach issues by starting at the baseline question as opposed to in the middle of the paragraph, which is where so many others' thoughts begin.

Roger Martin: I'm glad it feels that way, and while we're doing shout-outs, on the simplicity thing, I would give a shout-out to my dad, who's still alive, bless him. He is an entrepreneur, always seeking the simplest way of describing an answer. He was not highly educated. He was practical, became an entrepreneur at 18, and he always encouraged me to not complicate things. Make them as complicated as they need be but not one iota more. I think my love for figuring things out came from my mom and my desire to have a simple, straightforward solution came from my dad.

Deborah Midanek: What wonderful tributes to them. You have done a fabulous job combining their influences and then adding quite a bit of your own originality. Could you give us just a quick background on your journey through life as you moved forward independently of these two stalwart souls?

Roger Martin: I started out in 1956 in Wallenstein, Ontario, which is a hamlet of about, at that time, 50 people, a third of the way from Toronto to Detroit, in farming country in south central Ontario. My grandfather owned the general store across the street, and my dad started a feed manufacturing company called Wallenstein Feed and Supply Limited. I lived there for the first 18 or so years of my life. When I go back now, it is huge, just huge. It has 200, maybe 300 people now.

I went to a regional high school in the closest town, a town of about 7,000 people called Elmira, and had an adverse reaction to a guidance counselor. When I asked where to go to university, he said, and I quote, because I'll never forget this, "Well, Roger, it doesn't really matter. They're pretty much all the same."

Maybe I was a country bumpkin, but I wasn't that stupid to think that they were all the same, that Conestoga College, the two-year college down the road, was as good as the University of Toronto or McGill. I was a jock, for what it's worth. I actually was athlete of the year my senior year of high school and basketball player of the year and all that kind of thing. After the fact, I was thinking, what? Why would he give me this advice? He maybe just never looked at my transcripts or my grades and thought I was some kind of a dumb jock.

Anyway, it annoyed me enough that I, in that moment, said, "I'm going to go to some place that's not the same. I will show Mr. Conlon that they're not all the same. I'm going to go to ... " and some name had to pop into my head that represented lack of sameness. Since I was a country bumpkin, Princeton or Cambridge or University of Tokyo had no chance of popping into my mind because I'd never heard of them, but I had heard the name Harvard, and I knew it wasn't the same. So I said, "I'm going to go to Harvard. I'll teach Mr. Conlon that they're not all the same. I'm going to go to Harvard."

And so I applied and stunningly enough got in and went to Harvard College for four years undergrad and then I went to Harvard Business School immediately thereafter while they still allowed that. There were very few of us they allowed to go straight from undergraduate without work experience, but they still did.

Although, again, it was for not very good reasons, honestly. I had acquired a girlfriend at Harvard, and she was going to the Kennedy School [of Government], and I was a volleyball player. I was actually the captain of the Harvard men's volleyball team, and during my senior year, the coach told us that this was going to be his last year. He was going to coach a club team in Greece. I said, "Oh, man. I would love to coach the volleyball team." But I couldn't go back to my parents and say to my parents, "Gee, Mom and Dad, I've just gotten this Harvard degree, and I am now going to coach the Harvard varsity men's volleyball team and hang out with my girlfriend." How would that be? I just couldn't bear the thought of their disappointment. They would have been nice about it, but they would have been disappointed.

So I had to have a cover story. What in the world is a better cover story than, "Mom and Dad, I've decided to go to Harvard Business School to get my MBA"? And, "By the way, I will then be able to hang out with my girlfriend and coach the Harvard varsity men's volleyball team." So I did that. Then I met up with the bunch of guys who created Monitor Company with me. We grew that into a big global consulting firm. In 1998, I was minding my own business, consulting to a Canadian company that had on its board Rob Prichard, the then-president of the University of Toronto. He got it in his head during the assignment that I should become the next dean of his business school, the Rotman School of Management at the University of Toronto, and he's the most persuasive man I've ever met in my life. He talked me into it.

So, I took a 94% pay cut and became dean of the Rotman School of Management. Did that for 15 years, from '98 to 2013, and I just stepped down as a professor and am back to consulting to CEOs on strategy and writing articles and books.

Deborah Midanek: During those adventures, you've done a lot of thinking and writing about the corporation, about the process of making decisions, and about how corporations can learn from sports models. Let's start with this baseline question: What do you think the purpose of the modern public corporation is today, and has it changed?

Roger Martin: I don't think its purpose should have ever changed. I come from the school of thought that says the government gives this nice protection of limited liability to the corporations in America, and it's similar in other countries. In exchange, I think the job of the company is to make the world a better place. I honestly believe so, and I learned that from my father. You should both produce a product or a service that makes customers' lives better and in doing so employ people who you help to put food on their table and money in their retirement accounts and do it in a way that is beneficial for the planet.

If you do all these things, it's one of the highest callings you can imagine. I know being a teacher is great and serving your country in the armed forces is great, but I think if you take that as the purpose of the corporation, being an executive of a corporation is a great thing, too.

Deborah Midanek: Well, one of the things that strikes me is that it's also a profoundly creative position. That's what I find, having spent my life in the world of corporate turnarounds, that the opportunity to knit things together in a more logical way is really not about mechanics and physics. It's about biology and art and communication of a picture. Helping the corporation do those things you just mentioned, recover its roots, recover its connection to its purpose and its customers, is very creative. It's about biology and art. It is not nearly as much about spreadsheets as people tend to think.

Roger Martin: I couldn't agree more. It's a bit of an obsession of mine, the degree to which what's being taught in business schools, very influential because so many corporate executives in America now have an undergrad or graduate business degree, or both, is the primacy of analysis. You're taught in business school that unless you make decisions based on data analysis, facts, you are being a sloppy, slovenly executive. You must have analytical proof in order to do something.

The fundamental problem with that goes back 2,400 years to the guy who invented the methodologies we are taught in our business education. Aristotle in the 4th century BC was the first guy on the planet to describe a method for determining the cause of a given effect. That is the scientific method. It was formalized 2,000 years later by Bacon, Newton, Galileo, and Descartes in the Scientific Revolution, but it was all Aristotelian posterior analytics.

The interesting thing to me is that we accept that as a fantastic methodology created by this fantastic genius guy, but we ignore something incredibly important that he said about his method. He said, literally, in almost so many words, "About this methodology: this methodology is for the part of the world where things cannot be other than they are."

What he said is, if I let go of this stone, it will drop to the floor. It'll drop to the floor now, it dropped to the floor 10 years ago, five years ago, two weeks ago, yesterday, five minutes ago. It'll drop to the floor tomorrow, the next day, whatever. It'll drop to the floor in Africa, in Europe, in the US. It'll drop to the floor at the top of a mountain, in the bottom of a canyon. It's part of the world where things cannot be other than they are. There's a fundamental law that's unchanging that causes that to happen, and that is what my scientific method is for. It is for the part of the world where things cannot be other than they are.

Then he pointed out that there are parts of the world where things *can* be other than they are. Like my relationship with you, Deborah. If you started screaming and yelling at me, we'd have a different relationship than if you talk nicely to me. That's part of the world where things can be other than they are. Or, it's the part of the world where consumers can't be more than an arm's length away from their smartphone now, when in 1998, they didn't know what a smartphone was because it didn't exist.

Aristotle was clear. "In that part of the world, do not use my method." Full stop. Don't do it. Why would he say that about his beloved thinking method? Because he was smart enough to figure out that if you use the method of analyzing the past as if the future's going to be exactly like the past, it ain't going to work particularly well in the part of the world where things can be different. In fact, what will it convince you? It'll convince you that the future will be identical to the past, and then what's going to happen to you if you're a company and you keep on assuming the future's going to be the same as the past? Somebody will disrupt you and blow you out of business. In that part of the world, what Aristotle said was that rigorous thinking requires imagining possibilities and choosing the one for which the most compelling argument can be made.

Deborah Midanek: Just as you were speaking about Aristotle, I was thinking, hallelujah, the man allowed for the importance of imagination, and then there you used the word *imagine*. There are relatively few people who would start the conversation about the purpose of the corporation with the government grant of limited liability in exchange for furthering the purposes of the world; but for the first several hundred years of the existence of corporations, a large part of that charter was granted because the subject corporation was intended to be furthering world knowledge. It was a pretty direct correlation. As the charter became more of a commodity, where you could just go sign up in the Secretary of State's office, that grant became less valued, perhaps. Anyway, I'm getting off of the subject.

Roger Martin: No, no. I think it's a cool and interesting point. I think Aristotle would be very happy with that because he said, "In the part of the world where things cannot be other than they are, the purpose of human beings is to understand the causes of the current effects." And he said, "In the part of the world where things can be other than they are, the purpose of human beings is to be the cause of a new effect." Isn't that cool? It sounds as though that's essentially the deal the Dutch government made when it chartered the first limited liability corporation, saying we'll give you limited liability if you guys go out and cause a new effect: understanding, trading with, exploring East India. It's about the new, the creation of something that does not now exist, and that requires imagining possibilities.

If you imagine the possibility that there are lands over there, that it's not the edge of the earth and you're not going to fall off, but there are actually lands over there – you could sail to them. There may be interesting things that are completely unlike anything we've seen before over there. That requires imagining the possibilities. The interesting thing from an MBA standpoint is, you can't prove any of them in advance.

I like my philosophers. Charles Sanders Peirce, the great American pragmatist philosopher, pointed out that no new idea in the history of the world has been proven in advance analytically. How about that? How many times in your career has your boss said to you, "Well, that sounds like a good idea. Just go prove it and then we'll do it." All those clueless bosses who say those kinds of things do not realize that they're asking you to do something that's never been done before in the history of humankind. You can't.

You've got to go try stuff, which is why I'm so interested in the importation of some cool principles from the world of design into business. I work closely and am very good friends with David Kelley and Tim Brown and the cool guys at IDEO and other designers, some great designers from other firms, because they brought to the corporation the notion that you've just got to prototype stuff.

Make it cheap. Don't blow the entire corporate budget on trying new stuff. Try it cheap and quick. Figure out what works, what doesn't. Make it better, make it better, make it better. That's all consistent with Aristotle. What all the design folks don't realize is that their practice is consistent with what Aristotle said, while MBA programs are utterly inconsistent with what Aristotle said.

Deborah Midanek: If the corporation's purpose is to improve the condition of the world in some way and continue to sustain itself and its employees and its investors and its management and its board along the way, who is responsible for making that happen? Who owns the public corporation and what rights and responsibilities does ownership entail?

Roger Martin: The idea is, abstractly, that the owners of the company are the shareholders and the shareholders have that overall responsibility for serving the world as a limited liability corporation should. What they've done, essentially, in the modern world is outsource that to something called a board of directors that is responsible for the welfare of the corporation. But the relationship between the owners, as in the shareholders of the company, and the board has become so intermediated that the idea that the owners of the widely held publicly traded company can express anything useful has become difficult.

In the widely held publicly traded company, the owners of the company aren't even the owners. There's some notional idea that in representing the true owners, the guy or gal with a mutual fund at Vanguard or Fidelity or somebody with a pension coming their way in some number of years from CalPERS, that their wishes and desires are going to be expressed by these fiduciary intermediaries. Vanguard and BlackRock and Fidelity and State Street and CalPERS and CalSTRS and et cetera are going to give sage and wise advice and pressure and encouragement to a board of directors who will then, because of all that wonderful input, actually manage the company in the interests of the greater good. That's a set of logical leaps that I think are straight up unrealistic.

I guess the way I think about it is that there's this implicit assumption that the relationship between the owners and the company is like a committed marital relationship. It's long lasting. There's sort of mutuality of interest. There's talking things out and making the right decisions. But in fact, it's evolved to being not a committed, loving, long-term relationship, but anonymous sex.

I mean it is anonymous sex in the sense that Fidelity may show up on your share register this quarter as having 6.2% control. We don't actually know who Fidelity is. It's thousands and thousands of individual mutual fund investors, so it's anonymous in that respect. In the next quarter, they could show up with 3.2% or zero, and they didn't actually have to have a discussion about it. They got what they wanted, anonymous sex, and exited. The presumption is the parties behave like a committed, married, long-term relationship, and it's actually anonymous sex. What we get is the schism that comes from that. Disappointment, sadness, and STDs, lots and lots of that.

Deborah Midanek: Following along, what is the role of the board of directors, and to whom does that board owe its fiduciary duty?

Roger Martin: If you could get people on boards to be this way, it would be to have a commitment to doing the best for society that you can do. That means doing the best for consumers, customers, whatever they are, doing the best for your employees, doing the best for the environment. That means being able to say after you hang up your spurs as a director, say after 10 years, that in some small tiny little way, the world is a little bit better place than it was 10 years ago when I went on the board, because of what this corporation did.

That's what we should do at corporations. You could ask what about the poor shareholders? Well, I'm a subscriber to the Robert Wood Johnson credo, which he had engraved in granite in 1948 and still sits at the J&J headquarters. The credo says, paraphrasing, customers come first, employees come second, the communities in which we work come third, and last come the shareholders. However, if we do a good job with the first three, the shareholders will earn a fair return.

J&J went public for some tiny trivial amount in 1948 and the last time I checked was worth some $350 billion, so that credo may have worked. Shareholders don't get screwed if you take care of customers, take care of employees, and make the world a better place. Shareholders do just fine. Aristotle famously said, "If a man seeks to be happy, he's unlikely to end up happy. If a man seeks to lead a good life," by which he meant a life of virtuous contribution to his society, "he will end up happy." It's the same for shareholders. I wish that boards could take that credo as a responsibility and, as much as humanly possible, ignore chatter from the shareholders.

Deborah Midanek: What do we think defines the success of the board and how can we evaluate it? This leads to the next question, about your position that a public company board is a tax on investors. If we can't define their success, then it's absolutely a tax. Can we define their success?

Roger Martin: Here's the tricky part. I'll do a little bit of a digression before answering that question. In thinking about the world of business, I ask how two systems work. One system is the system that operates once a person is in a given chair. If there's a person in the chair, how do they do their job? What incentives do they have, what capabilities do they have, what governance mechanism runs them when they're in their job?

But there's another system that I think gets short shrift, which is the system that *gets the person in that job*. We can be very clear in specifying how we want that first system to work once the person's in the job, but we have a challenge in that we don't tie that assessment to how that person gets in that chair in the first place.

I'll give as an example how just cataclysmically horrendous the bond raters were shown to be in the global financial crisis. How many AAA rated tranches of subprime debt, which are never, ever supposed to default, defaulted completely and were utterly worthless? How could that possibly have been, people ask? Well, you have to ask the question: What do we want somebody in the chair at Moody's, Fitch, S&P to be capable of doing? We'd like them to be capable of analyzing the corporation, analyzing its capital structure both in detail and with inspired thinking to be able to come to a conclusion as to its credit quality, whether the instrument deserves a BBB- or junk or AA or AAA rating. We'd like them to be able to analyze companies, their risk profiles, the terms of bond issues, where they sit in the stack, how much of it there is. All of that.

Then you have to ask: How does a person with that set of skills get into that chair? There's a market for people with that set of skills who are really, really good at that, good enough to save us from the global financial crisis. What you find if you think about that, is that those people are also great at bond trading and they can make at least 10 times, probably 100 or even 1000 times what they can make sitting at a desk at Fitch or Moody's, by running the bond trading desk at Goldman or running their own bond fund, working at Apollo, whatever.

We assume that somebody sitting at a bond rating desk at Moody's, Fitch, S&P is really good at rating bonds, when in my view, the only thing we can know for sure about somebody who's at a bond rating desk at Moody's, Fitch, or S&P is that they're not very good at rating bonds. Otherwise, they'd be at Goldman, their own bond fund, or Apollo. It's the *impossibility theorem*, that if they have the skills we want them to have for that job, they will be in another job – and we've dotted the landscape with those folks. Again, after the global financial crisis, we said, "Oh, assets were exaggerated in value on balance sheets, so we will now have the auditors as part of their audit declare whether an asset is impaired or not."

Who's really good at that? Who's good at figuring whether an asset is impaired or not, when all you have to do is essentially look at that asset and be able to calculate with reasonable precision its expected cash flows up to infinity, then discount it back in precisely the right way to determine whether that's more or less than what's on the books. I know one guy who may be really good at that. His name's Warren Buffett, and he's not an audit partner at PricewaterhouseCoopers. He's worth $50 billion because he's really good at that. There are other people who are really good at that too, and they don't sit in Deloitte, PwC, KPMG. In asking them to determine which assets are impaired, we are giving them a job that they are, by prima facie evidence, by virtue of being in that chair, not good at doing.

This is a bit of a digression, but it gets back to boards. We don't teleport people into board seats. We don't have press gangs going around the streets forcing people to become directors. It's a voluntary act, and there's a selection process. What I argue is, we do not ask this question: What is it about that person that would cause them to say, "I will use my time and energy to do this thing"? Because of the logic laid out above, how can we believe that the person who is motivated to be in that seat will do that job well?

Deborah Midanek: The truth is, the way our system works is that it is often the easy choice that is made. To be as compassionate as possible to those people who are choosing directors, it is understandable that they will appoint people whose attributes they can understand. To me, the fact that it's taken a long time to add diverse points of view, diverse backgrounds to boards, makes great sense, because the people making the choices about who's on the board are most comfortable evaluating people who look like themselves.

Roger Martin: There's that, but you're talking about one direction. I'm talking about the other direction as well. What would cause a director, potential director, to say, "Yes, I want to spend however many person hours a year it is doing that thing versus the alternative thing."

I tend to agree with you that boards are typically made up of people who are like the people already on the board. I buy that argument, but if we want good governance, we have to have that person who is invited. Let's just say, for the sake of argument, that the nominating committees are doing a great job and they're inviting, let's just say, people who *would* do a good job. What causes that person to say yes?

I would argue that there are a whole bunch of bad reasons to be on boards, and I've heard all of them. There's only one good reason, but that's not a reason that I've heard very often, if at all. You could say yes because you think it's really good money. That would be one legitimate reason. Oh wow, the package is about $800,000 or $900,000 a year; that's better than the alternative use of my time and talent. If I spent those hours on an alternative use, I could make at most half that much, so it's really attractive. What's your motivation going to be, then, once you're on the board?

Deborah Midanek: Not to lose your seat. To fit in, to have people think that you're good at it.

Roger Martin: Exactly. A second reason is prestige. Serving on this board will raise my prestige. I can say, I'm on the board of General Electric Company. What'll you do? You'll make sure that you don't lose it, because then you'll lose the prestige you just got. If you run through the reasons why somebody would say yes, they're actually bad for everything that you, Deborah, would want that board to do. The only legitimate reason to be on a board that's actually good for the board is if you think that this is an act of public service, that the world is a better place to the extent that corporations are governed better so that they do good things for society. What percentage of board members you've met would say that's their motivation for serving on a board?

The answer is none, it's not viewed that way, and that if we're going to have widely-held publicly-traded companies, we have to honor and revere board members the way we honor and revere judges. Being a judge is a huge negative NPV [net present value] activity, right? If you were a super lawyer, super at what you're doing, you would make tons more working at Wachtell Lipton than you would being a judge. But in that profession, there is a view that among the highest public service things you could possibly do with your life is to sit on the bench and help us uphold and build the law over time. That's what we have to have for corporate directors.

I don't think we're going to get there for boards as a whole, but we could get there for chairs of boards. If you've got a good chair, they can slap around the directors enough to get them to be better directors. If you've got a crummy chair, you've got no chance.

Deborah Midanek: Where I have been able to be helpful is when boards are facing disaster and they don't know what to do, because the people who sit in those chairs are often uncomfortable having to step up and deal with it. That's where I have elected to participate, so I've served on lots of boards of troubled companies, and there I can have impact and I can help. I can help. I can help with the jobs, I can help with the customers, I can help with the environment, I can help with a lot of things because in the middle of that insanity, the situation is plastic. It's movable. You can reshape it, but you can't when it's going along in a very healthy, allegedly healthy, mode.

Roger Martin: You are part of the subversive minority, Deborah, and we need to make the subversive minority the majority if we're going to have good governance, in my view. You can see by your own experience that that's really hard. It's hard work. I'm totally, totally into hard work. In fact, I aim myself at the hardest possible work, but I can't make myself accept public board seats anymore, because it is such hard work to be that subversive a force; essentially, trying to subvert the norms of behavior on the board. That's really, really hard work.

Deborah Midanek: It *is* really hard work. Really hard work. My very first board, the board of the bankrupt Drexel Burnham, I learned that the men around me did not have the ability to hear my voice. It wasn't that they weren't willing to listen. It's just I realized that my voice is in a different register. The frequency of my voice is different. So I learned to project my voice by sort of throwing it at the ceiling so that the voice would come back down on top of them. I also led by asking questions rather than by asserting positions, because asserting positions would not have gotten me anywhere.

Roger Martin: And I would argue, sadly, Deborah, that if you were on the board of Drexel Burnham five or seven years before when it was the highest flying thing and you'd have been saying, "Guys, we're about to hit a wall. A bunch of you are going to be arrested," and so on, they would have said, "Give me a break. We're awesome. We are awesome and you're an idiot."

Deborah Midanek: Of course, of course. The diseases of affluence. But let's go back to the thread of this conversation. You are talking about seeing a world in which we find a way to position the chairs of boards of directors in such a way that they are seen as doing an important public service. Are you suggesting that we create a cadre of specifically credentialed chairs who have a certain kind of training, or a certain kind of imprimatur, or a certain kind of experience, or all of the above, and that it's from that pool that chairs are picked? What kind of mechanism are you imagining in this design thinking brain of yours?

Roger Martin: Well, it is a tricky question. I'm always into things that happen more organically than not. My own take on all the boards I've seen and board members I've seen is that there is no correlation between effectiveness and their previous roles. Oh, were they a CEO already or how much experience do they have in this industry? It is completely a psychographic thing. The question is: What is their way of being in the world as a human being?

Any kind of categorization scheme that makes it seem like we're going to have to pick specific features is going to be hard. I guess I would just hope that there could be a movement that says, "We need these people and we need them to be this way," and people start emerging organically as great directors.

Of course, we do know that there are people out there who I think are great directors, and I think they need to be celebrated more. We may have a 25-year migration path toward having essentially that cadre. I would love to see that group of directors, of chairs, become a bit of a club; one that admits people that they watch on boards behaving the way they think they need behave. So if you're a member of that club, even though that label has some bad connotation, but just go with me, people will seek you out to be a chair because you have that kind of stamp from peers who are doing it the way you're doing it.

There's lots of thinking that would have to happen on this front to say how we could accelerate that and I think you'd need some leadership from the big owners of equity capital and the big investment managers, maybe even the pension funds, in order to push for that kind of person being the chair of the board.

Deborah Midanek: Well, you know, Roger, it seems to me that you just retired from being a professor. You have greater clarity of thinking than many people around this issue. I nominate you to be the person who figures out how to create that club. Seriously, you have the power of the pen and you have the power of the brain, and you have a history of talking about integrative thinking, design thinking, and solutions-based processes. What can we do to make this happen? The existing infrastructure around boards of directors is not going to do the job.

Roger Martin: Right, right. It's the wrong kind of club now. Agreeableness is the number one criterion of membership in the club now.

Deborah Midanek: I think you may be right that it has to start with investors, but I'm not sure that they actually really understand the job of the board.

Roger Martin: You're right, you're right. I think it's got to start with people committed to and practiced at being a great director. I think you should do it.

Deborah Midanek: But I'm outside the system.

Roger Martin: I think about too many things, but it would be a 10–20-year project. I think it's the only thing that will save the widely-held publicly-traded company from going into the ash bin of history as something that we tried but didn't work and we'll go back to what we had in the 20s and 30s where there will be semi-public companies, with people saying as John D. Rockefeller did, "You can buy some shares, but I'm in charge, I own this."

Deborah Midanek: That's happening. Look at Carlisle and KKR and so on. That's the world that they live in.

Roger Martin: Or Facebook or Google.

Deborah Midanek: Absolutely, those guys too. I don't know whether you want to call them benevolent, but these same dictator structures are in a position where in many ways they have way more influence in the world than governments do.

Roger Martin: Oh, absolutely.

Chapter 11
Why things don't work as they're supposed to, and what to do about it

Nell Minow

Nell Minow, is currently Vice Chair of Value Edge Advisors and was previously co-founder of GMI Ratings. For the 10 years before, that she was cofounder and editor of The Corporate Library, an independent research firm that rates boards of directors of public companies and compiles research, study, and critical thinking about corporate governance. Its board effectiveness rating allows investors and analysts to evaluate governance as an element of investment risk. Special reports and studies include reports on CEO employment contracts, related transactions, and CEO compensation.

Nell was formerly a principal of LENS, a $100 million investment firm that bought stock in underperforming companies and used shareholder activism to increase their value. Before that, she served as president of Institutional Shareholder Services, Inc., a firm that advises institutional investors on issues of corporate governance, and as an attorney at the Environmental Protection Agency, the Office of Management and Budget, and the Department of Justice.

She has written more than 200 articles about corporate governance as well as chapters in treatises on executive compensation, annual shareholder meetings, and in the books *Law Stories, The Dance of Change, The Financial Services Revolution, Leadership and Governance from the Inside Out,* and *How to Run a Company.* She is co-author with Robert A.G. Monks of three books, *Power and Accountability* (HarperBusiness 1991), the textbook *Corporate Governance* (Blackwell 1995, 2001, 2004, 2007), and *Watching the Watchers: Corporate Governance for the 21st Century* (Blackwell 1996). She taught corporate governance to MBA students at George Mason University for five years. She is also a well-known film critic.

Deborah Midanek: Nell, thank you for taking time to talk. You have been an opinion leader in corporate governance for a long time. How did you get so deeply involved in governance? How did you build your life?

https://doi.org/10.1515/9783110670004-012

Nell Minow: Well, I was working for the government at the Office of Management and Budget, and I loved that job. I saw myself doing that indefinitely, being a lawyer in the government. While there, I met a man who was also working for the government, for the then-Vice President, George H.W. Bush, and his name was Bob Monks. I had heard about him before I met him. I'd heard that he was like Lord Byron: mad, bad, and dangerous to know. I was intrigued.

We met at one of those meetings where everybody around us was saying things that made no sense whatsoever; we caught each other's eye, and realized we were on the same page. We got to know each other a little bit. He then joined the Labor Department, where he ran the ERISA [Employee Retirement Income Security Act] program for a year. I met with him again there, and by that time, pregnant with my second child, I was working three days a week. I saw Bob and he said, "I'm starting a new company, called Institutional Shareholder Services. We're going to advise institutional shareholders on corporate governance."

I was eight-and-a-half months pregnant. The only words I recognized in that sentence were we and advise, not familiar with any of the other words. I could barely get out of the chair where I was sitting while talking to him, and I said, "Well, I'm having this baby next month. I really can't come to work right away, and when I do come to work, I'm going to need to work no more than three days a week." He said, "That's great. It's a start-up. We really couldn't afford you full-time. Why don't you take nine months off and join us next fall?"

I said, "Okay." Even though I'd never thought about leaving the government, and I had no idea what he was doing, I liked him very much. I knew I'd learn a lot from him. I really wanted to work three days a week. So when he explained what it was that he was doing, I said to myself, "This is great because there's no way that the entrenched business interests are ever going to let this grow. We will think great thoughts, and we'll file amicus briefs, and we'll write op-eds. This will never become such a successful company that I will have to work full-time. So, I'm good."

I went off, had the baby, and he would send me updates by regular mail on what he was doing. I arrived in September, the day after Labor Day, and he said, "Okay, everything I told you about what we're doing here is out the window. I've spent nine months visiting every institutional investor in the country, proposing to them what I wanted to do. Every one of them said, 'I have no interest in what you're doing. I don't even want to talk to you. Leave my office immediately.'"

But, he said, "A couple of them said something very intriguing. They said, 'I hate what you're doing. I don't want any part of it, but what I would like is some advice on how to vote proxies,'" because, you know, for 30 or 40 years, proxies have been voted, when voted at all, for the unopposed candidates for the board, and to approve the auditors. There's really never been anything particularly interesting on a proxy.

But we were in the middle of the era of LBOs, hostile takeovers, greenmail, and entrenchment. There were these unprecedented, hideous battles between management and the raiders. Shareholders were in the middle, and they were getting very upset about it. The year that I arrived was the year that Marty Lipton created the poison pill, and every company in America was adopting them without shareholder approval. That created an opportunity. So, he explained to me, "We're going to start a business where we're going to give people advice on how to vote their proxies."

"That's a much better business because what you most want in a business is something that is not tied to your hours. Once we create the advice, we can sell the same advice over, and over, and over without doing any extra work, and all we have to do is run the Xerox machine," I said. "What's really great about it is that normally when you're talking about the investment world, there's a premium on exclusivity. If you're giving buy-sell advice, you don't want your competitor to have that same advice. But on voting proxies, you do want everybody to have the same advice. Your vote is meaningless unless you can get enough people to vote with you. So our customers are going to be our best salespeople. That's a very good business."

A college classmate of Bob's became our first customer. For the next two years, we had, I think, a total of three customers. On February 23rd, 1988, however, the Labor Department issued a ruling called the Avon Letter, which said that the right to vote was an asset of the pension plan. That was a real turning point for us. Recently, as a matter of fact, the Chamber of Commerce has asked them to rescind that letter. We went from three clients, to nine clients, to 27 clients and were growing exponentially. Then we had the dream moment where a very, very large institutional investor literally walked in the door and said, "If you can expand to cover all 6,000 companies in our portfolio by next proxy season, we will pay whatever it costs to get you there."

My first phone call was to the landlord, and after that, that's what we did. That's how ISS got up and running and that's how I got involved in corporate governance. It was completely happenstance that I happened to meet Bob, and he happened to be a great visionary, and I happened to want to work three days a week.

Deborah Midanek: Yet something beyond the fact that it was a great business model kept you engaged in it through those 18 years and well beyond. Was there something in particular that fascinated you, that really got your attention?

Nell Minow: I currently have three blogs and five Twitter accounts because I like to do a lot of different things at once. It occurred to me, in retrospect, that all of my jobs have had one thing in common, and that is I'm really interested in why things don't work the way they're supposed to.

Before I was in this business, I was in the government looking at domestic regulatory programs, trying to figure out why they didn't do what they were supposed to do. I started out at EPA, and then I went to OMB, which is kind of quality control over all domestic regulatory programs.

Somebody says, "You know what? There's proof that having pets helps seniors and disabled people have healthier lives, so, government, go make a rule that allows pets in subsidized housing."

That seems very straightforward. How hard is it to do that? Well, you end up with an 80-page rule because people will think up things that you could never imagine, and you have to put in the rule such things as "No pet bigger than this," and, "No pet that's been determined to be dangerous." So something as simple as that becomes complicated to implement and creates unintended consequences. So I've been very interested in why things don't work.

That's also how I became a movie critic. I love movies. Everybody wants the movie to work: the directors, the producers, the actors. When it doesn't work, it's interesting to think about why it doesn't. Everybody wants the corporation to work, and then it doesn't. It is interesting to think about whose resources are being diverted for a purpose that is not what was intended.

I studied Shakespeare at Sarah Lawrence College, and then I went to the University of Chicago Law School, and you can't graduate from the University of Chicago Law School without a grounding in economics. So I knew about agency costs, and I knew about sunk cost. That really helped me to understand what the problems were in these companies we're looking at.

The other thing is something that Bob and I didn't talk about for perhaps the first 15 years we were working together. But it turns out that another big motivating factor for both of us is that we really hate bullies. We don't like people who try to push other people around. So that was also a big factor. I didn't like to see CEOs abusing the process. I believe in the free market. I believe in market forces. I don't like people who try to subvert that.

That made it fun. About once a year, Bob would take me out to lunch, and he would say, "Let's talk about you. What do you want? What do you want for yourself?" He was hoping is that I would say, "Well, my kids are in school now, so I can work full-time," which I never did. What I said to him is, "Look, I only need three things from this job. The first is I need to feel like I'm on the side of the good guys, because when I wake up in the morning, I always ask myself, 'Why should you get out of bed?' Unless I have a good answer, I don't get out of bed. So, my good answer is doing something to make the world a more just place.'"

The Jewish idea is that the purpose of life is tikkun olam, to heal the world. That was the first thing that I wanted. I said, "The second thing that I want is to learn something new every day, or I get really bored." Bob is kind of the same way. Bob and I keep starting these companies and selling them because once they're up and running, they're not that interesting anymore.

The third thing I said was, "I have to work three days a week. When I work three days a week, happiness results. When I work three days and one hour a week, misery results." Many people can work full-time and have children, but I am not such a one. When my children did grow up, instead of working full-time with Bob, I started a second career as a movie critic.

Deborah Midanek: Those comments provide a good on-ramp to the critical question, which is: What, to your mind, is the purpose of the modern public corporation? Your reference to the Old Testament, heal-the-world value system, may be an important lead-in to that question.

Nell Minow: The purpose of the corporation is to provide goods and services and jobs and returns for investors. As originally designed, it is one of history's greatest miracles. It has done all of those things. Unfortunately, too often that has been subverted and, as I said, the assets have been diverted.

But when it does work, when you think about the great corporations, and all of the great things that they've brought to us, including the technology we're talking about right now, and the electricity and water in the buildings that we're in, and the cars that we drive, that's terrific. That's exactly what they're supposed to do. No other entity has done that job as well.

It means that I can get the benefit of providing those goods and services as a shareholder of a company, without having to work at it or invent it. That's what the purpose of the corporation is. Yet the corporation's most significant asset is the idea that it can live beyond the life of any individual. Before the idea of the corporation, I had my little company, and I ran it myself, and when I died, it was gone. Somebody else had to start their company.

So the central idea of the corporation is that it lives beyond the human lifespan. And yet we have a chart in our MBA textbook, that Bob and I wrote, that I refer to as the Ozymandias chart, that shows the largest companies in the country by market cap, by decade. So, we have columns, 1960, 1970, 1980, 1990, et cetera, and anybody who has lived in this country will not be surprised to hear that there are companies in that most recent column that didn't exist at the beginning of the chart, that didn't exist even 10 years ago. There are companies like Facebook and Google and Apple that now take the places that were once taken on the chart by companies like Kodak and Sears.

So, in theory, companies live forever. In reality, not so much. Why is that? Well, that's part of what corporate governance is about. Why, with all of the benefits of the corporate structure, why is it that so many companies become sclerotic, become inbred, become hidebound, become unable to survive disruption?

Deborah Midanek: It is relatively recent that the actual work of the board of directors has begun to be codified and this whole question is at the heart of what I'm trying to get at, which is: What is the job of the board of directors?

I'll tell you what I think it is. I think it is to be the guardian of that perpetual life of the corporation. I do think it is to be a fiduciary to the corporation and not to the shareholders directly, because to try to be the fiduciary for the shareholders directly is a recipe for constant frustration.

Nell Minow: Oh, I'm not going to agree with you on that.

Deborah Midanek: I know you're not. But I want to see how your mind works on it because, to me, preserving the health of the corporation *is* serving the shareholders.

Nell Minow: How about if I put it this way? To me, serving the shareholders is preserving the health of the corporation, and the only way, the only way to preserve the health of the corporation, because serving the corporation always, historically, translates into entrenching the management.

Deborah Midanek: I agree with you, and the issue, to me, is that the flaccid board that doesn't understand its job and allows board meetings to be nothing but a kabuki dance doesn't hold management accountable.

Nell Minow: That's why they have to be fiduciaries for the shareholders, because if you tell them that that's their job, then they will do that. Then they will hold management accountable, and they will stop creating idiotic pay plans, and they will act on behalf of the theoretical, and now more often than not, real permanent shareholder.

You cannot show me a time when boards have said that they've acted on behalf of the corporation and not the shareholders, that it hasn't redounded to the benefit of the insider executives and not to anybody else. Every time they use that language, that's what it has meant in real life.

Deborah Midanek: I find it deliciously ironic that the ESG movement driven by institutional shareholders may allow the board to be able to focus on long-term sustainability. What do you think about that?

Nell Minow: I find that to be the natural evolution. The last time the Business Round Table talked about the importance of stakeholders was when I first got into this field in 1986. Why did they do that, and why did they get stakeholder laws passed in almost half of the states? It was as an entrenchment device. It was because they wanted to be able to say, "Well, this offer that's coming into us would be beneficial to our shareholders, but where would the Girl Scouts have their cookie drive, if it wasn't in our corporate headquarters?"

So, I'm very, very, very, very skeptical of their renewed focus on stakeholders. I think that the ESG initiatives are very powerful and are the fastest growing area of investment. But I think the ESG initiatives are a reflection of the antiquated generally accepted accounting principles, which are really 19th century accounting principles to determine the value of companies, when overwhelmingly today their assets are intellectual property and human capital, not reflected accurately on the balance sheet at all.

Deborah Midanek: Going back to that time in which you were getting involved in this, what we had then was the wages of a long period of high inflation, and a particularly acute demonstration of the archaic accounting rules. The reason all those takeovers were going on, reduced to hyper simplicity, was that assets were undervalued on balance sheets, so raiders could come along and buy the company with the company's own assets financing the debt.

Nell Minow: Exactly.

Deborah Midanek: It was a crazy time, and in another irony, Drexel Burnham and its singular ability to finance hostile takeover activity ended up spawning the rise of the independent director. The independent director is not there because of some argument that they're going to add economic value, but they are needed because in the eyes of various courts management cannot supervise itself. The courts found they could uphold Mr. Lipton's poison pills if they believed there had been a process in which disinterested directors separately reviewed what was going on.

Nell Minow: In fact, interestingly, the Delaware courts, which typically have stayed very, very far away from the issue of executive compensation, are allowing a trial to go forward on compensation at Tesla, specifically because the compensation committee was not independent.

Deborah Midanek: Tesla is just such a wonderful example of . . .

Nell Minow: Everything.

So, I think ESG is just a recognition that 19th century accounting principles based on equipment and real estate are not accurate reflectors of the investment opportunities and risks that companies present.

Deborah Midanek: That is absolutely true, but that then puts, I think, a premium on the board of directors being effective in carrying out what I perceive to be its job, which is guardianship of the perpetual life of the corporation – I'm perfectly happy to say on behalf of the shareholders, which I believe is true.

They need to protect the corporation because the rest of the world does not understand the fact that 85% of corporate value is intangible now.

Nell Minow: It's up to them to try to disclose that. In fact, Leo Strine published a piece this week that was really shocking, you know, given who he is, and he said, "Companies need to do a better job of disclosing their human capital and other ESG data."

As I said, I am a great believer in free markets. This is the market saying, "We need this information in order to make the market-based decisions that it is our job to do, both as fiduciaries for our clients and in the role that we play in the economy. We are not getting the information we need to do our jobs."

Deborah Midanek: I do not disagree with you in any respect on that. It's those same accounting rules that have moved the world to valuation on a mark-to-market basis, that we can argue forced institutional investors and companies into chronic short-termism.

Nell Minow: That and fees.

Deborah Midanek: I also know that, even if you're trying to move everybody toward a longer term framework, as Marty Lipton and others who are promoting the new paradigm for corporate governance are seeking to do, that the institutional investment manager can be replaced in a heartbeat, if his quarterly numbers do not add up. He has got to be compared to his peer group, and to the indices, and all the rest of that stuff, unless you're all in the world of indexing.

Nell Minow: Which, increasingly, everybody is.

Deborah Midanek: Right.

Nell Minow: Nobody, nobody, nobody has looked at the impact on the capital markets of having a majority of the stock market passively invested. Bob Monks has done some fantastic research on that, showing that companies primarily held by index investors underperform, et cetera, et cetera.

Deborah Midanek: I laugh when I see Larry Fink of BlackRock putting out his letters, because I'm thinking, "Yeah, you're sitting on this big pile of indexed assets. You have a bully pulpit and you're using it well, but you're the ultimate pragmatist." What's in it for Larry?

Nell Minow: By the way, there was a report that just came out last week showing that BlackRock does not put our money where their mouths are, and that they consistently vote against even advisory-only proposals on climate change.

Deborah Midanek: Moving on, what defines success for a board? How can they measure whether they're doing their job well, or not?

Nell Minow: You know what? It's like any other big job. it's like raising kids. You won't know until 10 years from now how you did. It's important that they know that that is how they'll be measured, which is why I'm extremely hardcore on stock ownership, and I don't think that board members or executives should be allowed to sell their stock for five years after leaving the company.

Deborah Midanek: There's another question to that, which is how much should they own?

Nell Minow: A lot. In terms of their own personal net worth, a very meaningful chunk. We have a quote in our book from a board where every director had at least a million dollars in the stock, and one of them said, "You never saw the pocket calculators come out so fast." Those are people who are really invested.

Many, many years ago, I went to an annual meeting and when it was the time to vote for the directors, I raised my hand. I get the eye roll. I have teenagers, so I'm impervious to the eye roll. They asked if I could wait until after the meeting to ask my question. I said, "No. I need to know the answer to this question before I decide whether I'm going to vote for this board. I want each member of the board to get up and tell me why this stock is a bad investment, because no one on this board has more than 100 shares. I have five million shares on behalf of my customers, and I would like to know what I'm missing." So the company voted to give each of the board members a thousand shares. That was how they responded to my question.

Deborah Midanek: Well, you're right. The corollary to that is that they have to be in a position where they can't sell it. Because otherwise, we're upping the ante on short-termism.

Nell Minow: Well, one of the things that I've been working on for the past year, that has just made me crazy, is share buybacks. I have no problem with buybacks theoretically, when the theory of buybacks is that you buy back stock when you have excess cash, and the stock is undervalued. But last year there were a record number of buybacks, mostly at 10 companies, and the stock was at a high. The stock market as a whole was at a high. None of the companies adjusted their EPS targets and incentive compensation to reflect the buybacks, which makes me furious.

Deborah Midanek: Because they were using the buybacks to meet their earnings target.

Nell Minow: Exactly. There's data showing that companies otherwise unlikely to meet their earnings targets were more likely to do buybacks. Furthermore, many of the boards allowed the CEO to sell into the buyback, which is a very bad mixed signal. They're supposed to be telling the market that the stock is undervalued, which is why they're buying it. Because you shouldn't be spending any corporate money on anything that isn't a good deal.

That's the idea. So they're buying back stock, they're saying that it's undervalued, and yet the CEO is selling into the buyback? That's ridiculous. The CEO's getting a triple dip. He's hitting the EPS targets, so he's getting his bonus, and he's getting the benefit of the rise in the stock price from the buyback, and he's selling his stock into the buyback. That's crazy. There's also a survey I quoted in one of my articles that asked directors, "Why did you approve the buybacks?" The directors had no idea.

I was arguing with the chairman of a comp committee once about a comp plan, and I said, "You paid out the bonus even though he didn't meet the targets," which seemed like an obvious comment to me. He said, "Well, yes, but he made some very difficult decisions that are going to pay off in the long run." I said, "Great. Guess when we're going to pay him for that?" I know you're going to pay him then. So, you're going to tell me you're paying him twice for the same thing?

Deborah Midanek: So where is a board that's doing the job well? Can you point to one? While you're thinking about that, I'll tell you that my main analogy, and I'm sure it's yours, for how you operate as a member of the board, is to conceive of yourself as a parent. Right?

When the child is small, and it's an early stage company, you're trying to make sure that they have the tools they need to grow, they've got the right vaccinations, you know, they've got the right beginning education, and they're not allowed to use their own judgment at all. Right?

Over time, you're moving the fences back to make sure that they're learning to use their judgment, but you have an eagle eye on them, constantly, about whether they are performing properly. To me, this is an obvious analogy, and it goes right by so many people sitting on boards.

Nell Minow: I completely agree with that. The answer to your question is the only boards that I know that do an excellent job are the boards dealing with catastrophe. Because, believe me, I've spent a lot of time thinking about why it is that some of the most capable, accomplished people in the country do such a bad job as directors.

I consider myself kind of an anthropologist of the boardroom. It helps to be a woman because you're already an outsider, and they're treating you differently. You might as well take advantage of it. My view as an anthropologist is that the one quality that is most prevalent in the people who are accomplished enough to become corporate directors, is that they have a genius-level ability to size up the norms in any situation, and seamlessly adapt to them. If, therefore, they walked into their first boardroom and everybody was putting their coffee cups on their heads, they would just sit down and put their coffee cups on their heads.

Over and over, and that's a wonderful quality to have, and it hugely contributes to the success these people have had. Over and over, we hear things like what the directors at Enron said, when asked after the fact to explain why they agreed to waive the company's conflict of interest rules and permit the outrageous self-dealing structures. They all said, "Well, nobody else said anything."

That's not conducive to very good oversight, unless things go very badly. Because I will say that directors generally have a very, very strong sense of integrity, and when things become catastrophic, they have almost always stepped in and done the right thing. We see that now in WeWork. But when things are going well, boards are terrible.

Deborah Midanek: As Hyman Minsky, the economist, said, "Stability breeds instability." That's when all the diseases and pathologies are being planted, and nobody's really looking because they're patting each other on the back.

Nell Minow: Yes. I like that.

Deborah Midanek: Having sat on a number of boards, I know it's very difficult to be an outlier and be heard. You need to speak from the center of the discussion, and move it incrementally toward the direction you want to go in. If you take an extreme position, you put yourself in a position where you're in a win-lose with the other people in the room, and you're most likely to lose. I believe Mr. Monks has done this once or twice.

Nell Minow: Bob was on a board where he thought the board was very dysfunctional, and he kept asking questions and making everybody uncomfortable. Finally, nobody would listen to him.

Eventually, he said, "Ugh, how about if we bring in someone to do a board evaluation?" They said, "Okay." So, he thought, "All right. That way, everybody will feel comfortable raising their concerns, and it's going to be … I'll finally get some traction here."

The person came in to do the board evaluation, and the conclusion of the evaluation was that everything was great except for this one troublemaker, who should be removed from the board. That board was Tyco, which became involved in this massive fraud, and the CEO went to prison.

I talked to a guy who was on the board of General Motors when it was listed in surveys as the most admired board in the country, even though it was on the way to complete and total disaster. He said, "The board materials would be delivered by forklift," and then he would go to the meeting, and it would be presentation, presentation, presentation, pick up your new car, and go home. He said, "On the agenda, there was never any time listed for questions or discussion."

When people ask me how to make boards more effective, there are two things that I recommend. One is that you assume going in that everybody's read everything, and 100% of the time is for questions and discussion. Two, that someone other than the CEO controls the agenda and the quantity, quality, and timing of the information that is sent to the directors.

Deborah Midanek: The work of the board is very different from the work of the company, and the leader of the board has a big job to do in being sure not only that that work is done and that the agenda is appropriately developed, reflecting lots of different points of view, but that person is also supposed to be getting the value out of the diverse opinions that are in the room.

Nell Minow: Exactly. It's the most underused asset in the company. You have these extraordinary people, and you are treating them like potted plants.

Deborah Midanek: Absolutely! They allow it. My husband, who studied Roberts Rules when he was in eighth grade, and has been chairman of various companies, and said, "I knew Roberts Rules well enough that I could assert my position and nobody knew whether I was right or not. So I could control any meeting." But here's my favorite. "I'm sorry. We don't have time for that because so and so has got to run to catch a plane."

How often have you heard that? I am thinking, "What? We have got so much money and so many people who have dedicated so much time to being here, and you're going to torpedo the whole thing because somebody has to run to a plane?! Let them run to the plane!"

Nell Minow: Yeah. We'll miss you. Bye.

Deborah Midanek: I also saw a college classmate of mine who had been an early partner of one of first LBO shops. I said, "Hey, talk to me about corporate governance." He looked at me, and he said, "I don't care about corporate governance. There is one sentence that I will offer you, which is that you have to have people on the board who have the experience, the ability, and the courage to tell the CEO when the CEO is dead wrong. If you don't have that, there's no point in any other thing." I thought that was pretty efficient.

Nell Minow: The CEO is going to be surrounded by people who tell him how wonderful he is all the time. Somebody's got to be there to counter that.

I will say this about KKR. KKR taught me the single most important lesson that I learned in my first year of working in this arena. As we have said that was the middle of the LBO era. At the time, the CEO of RJR Nabisco had 22 golf club memberships that were paid for by the company, and of course, the jet and all of that. When KKR came in, the very first thing he said to them, reflecting his priorities, was, "I hope you guys aren't going to make a fuss about my country clubs, or the plane, or anything like that." They said, "Actually, we are." He said, "Why?"

Deborah Midanek: Because we have to pay all those investment banking fees.

Nell Minow: They said, "Because it's our money." To me, that was the big light bulb moment because why is it that the debt guys get to say, "Because it's our money," when the equity guys never get to say, "Because it's our money." That's what I have spent the rest of my career doing, on behalf of the equity guys, saying, "Because it's our money."

Deborah Midanek: As a restructuring person, when I have creditors that want to do an all equity plan, which means the creditors own 100% of the company when it comes out of bankruptcy, I have counseled them, "Do not do that. Keep at least $10 million in debt, because then you will have greater rights to sit at the table."

Nell Minow: You shouldn't. You shouldn't.

Deborah Midanek: Back to Drexel and the LBO days, the idea behind using bonds to acquire companies was that that was the cheapest form of capital, because you got to deduct the interest. It wasn't that Milken was a debt maven, it's that he was saying, "Hey, this is a really cool way to buy companies because it's cheap."

Nell Minow: Again, that's a function of the tax law. The same thing was true with why everybody all of a sudden started giving insane amounts of stock options, because the company didn't have to expense them. I always say that is Exhibit A in the law of unintended consequences.

Deborah Midanek: I think that, despite your very nuanced command of what is going on and what the pressures are in America's boardrooms, I'm hearing someone who is fundamentally bullish on the future of governance. You think it's getting better, do you not? Because the shareholders are more able to be effective in having their voices heard.

Nell Minow: Yes and no. I have kind of a Dickensian best of times, worst of times view on it, because some things are so much worse than I could have imagined, but so many things are so much better. I mean, when I got into this business, OJ Simpson was on five boards, and he was on an audit committee.

There was a company where the CEO's father was on the compensation committee. The CEOs of Cummins Engine and Inland Steel chaired each other's compensation committees, and generally speaking, directors felt very comfortable saying to me, "The job of the director is to ask in case of emergency," and I would say, "No, no, no. The job of the director is to prevent emergency."

At that time, there were people who served on 10 boards; Frank Carlucci served on 30 boards at the same time. He averaged a board meeting a day. A lot of that is gone.

When Bob and I, during the slow years, made lists of how we'll know when we've succeeded. One thing on the list was that corporate governance will be taught in law schools and business schools. Well, that is finally beginning to happen, and they're using our book.

So corporate governance is a field now, a presence now, it's understood that it's important. A lot of stuff is much better than we ever hoped. On the other hand, the other thing beside buybacks that I've been spending my time on is the dark money behind groups like the Main Street Investors Coalition, which has nothing to do with Main Street or investing, and is not a coalition. It's funded by the National Association of Manufacturers to extinguish shareholder rights.

They have been extremely effective at the SEC, and now the Department of Labor. They got Trump to issue an executive order. They're spending a fortune. They're spending a fortune trying to stop everything that we have achieved so far, including, as I said, the 1988 Avon ruling.

Deborah Midanek: So, last question, given that it's a Dickensian situation, the best of times and the worst of times. What do we do from here to improve it? What do we do? Because our corporations are remarkably important.

Nell Minow: Our corporations are remarkably important, so are institutional investors, and we need to pay more attention to the role that they play in our capital markets. Nobody thought about the effect that the switch in the 1990s from defined benefit pension plans to defined contribution plans would have on the capital markets.

We were much better off with the idea of large fiduciaries who are permanent holders, and who are ideal proxies for society as a whole. For pension funds, 30 years from the day that a dollar comes into the plan it has to be paid out. We need to focus much, much more on the governance and the responsibilities, and the performance, and I mean not just financial performance, but governance-related performance of the institutional investors.

Deborah Midanek: One of the things that I find interesting about looking at the new paradigm for corporate governance, and so on, is that whether you believe that the actual bargain that is being proposed there is possible or not, it certainly elevates the dialog. But it also highlights the fact that there is a fairly small number of huge corporations in this world, and there is a remarkably small number of huge institutional investors, whether they are the public pension funds, the ultimate fiduciary, or whether they are the intermediaries like BlackRock. It's a tiny, tiny number.

So that may bring us full circle back to the point where it's possible for them to actually talk to each other, and hammer out some version of a paradigm for governance. What do you think?

Nell Minow: Yes. I would underscore that by saying that only corporate governance can solve the problems facing the world right now, because these corporations that you've just described transcend any kind of jurisdictional boundaries.

And so do the consequences of their actions. You know, Walmart's operations in China create much air pollution. Their decision to look at that as an issue did more to help the issue of climate change than any ruling by any government or the Paris Accords.

Only investors and corporations transcend jurisdictional boundaries and, therefore, it's absolutely essential that they work together on these issues that affect the entire planet.

Deborah Midanek: That's one of the reasons that I care enough to spend my time on governance matters. The corporations and the investors are the world's best hope. As an aside, one thing I have found in boardrooms is how ridiculously uninformed directors as a whole are about the functioning of capital markets.

Nell Minow: Yes, that is definitely true. They can read a balance sheet but they don't have any understanding of macroeconomics.

Deborah Midanek: Right! So what they are is putty in the hands of people who tell them what their shareholders want.

Nell Minow: Absolutely. I talked to one director who said that the CEO talked to the board about going from a quarterly dividend to an annual dividend, and you know exactly what was on that PowerPoint. They all voted yes, okay, fine.

Then they went to the annual meeting and this was a real widows-and-orphans stock, and people got up and were crying at the annual meeting because they were so upset about this. She said, "No one ever said anything to us about that. They said the shareholders are going to love this."

I think IR [investor relations] departments are really useless. They see themselves schmoozing securities analysts. I talked to one IR guy years ago, and he said, "We do this on the buy side, we do this on the sell side," and I said, "And who's responsible for the hold side, because that's the side I care about?"

Deborah Midanek: We're preaching to the choir, which is to say that the design of investor relations, which took root in the 1950s, was completely wrong-headed. It probably took 40 years for anybody ever to connect the dots between investor relations and the board.

Nell Minow: Right.

Deborah Midanek: I can't tell you how many times, as a director, I have asked for conversations with the shareholders, and been rudely dismissed because after all, that is something directors simply do not do, because they simply can't be trusted to offer a limited and consistent message.

Nell Minow: Absolutely. Reg FD, Reg FD.

Deborah Midanek: You trust me to sit in this chair and make decisions with respect to this company, but you don't trust me to have the discretion to know what I can talk about with a shareholder and what I can't? Okay, then go with me to the conversation with the shareholders.

The design issue here is that we're supposed to be thinking about the shareholders and making these decisions on their behalf. How can we do that if we don't know what's on their minds?

Thank you so much, Nell.

Nell Minow: It's been a pleasure. Let me know if I can do anything else.

Chapter 12
What we need to do is listen to each other

Michael Useem

Michael Useem is the William and Jacalyn Egan Professor of Management and Director of the Center for Leadership and Change Management at the Wharton School, University of Pennsylvania. He is also a prodigious contributor to our thinking about organizations, management, and change.

Professor Useem has completed studies of corporate organization, ownership, governance, restructuring, leadership, and teamwork. He is author of *The Leader's Checklist* (Wharton Digital Press, 2011); co-author of *The India Way: How India's Top Business Leaders Are Revolutionizing Management* (Harvard Business Press, 2010); co-author and co-editor of *Learning from Catastrophes* (Wharton School Publishing, 2009); author of *The Go Point: When It's Time to Decide* (Random House, 2006); the co-author and co-editor of *Upward Bound: Nine Original Accounts of How Business Leaders Reached Their Summits* (Random House, 2003); author of *Leading Up: How to Lead Your Boss So You Both Win* (Random House, 2001); *The Leadership Moment: Nine True Stories of Triumph and Disaster and Their Lessons for Us All* (Random House, 1998); *Investor Capitalism: How Money Managers Are Changing the Face of Corporate America* (HarperCollins, 1996); *Executive Defense: Shareholder Power and Corporate Reorganization* (Harvard University Press, 1993); co-author of *Change at Work* (Oxford University Press, 1997); *Turbulence in the American Workplace* (Oxford University Press, 1991); co-editor of *Transforming Organizations* (Oxford University Press, 1992); co-author of *Educating Managers* (Jossey-Bass, 1986); and author of *The Inner Circle: Large Corporations and the Rise of Business Political Activity in the U.S. and U.K.* (Oxford University Press, 1984).

In addition to his writing and teaching, Michael has presented programs and seminars on leadership and change with Abbott Laboratories, Accenture, ADP, American Express, Amgen, Berkshire Partners, Canadian Imperial Bank of Commerce, Cargill, CEO Academy, China Minsheng Banking Corporation, Citigroup, Cisco Systems, Citic Bank (China), Coca-Cola, Columbia Energy, Comcast, Computer Sciences Corporation, Daimler, Deloitte, DuPont, Entergy, Eli Lilly, Estee Lauder Companies, Federal Executive Institute, Fidelity Investments, GlaxoSmithKline, Goldman Sachs,

https://doi.org/10.1515/9783110670004-013

Google, Grupo Santander (Chile), Hartford Insurance, Hearst, Hewlett-Packard, HSM, IBM, ICICI Bank (India), Intel, Johnson & Johnson, Kimberly-Clark, KPMG, Liberty Mutual Insurance, Lucent Technologies, MassMutual, MasterCard, McGraw-Hill, Medtronic, Merck, Microsoft, Milliken, Morgan Stanley, Motorola, National Football League, Navigant, The New York Times, Nokia, Northrop Grumman, Novartis, Penske, Petrobras (Brazil), Petroleos de Venezuela, Pew Charitable Trusts, Pricewaterhouse Coopers, Raytheon, Samsung, Securities Association of China, Siemens, Singapore General Hospital, Sprint, 3Com Corporation, Thomson Financial, Toyota, Travelers, Verizon, United Healthcare, United Technologies, U.N. Development Programme, U.S. Department of Justice, U.S. Department of Veteran Affairs, U.S. Marine Corps, U.S. Military Academy, World Economic Forum, and other organizations.

He has also consulted on governance with Fannie Mae, HealthSouth, Tyco International, and other companies; and on organizational development and change with the U.S. Agency for International Development, U.N. Food and Agriculture Organization, Organization of American States, and other agencies in Latin America, Asia, and Africa.

Michael Useem's university teaching includes MBA and executive-MBA courses on leadership and change management. He also edits the bi-monthly electronic bulletin, *Wharton Leadership Digest*. He holds a B.S. from the University of Michigan and an M.A. and Ph.D. from Harvard University.

Deborah Midanek: The first question is this: Professor Michael Useem, who are you and what makes you tick?

Michael Useem: I'm on the faculty of the Wharton School of Business at the University of Pennsylvania. A while back I became interested in senior management and large companies, and I began to write about and teach courses on corporate leadership. But of course you can't think about business firms and executives and understand how they operate without also looking at their governing boards.

Were you an undergraduate or an MBA at the University of Pennsylvania?

Deborah Midanek: Well that's a deep dark secret. I did start my undergraduate career at the University of Pennsylvania when it was still the College for Women. I lived over the mail room in Morgan Wilson Memorial Tower. I watched the White Tower that used to be at 37th and Spruce be demolished and then the Ant Farm, aka the Wharton School's new home, Vance Hall, being built. I finished my degree at Bryn Mawr and then returned to attend Wharton for my MBA.

Michael Useem: In my own case, I now primarily teach MBA students, executive-MBA students, mid-career managers, and company executives and directors. In those programs, I couldn't do justice to the issues of company compensation, decision making, shareholder rights, and other topics without giving a lot of thought to how boards are put together, how they operate, and what they stand for.

Deborah Midanek: Did you reach any conclusions? Is there a particular aspect of it that puzzles you, fascinates you, confuses you?

Michael Useem: My own thinking today still dates back to an early research experience in which I interviewed chief executives and board members of major US companies and British firms, primarily in New York and London. British directors, for example, were much more comfortable with the Conservative Party in London than company directors over here were comfortable with American politics at all, and that difference affected how companies operated. Until then, I hadn't really thought about governing boards and how they influence company behavior.

Upon talking with those chief executives and board members, including the CEO of Chase bank in the US, for example, and the top people for National Westminster bank in the UK, I discovered that governing boards often played a significant role. Though boards of directors have sometimes been dismissed as inconsequential, I concluded that they could be very impactful. As a result, I became interested in how boards operate, how they work with top management, and how they bring value to their enterprise.

Deborah Midanek: So do you think that it is clear that they do add value? How do they do that? There are people who would argue with you about that.

Michael Useem: Sometimes boards add little or no value. As part of that early study, I sat down, for instance, with the chief executive and chief financial officers of the then-large American conglomerate, ITT. It made everything from Twinkies to telephones. The ITT executives made an implicit case that their directors added little value to what they, the company leaders, were thinking or doing. The CEO and CFO reported meeting periodically with their board for 90 minutes over lunch and, near the end, the directors by custom would politely return their napkin to the table and collect a check from beneath their plate for attending the noontime meeting – a fitting conclusion for the largely perfunctory gathering.

But consider the governance reforms enacted after the failures of Enron, WorldCom, and Tyco in the early 2000s. Since then, American boards have been on a two-decade-long march toward greater oversight of and stronger partnership with top management. If properly composed, if of the right size, if supplied with the right ingredients, directors today are better at keeping companies from going off the rails and also serving as sounding boards and strategic partners for company executives, providing informed advice and counsel. As a consequence, boards today are more widely expected to add value, and when they fail to do so, shareholders and regulators have become quicker to intervene. Consider the failure of executives of Wells Fargo Bank to prevent their sales force from creating false accounts for customers when pressured by its compensation policies to do so. This led the bank to forfeit billions in financial penalties and badly lag other major banks in the growth of its market value.

In response, the Federal Reserve forced the Wells board to fundamentally restructure itself to prevent such malfeasance in the future. The Fed has, for instance, pushed the board to be smaller, more diverse, and stocked with directors who understand enterprise risk management. The directors can now better press for and evaluate steps that Wells executives are taking to ensure that the bank's customers are not improperly served again.

For the past 20 years, boards have been on a long march to become more engaged with management, more effective in guiding management, and more able to add value to management. Governing boards have moved well beyond their fiduciary obligations to helping companies be better led.

Deborah Midanek: You're absolutely right that Enron, Tyco, WorldCom did precipitate Sarbanes-Oxley and renewed focus on the board. Then we have the financial crisis and further indications of the distance between the board and the reality of a number of companies' operations. That 20 years has indeed been full of change. You also mentioned Jensen, who wrote with Meckling that seminal paper in 1976 talking about the agency theory of the board, following Milton Friedman's paper that the business of business is to earn a profit. Combined with high inflation, with the takeover movement in the 70s and so on, those things did have a major impact on corporate governance. Focus shifted from the idea of the board as the compadres of the CEO, offering advice and access and connections and so on, to the monitoring role.

We moved into something called shareholder primacy, where big investors got bigger and bigger, so they pretty much have to own the shares of most large corporations. The idea that the board was responsible to the shareholders directly became widespread.

Michael Useem: You've summed it up very well.

Deborah Midanek: Well, I spend a lot of time thinking about it, to tell you the truth.

Michael Useem: This is an American story more than elsewhere, and the essence of it is to place shareholder primacy at the center of the more engaged board's attention. In consonance with the influential works by Michael Jensen and Milton Friedman, many were making the argument that boards had to become more engaged in protecting and advancing total shareholder return – but only that. If you talked to directors and executives and suggested more diverse concerns beyond just TSR – e.g., that boards ought to be focusing on climate change or living wages – it was heretical. But during the last a couple of years, the Business Roundtable and institutional investors have finally pushed the pendulum the other way, arguing that directors and executives should focus on a host of stakeholders, not just investors, and on the long-term, not just the quarter.

Deborah Midanek: Yes, indeed, that shift feels recent and widespread. It is true that 20 years ago focusing on ESG was considered heretical. No board member can afford to be considered heretical because once you're identified that way you lose all chance of influencing the whole group, which is the only way you can get anything done. ESG was seen as a wild outlier, and not about the core of governance. It's fascinating to watch these very same investors that were pushing for shareholder primacy, now pushing ESG, which has become a proxy for corporations taking a long-term view. It's so interesting to watch, isn't it?

Michael Useem: I'm a little bit skeptical of how far directors will be willing to change company focus, but the very strong statement in 2019 from the Business Roundtable will, if followed up by directors, make me more optimistic that boards will become more diverse in what they're pushing top executives to do.

Deborah Midanek: That leads me to confront the basic maxim since Jensen and Meckling wrote their article: that the goal of the board is to maximize shareholder value. If you sit and think about what that means, you realize that it is a conversation stopper. You can't argue with it, but what does it mean?

Michael Useem: It's a great point. Let's just dwell for a second on what that means tangibly. Let's say the chief executive of a major US publicly-traded firm said to me, I've read this Business Roundtable 2019 statement and I want to work with the board to enact it. What does that mean in terms of how we structure executive pay? Who do we bring on the board to better serve multiple stakeholders? What new board committees should we have? Should the status of the chief of human resources at the company be on a par with the status of the chief financial officer? I think the next five years will be riveting as many directors and executives realize that the pendulum is swinging back, and as they try to figure out what it means for what they have to do.

The recruiters of executives and directors will also have to work through what kinds of new directors will be needed. Companies will want fresh faces that know not only how to run a company but also how to make for more sustainability and less inequality.

Deborah Midanek: It is very interesting because if you argued that maximizing shareholder value was an inadequate description of the goal of the board, it was the equivalent of the kind of heresy you've mentioned in about talking about climate change. What that narrow focus did, and I hope it is past tense, is force everyone to default to the nearby share price as the best measure because everything else was subjective.

Michael Useem: Yes, certainly.

Deborah Midanek: Exactly. So you end up with this solipsism where the shareholders, in pushing this idea of shareholder primacy are to some extent shooting themselves in the foot. In insisting that maximizing shareholder value was the goal, and that the directors represent only them, what they may have been doing is reducing the board's ability to focus on long-term investing. Thus, to me, the next question is a really important one, which is to whom does the board owe its fiduciary duty?

Michael Useem: You raise a good question for which there is no sure answer. We can look at what the state of Delaware expects where so many companies are incorporated, but I think we also have to look at how companies and boards actually operate. I believe it's useful to study who actually goes on a board, and when annual director reviews are conducted, what questions are they asked about the contributions of the other directors?

If you look at the list of questions in typical board self-evaluations that each director is asked to answer about the other directors in the room, they tend to be, "Does this director perform as a fair adviser on business matters?" as opposed to, "Does this director optimize shareholder return for the company?" Or "Is this director good at identifying strong talent when the CEO brings in a CFO candidate?" instead of questions such as, "Has this director significantly contributed to the quarter's earnings per share?"

Lots of voices weigh-in on what directors should do, including the courts in Delaware, the Securities and Exchange Commission, the New York Stock Exchange, institutional holders, activist investors, governance raters, and academic researchers, but in watching directors in action, I am impressed with how they themselves have moved in recent years toward greater focus on their service as trusted advisors of the CEO while at the same remaining tough-minded overseers of the chief executive.

Deborah Midanek: In a recent conversation, a respected investor told me that, "I don't have time to talk about corporate governance. The only thing that I want to know about somebody who serves on a board is does he have both the courage and the knowledge to be able to tell the CEO when the CEO is full of %&#@?"

I thought to myself, that's a very efficient description of the need. So what you are saying, I think, is that the monitoring role could have been looked at as more passive in terms of looking at checklists and being sure that compliance in the biggest possible sense was being addressed. But that in this more active working partnership with the CEO about strategy, capacity, avoiding catastrophe, the board has a much more active and engaged position.

This can be seen as going back to the design that was believed to be prevalent in the 50s and 60s, that the board members were advisors to the CEO and were his trusted people. That question of trust is the really important intangible here. The people who are doing this job need to be able to engender trust between themselves, and between themselves and the CEO, and between themselves and the big shareholders.

Michael Useem: Put yourself in the position of the current chief executive of, let's say, General Electric. You certainly want to have total trust with everybody in the boardroom. You also want them to know what the heck they're talking about. For that reason, my intuition from hearing many executives and directors speak about the issues is that a great director is somebody who has served as the CEO of a company of similar size in the last 10 or 15 years. You can likely get more from that person than from anybody else with other kinds of professional backgrounds. For the board's inner circle of the most important directors, I think you cannot do better than relying on the former CEOs.

Deborah Midanek: Like so many things in this our discussion, it cuts both ways. The model of the CEO as the most attractive board member has been the dominant model for some time. But the flip side of that is that you don't necessarily get the diversity of thought from that person that is valuable in terms of risk protection.

Michael Useem: Totally.

Deborah Midanek: It is still the case that despite major changes and much progress, the average age of the public company board member falls in a very narrow band of say 63 to 65, The gender is typically male and ethnicity is white. I'm in that age range and have great sympathy for the fact that this is the way boards have evolved. I understand it, but nevertheless, if everyone is seeing the issues through a similar lens, they're going to be blindsided.

Michael Useem: If you step back and ask, what exactly is a board? Well, it's at least an advisory and sometimes decision-making group. A team may be a little bit slower if it's more diverse, but it is almost always better for the quality of the decisions that come out. If I were putting a board together, I'd like to have three or four former CEOs, but I also definitely want the remainder to be non-CEOs. I want somebody who's had technical expertise about how to think about science and engineering in such areas as climate change and product development. And if you have gender diversity, the research confirms that you again have better decisions coming from the board.

Let's turn that upside down: should you see a board that's all guys in a limited age range that mostly come from the same metropolitan area, you might well think, "Here's a company that doesn't believe more diversity in thought is better for producing whatever product they're making," and therefore short the stock. To put that back in the affirmative, we now have additional criteria for evaluating a board's composition from what had been dominant even just five years ago. We now want directors of many different stripes, including those of varied age and gender and color and experience.

Deborah Midanek: Having served as a CEO, a board like that requires a great deal more work. CEOs can speak to each other in a certain shorthand, they have been in the chair, and as you said above, confront issues with a degree of understanding. People that come from very different walks of life and from different experience bases require a lot of original effort to establish a common vocabulary and an understanding of what they need to learn. So what often happens is that these new people act as if they're a guest at a state dinner unfamiliar with which fork to use. So they watch the guy next to them to see which fork to pick up.

Getting that group of diverse people to be able – clearly and easily and candidly – to communicate with each other takes a lot of work. So this leads to the question of board leadership. You mentioned that the lead director has become a very substantial role. Do you think that responsibility for running the board and running the company should be separate roles?

Michael Useem: Historically, I think the board wasn't much "managed" and the chair handled what *was* managed in a limited and informal fashion. Now, the board chair and lead director spend much more time on the mechanics of how to lead a good team. Do you have a strategic agenda? Is strategy on the table at every board meeting? Does everybody speak at the table? Are there any underperformers in the room? These would not have been active topics when boards were more passive. But now boards are more autonomous, more powerful, more impactful. Look at what lead directors do these days in terms of the hours they devote to their board. It's become a very big and very time-consuming calling.

Deborah Midanek: It is.

Michael Useem: It's a big deal, right?

Deborah Midanek: Yes. Not broadly understood by those people that aren't familiar with what goes on in the board.

Michael Useem: The role of the lead director is still one of the great secrets of corporate governance. What exactly is a lead director and what do they do that the board chair does not? I find that I have to explain that to many audiences.

Deborah Midanek: That brings us to another point, which is that a lead director is a creature of the huge shift over the last 50 years to favoring independent directors to an overwhelming extent. So the lead director is by definition the leader of the independents, if not the leader of the whole board. Do you think that independent directors have been overdone? Do you think that they are useful?

Michael Useem: I think we're better off with the new model. Typically, an 11-member board includes one insider, the CEO, and 10 independent directors. If you have 10 heavy hitters from the outside on your board, I think you're getting good value. If some of them are significant shareholders, so much the better. If you have big stockholders who have not had management experience, however, the company may perform less well.

Major shareholders on the board without personal management experience, I infer from the research, are less able to serve as trusted advisors of the chief executive and his or her top team. They are less likely to know whether a given acquisition or a new compensation plan is good or bad, or if a proposed legal settlement ought to be accepted – because they've never had to face those questions. They have a huge financial interest in the enterprise, but the lack of prior business leadership experience hampers them, even though they're very close to the company if they inherited their ownership stake from their parents who founded the firm.

Deborah Midanek: I'm living through that circumstance right now. What happens is that those people don't know what they don't know, but they know that they don't know a lot, so there is a lot of insecurity. This can lead to rage and finger-pointing and weird behavior because they're terrified.

Michael Useem: Just to put a fine point on that, I think you probably follow the Spencer Stuart annual survey of large-company board practices. It shows that here has been a steady movement toward a board size of about 10 or 11 members on average. One insider and 9 to 10 outsiders, and three required board committees, all composed of outsiders. I think it will be *the* model we're likely to see, for good reason, for quite some time. In my view, it optimizes the board's ability to serve as a trusted advisor to, and partner with, top management.

Deborah Midanek: How do you think the board can acquit itself of its responsibility to nurture a strong and positive tone at the top along with an ethical corporate culture? Do you think that is a byproduct of what you're talking about in terms of robust processes ensured by disinterested people?

Michael Useem: That's a really important topic. Let's go back to Wells Fargo Bank. I think that's why the Fed has come down so hard on the Wells governance scheme. The Fed forced the Wells board to contract, and separated the board chair from the CEO. Elizabeth Duke, who had been a governor of the Federal Reserve, has been brought in as the chair. The Wells annual proxy statement describes at length the many steps the board has taken to improve the tone at the top. And the Fed had said, until the board improves the tone at the top by recruiting the right non-executive chair, by creating the diversity that ought to have been on the board all the way along, by conducting annual evaluations of directors that make sense, by rotating committee chairs, by creating a separate risk committee, you cannot grow. While each of those factors in and of itself won't make that much difference, taken together it is clear that the Fed is trying to make certain that there is now the right tone at the top.

I think it's within our grasp to set the right tone at the top if the directors are the right directors and if they act in concert. If they don't pay attention, however, as evidently the earlier Wells board had fallen short, then we have a new problem, called crisis or even survival. Boards are fortunately now beginning to tangle with ensuring business continuity and enterprise risk management.

Deborah Midanek: It's quite fun to listen to you because I think that you are on the bullish side of the spectrum as far as improvements go in the current corporate governance model. You think that the stewardship structure works and will be getting better.

Michael Useem: Yes, for sure.

Deborah Midanek: So what else can we do to make it better? Because if 500 corporations are as dominant as the World Economic Forum says they are at 70% of world output, while government is having a much harder time making its will felt, corporate behavior will determine the future of our world.

Michael Useem: Unequivocally.

Deborah Midanek: So what do we do to make it even better? One thing someone suggested is, if the chair of the board is a really, really important role, how do we make sure that the right people are serving as the chair? We need those people to be doing it not just from the point of view of improving the value of the shares, but from the point of view of improving the company's contribution to the planet.

Michael Useem: I again refer to the Business Roundtable's 2019 proclamation, which did not call for government regulation. Instead it basically said, "Come on everybody, pull your socks up and let's together make a better world, not just more shareholder value." I happen to be in that camp of thinking, that changes of this magnitude in business will only come out of a collective of people like those in the Business Roundtable at the World Economic Forum, and that no single voice is going to change much of anything nationally. But when we see 181 CEOs signing on to the Business Roundtable agenda, and 2,500 people attending the annual meeting of the World Economic Forum in Davos, and large institutional investors like Vanguard and BlackRock all moving in a similar direction, I tend to be on the optimistic side.

For me the Business Roundtable declaration was especially powerful because it went against what executives, directors, and investors had been saying for 40 years. In the past, the American mantra has become that the purpose of the corporation was to ensure high shareholder return, period. Everything else was secondary. But no longer.

Five years ago, CVS abolished tobacco products from its stores. It took a $2 billion hit to its stock price as the Street didn't understand the decision. The CEO, Larry Merlo, obviously gave it a lot of thought, reviewed it with his top team including the head of tobacco products, and spent a lot of time with his board. We interviewed him for a book we recently completed and came to learn the inside story. He said that for the longer term, we want CVS to be a health company and not a convenience store. We're going to lose money short term in this conversion. And since I'm the CEO, I'm going to lead the very difficult change. I can't do it by fiat any more than Donald Trump can tell companies to leave China. What I can do is build a coalition of the willing. He had to get buy-in from the board members, from the top executives, from the stores, and from franchise operators, and in the end he did, changing both the identity of CVS and public health. He made the change happen. It didn't come as an edict from a state capitol or the SEC, but by seeing where the world should be going.

Deborah Midanek: He's got courage. A critical question is how do we help the leaders of companies and leaders of the board to grow that courage, and deploy it and do that well in this crazy changing world that we're living in. And unfortunately that's the question that has no answers, right?

Michael Useem: We believe that we can work with all managers, executives, and directors to strengthen their courage along with every other element that defines how leaders lead. It is a challenge to do so, but a well-crafted leadership development program can do so.

Deborah Midanek: We'll just keep on holding up examples as you just did. Leading by example is the only way to go about doing it. I have an opinion about why this is possible now. In what may be another example of the "coalition of the willing," consider Marty Lipton and his new paradigm for corporate governance, his method of building alignment between investors and companies driving toward long-term value. That may be made possible by the huge role that index funds now play. Our big investors are inevitably invested in the shares of every big company. The effort they would have to go to to change that is very high. So they're left with having to be involved in governance as a way to protect their investments.

Michael Useem: In fact, I have been remiss in not sufficiently emphasizing the role of the BlackRocks, Vanguards, and other institutional investors as a part of the story here. Laurence Fink of BlackRock, William McNabb of Vanguard, and many others have been out front in advocating many of the principles that the Business Roundtable recently embraced. The premier funds have been a force for affirmative change, along with the Business Roundtable and the advocacy of a group led by attorney Martin Lipton. There are voices and forces that have fortunately been coming together for the past several years.

Deborah Midanek: There are even a great many in the legal community that just don't understand.

Michael Useem: I think people are increasingly being drawn to the governance arena who weren't in it before. A better phrase than "coalition of the willing" to describe them is a "coalition of the eager." Klaus Schwab, the founder and executive chair of the World Economic Forum, has been actively working in the same direction. I think we're going to end up with an even better governance scheme in the years ahead, and your new book is extremely timely in light of this shift.

Deborah Midanek: It's funny that when I started my first book, calling it *The Art of Governance*; but when I was halfway through it, the Wells Fargo actions by the Fed came out and I realized I was not writing about the art of governance. We are not living though gentle improvements, but are in the midst of a revolution. So I changed the title to *The Governance Revolution*.

Michael Useem: That has really been the point of our discussion. You're part of the movement, and it has indeed become a revolution. Great that you are getting those ideas out to help guide everybody's thinking.

Here's where I think the rubber's going to meet the road. When companies seek new directors, I predict we'll see that search firms are going to begin to hear a different mantra: "We want people who know how companies run, we want them to know how to make money, but we don't want people in those categories who also don't know about employment compensation schemes and what communities want and how supply chains work." These are the facets of being a board member that didn't count so much in the past, but I think that's where we are going to see some of the biggest change in the next couple of years in line with the new governance paradigm.

Deborah Midanek: I hope so. Because if I go back to your comments about the most critical core board member being a fellow CEO, that is shorthand for the fact that you need people on the board who are experienced, tested, and have the judgment and wisdom to work across different categories of endeavor. So the easiest way to express that is to call that a CEO. But to me the skills matrix that has driven a lot of board recruiting in the last umpteen years has always worried me because, while important, it emphasizes a divide and conquer approach. It's putting people in little silos when you need those various skills but what you really need is judgment and wisdom. You can acquire whatever the technical skills are that you may need if you have judgment and wisdom, but if you *don't have* judgment and wisdom, those technical skills are not going to carry the day.

Michael Useem: I totally agree.

Deborah Midanek: I have spoken like the turnaround manager that I am.

Michael Useem: Here's another way to make the same point. Let's say you are on a board's search committee to recruit three new directors. A good question to ask yourself when you interview them is to evaluate whether a year from now, when you conduct your annual evaluation of the board members, are they going to be star performers, or are they going to suck the air out of the room? I think the answer to that has much more bearing on the company's future than it would have had in the past.

I think the same revolution is slowly coming to other national settings. It's got a long way to go in China or India. But the winds of change, partly driven by the BlackRocks and Vanguards that have so much of their money invested abroad, are pointing in the same direction. I think we're seeing this is not just a US revolution.

Deborah Midanek: In fact, there are some ways that non-US companies are ahead, focused on the environment and the climate change issues. I love the fact that these are now easily considered global issues as opposed to single nation or market issues.

With that I must say I really appreciate your time. Thank you so much for investing your time and thought in our discussion.

Michael Useem: It worked well for me too, and I especially appreciate two things. Your questions have been great, and above all you are putting a lot of thought into creating an actionable set of thoughts on a really important topic.

Chapter 13
Clarity on the board's role can be transformative only if it is honest

Paul Halpern

As Chief Investment Officer for private equity firm Versa Capital Management, **Paul Halpern** has responsibility for day-to-day oversight and supervision of the content, quality, and implementation of Versa's investment process, including transaction sourcing, due diligence, underwriting, and execution.

He is a member of the firm's Investment, Portfolio, and Management Committees, and is currently Director of Versa's portfolio companies Allen-Vanguard Avenue Stores, Bell + Howell, BridgeStreet Worldwide, Civitas Media, Hatteras/Cabo Yachts, Polartec, Silver Airways and SynCardia Systems.

Mr. Halpern received a J.D. from Stanford Law School (with distinction, law review, and Order of the Coif) and his B.A. from Reed College (Phi Beta Kappa). He has been a member of Versa and its predecessors since 1995.

Deborah Midanek: Paul, thank you for your time. There is a debate going on in the world about who's controlling the corporation and its wealth. I am sure that you have a lot of opinions about that. Can you tell us a bit about your background? How you came to have the opinions that you hold?

Paul Halpern: I went to law school, studied all the usual things there, and went directly into bankruptcy and creditors rights practice where I spent six years representing middle-market debtors in Chapter 11 cases. Then I moved into the crisis management business where I was managing companies that were in transition, where secured lenders were taking the keys away from shareholders after defaults and other problems. They needed a management team to come in and take the roles of both board and management to work out the situation.

From there, my group and I started acquiring companies that were in special situations and then raised the first in a series of funds focused entirely on making control investments in distressed and special situations in middle-market companies in

https://doi.org/10.1515/9783110670004-014

North America. That's what I do now. When it comes to my experience as a board member, I have been a board member of all the portfolio companies of Versa Capital at one time or another, usually during most of our ownership. That's a total of 18 companies over time. We wound up merging one of our portfolio companies into a public company where I had the pleasure of being on a public board for the first time in my life.

On that board, I was on the finance committee and the audit committee and was a fairly deeply involved board member. That experience was very interesting because it taught me a lot about what I thought was wrong with public board structures. I'm also on the board of an independent school called Friends Central School. It's a Quaker school and that's very interesting because they bring a different perspective to how a board operates. This particular institution has a great deal of clarity about what a board's job is, which has been very enlightening in thinking about my job as a board member in both my portfolio companies and public boards.

My non-profit experience has been helpful because that institution has done a good job of being very clear with board members because it has a larger board and various motivations for making people part of the board. Board members may play other roles in the institution. So, if you're also a parent of a student at the school *and* sitting on the board, you really want to be clear with that parent about what their job is as a parent and what their job is as a board member. And how not to cross them up.

For that institution, there are three things the board has to do, three and only three. Those three things are: to select and support the head of the school, to define and then monitor implementation of strategy, and to provide representation of the school to its stakeholders. That's it. Everything else we do is either part of one of those things or a distraction. And the desire to get distracted and do the head's job for him or do the admission director's job for her or do the development director's job is enormous and always mistaken. When I take that to my portfolio as a private equity owner, there are things we do as shareholders and things we do as directors, and those tend to get blurred. At our firm, for example, we generally keep capital markets activities here at the firm rather than in the portfolio company.

When I think about my board role within our portfolio, I'm usually thinking about our periodic reviews with management of what they're doing and how they're doing it. This starts at the end of the year as budget, and then begins immediately thereafter with strategy and execution monitoring, but actually has a longer cycle that begins with our acquisition and ends with our disposition. The problem with what I've said and the problem with this division of responsibilities is that strategy is a lot easier to name than define and it's not very well bounded.

Deborah Midanek: If that's true in the private equity format where you have a large measure of control, it is even more difficult in the public company format as you have no doubt discovered.

Paul Halpern: I have to say that my experience in a public company format is that the board's number one role seems to have become to fulfill the process requirements externally imposed by regulation. My experience is that the substantive job of a board of selecting and supervising and supporting management is inverted. And the job of setting strategy is in the hands of management and sometimes a board is informed. I would have to say that the company I served increased in value and went through a transition in its leadership while I was there. But what the board did was primarily fulfill the obligations simply of having a board.

It was a very interesting experience. I mean, I was on that board because my fund was a significant minority shareholder and for some reason that meant I was considered interested and not a reliable participant in board deliberations – which was through the looking glass to me. Because I looked at these independent directors, all of whom had great resumes and did a bang-up job of doing what they were being asked to do and thought that they lacked the direct incentive to increase value. They were looking at value increases that were a small fraction of the value that I was trying to create and defend for my investors. It was pretty bizarre from where I stood.

Deborah Midanek: Where did that way of functioning come from?

Paul Halpern: I viewed it as an agreed upon modus operandi that had been developed by management and the independent directors. Everybody seemed to think that was the way it ought to go, and no one was interested in rocking the boat.

Deborah Midanek: You mentioned independent directors. So the legal concept was that the management director cannot supervise him or herself, that certain decisions such as mergers in which management has a lot at stake are best made by disinterested parties. What do you think?

Paul Halpern: Yes, I went to law school at the very tail end of all of that, when most of the law was settled, and the notion that management wasn't a good decider, made a great deal of sense to me. Because management has their own incentives and you've got all kinds of agency problems there. But considering actual shareholders to be too interested to have a reliable view has always struck me as pretty damn strange.

Most independent directors are interested in serving on more boards. Everybody has an incentive. The simplest incentives to find are the economic incentives. It makes perfect sense to say management's economic incentives are often adverse to those of the company. That's a problem. But to think that you can hire somebody whose job it is to sit on a board and not be too intertwined with management and have them have an incentive to supervise management is not the best answer. Their incentive becomes getting selected to serve a board of a bigger and better corporation when this gig runs out, or as their second board, or as their third board. You have to ask whether that incentive is better for the company and shareholders than management's self-interested incentive would be.

As a private equity owner, I don't trust board members in general who aren't aligned, as in invested in the company's success. Although we use independent directors for industry expertise when we can get them and when we can get someone who will be useful. That has some value in some circumstances. It's really hard to find people, especially for lower middle-market companies, who are going to be good value.

In our medical device board, we've created an advisory board. They're great in that business. But for most of our businesses, if we say we want to form an advisory board, people would look at us oddly. Outside director is a role that people do and they have resumes for it; search people will help you find them. The hard part is figuring out a way to have them truly add value.

Deborah Midanek: That goes perhaps to the question of organizing the leadership of the board. I do believe, even in your private equity company, that the work of the board is different from the work of managing a company.

Paul Halpern: We look to our CEOs primarily for the skill of managing the business and only secondarily for the skill of presenting the business to non-stakeholders. If we have a CEO who has very strong skill in presenting the business to customers, then he's likely to have very strong skills of presenting the business to lenders or co-investors or new buyers of the business. But other CEOs might not. And so what we do, and I'm ambivalent about this sometimes, but we as the fund manager provide the people directly involved in the preparation of the materials used for board meetings.

At the beginning of our ownership of the company, we get heavily involved in managing cash. We may be less involved over time, and, similarly, the question of how to structure and compensate the executive team is something that we might be more involved in when things are at a more formative stage and less involved in later. We take responsibility for what gets presented every one, two, or three months when we meet as a board with management, because that isn't necessarily a focus that management needs to make the business successful as a business.

But it is certainly something we need to be able to do to make ourselves successful as investors and owners of businesses. That's the beginning of a window into that question of who has what job and where does what expertise need to reside. At a big corporation you could even imagine a board having staff to develop those materials.

Deborah Midanek: In having your fund manager involved in developing materials for the board meeting, you could argue that Versa is serving as de facto chairman of the board.

Paul Halpern: Yes, absolutely. It is usually the case that the person who is chairman of the board is a Versa person.

Deborah Midanek: In contrast, how does this preparation for the board meeting happen in the non-profit and the public company? I think you're probably going to tell me that management sets the agenda.

Paul Halpern: Yes. They negotiated with the chairman of the board who comes in, convenes the meeting and turns it over to the CEO. Then all of the strategy work gets handled that way. Then the compliance stuff gets turned back over to various board members for the board housekeeping work. As a shareholder in public companies, I am coming around to the view that shareholder democracy is broken but very fixable.

Deborah Midanek: Okay. What does that mean?

Paul Halpern: I don't own any individual equities because I went to business school, where they taught me to own the whole market. I didn't take the class where they told me how to pick individual equities in public markets. In public markets, what I own is a small piece of the ownership in a large number of companies, because I'm a Vanguard investor, among the very largest. Right now we have a system where those votes are exercised in accordance with an abstract set of views about governance entirely separate from the realities of any particular business. That to me means that shareholder democracy is broken because the largest shareholders aren't participating in the game in the way that they're being counted on to participate.

They don't own the holdings and they are evaluated not on the amount of resources they can put into being better holders, but on the amount of resources they can avoid spending on owning those holdings for someone else, which is great. I mean, it's exactly what it ought to be.

The solution is readily apparent. The technology now exists to make it possible for ETF holders to exercise their votes and do so easily because they're looking at their screens and evaluating their investments all the time anyway.

The beneficial owners of the ETFs or the investors in the mutual fund could have the power to pro-rata exercise their votes. And that could go with any degree of education or information dissemination or lobbying or whatever else that one wanted to do. If Fidelity does it better than Vanguard, then I'll wind up moving my money to Fidelity. And if Vanguard does it better than BlackRock, then I'm likely to move my money to Vanguard. I think that is something that nobody's looking at, but it seems like a slam dunk. Once you actually democratize shareholding to open up share voting, you can restore shareholder democracy, whether through advisory resolutions or binding resolutions or votes or whatever.

If some CEO starts using his job as head of a Fortune 10 company to go around and tell communities that they should do this and do that and the shareholders think that's a bad idea, they're going to say so. On the other hand, if a CEO gets up on his hind legs and says, it's not my job to care about the environment, it's my job to care about shareholders, the shareholders would then have the opportunity to disagree. It is a small flaw in the way we've organized share ownership, but it's a solvable problem. It's just when you think about it, you and I could design the app and the database to let you and I vote our mutual fund shares.

Deborah Midanek: But you and I are not representative of the great mass of owners of these things.

Paul Halpern: You could very well find that most people just don't bother, the voting season comes around and they treat it the same way they treat the first Tuesday after the first Monday in November. But that's got to be progress because then they're deliberately ignoring the issue as opposed to ignoring the issue because the most efficient method for them to own the shares gives them no option.

Deborah Midanek: I'm intrigued by what you're saying because indexing is so dominant now. It's such a big piece of our capital markets and of the holdings of our big, "institutional investors" – who are really not institutional investors. They are intermediaries, the BlackRocks and the Vanguards and so on. I mean, the state and public pension funds are also intermediaries, but they are intermediaries with a much longer term responsibility for the assets they are working with. But what an interesting idea, because you could actually ultimately apply it to the pension funds as well.

Information is now out there, everywhere. Maybe it is time to start to use technology to allow the underlying investors to vote.

Marty Lipton and others connected to the World Economic Forum are leading an effort called the "new paradigm in corporate governance" which envisions an alliance between major institutional investors and major issuers of shares to agree on long-term behavior. The bargain contemplates that if corporations will focus on the long-term best interests of their enterprise, then the institutional investors could agree also to focus on long-term share price growth, and support the company in the face of short-term challenges. I look at that and say, it's a great model. It's wonderful because it'll foment discussion among the players, but what it will not do is work. Because those guys that purport to be institutional investors are not institutional investors, they are simple custodians of units owned by others.

Paul Halpern: Yes, this is just a plot to disempower the activist. I think that calling a shareholder an activist because they have an opinion about how they're going to make their shares more valuable suggests a certain prejudice against the actual owner, because at least that person has money in the game.

Deborah Midanek: There are many ways to look at that too.

Paul Halpern: There's is no question that a strategy built on buying shares and then getting disproportionate treatment relative to other shareholders is destructive of value.

Deborah Midanek: Many activists have good ideas, but they don't have a corner on good ideas and generally they don't have very big staffs. They don't have anything like the resources of the corporation they're investing in has. Therefore why not learn from the activists how to think this way about how to maximize the value of your balance sheet. Why not welcome these ideas and get into a discussion with them about how to find multiple sources of value? That does not mean that the company must take all the actions suggested. It does seem useful to be open to the ideas and seek to find value in those ideas that might be realizable.

Paul Halpern: So, part of it, there's connection obviously between the disproportionate power that the activists have developed and, what would you call it, disempowering of actual shareholder democracy? Management teams successfully managing their businesses are expected to generate overwhelmingly positive votes every time there's a vote. So anybody who says, "I'm going to vote in a negative way," suddenly gets ridiculously disproportionate power just because there's going to be something in the "no" column. That is not a sign of robust debate, and the thorough processing of alternative ideas. It's a sign of enforced groupthink. Which might or might not be great within the ranks of a business, but it can't be right at the top level where strategy and management selection are supposed to go on.

Deborah Midanek: Groupthink is a serious threat. Because an individual voice in that setting of 7 to 11 people cannot take an extreme position and be heard. You have to learn to float your views to slowly and gently move the group in the direction that you want to go without ever having it be seen that you took a position in one direction or the other. Because if you are an outlier, you get discounted immediately.

Paul Halpern: I agree with you about that. I'm not sure I agree with you that there is a path to soft influence, because my experience is that the hard ground moves before soft influence can begin to have an impact.

Deborah Midanek: That is very true, which brings us back to the question about board leadership. The leadership, whatever form it takes, must insist that all voices be heard, that you don't have what amounts to bullying by the dominant voices, precluding the other voices from having their time.

Paul Halpern: Well, this is hard enough in a private board where everybody has a stake and works together frequently and is sort of locked in together until a liquidity event, so it's a seriously difficult thing to hope to get from a board.

Deborah Midanek: It is a very difficult thing. And but it does seem to me that a lot of what we have talked about seems to come back to the question of whether we desire active or passive board leadership. In your private equity portfolio company model, your firm as the manager is serving as the board leadership. The board leadership in your public company example appears to have been willing to develop a board process that reflects the wishes of management and focuses board energy on compliance. Then there's the non-profit one, where there seems to be an active leadership model aimed at being sure that the various parties understand the multiple hats they're wearing and which hat they're supposed to wear to the board meeting.

Paul Halpern: Yes, absolutely. And it's a very different experience because the task of identifying strategy and creating improvement and greatness is similar, but the stewardship responsibility for an institution that's in its 175th year weighs more heavily. I think that does a good job of making all stakeholders involved in the board process more sensitive to their roles and the consequences of what they are doing in both short and long term.

Deborah Midanek: You're saying that the longevity of the organization has an effect? To me the classic definition of the role of the board is to be the guardian of the perpetual life of the corporation. The corporation is a person under the law but it doesn't have arms and legs, but the board needs to be the arms and legs and animate the corporation and keep it healthy.

Paul Halpern: I would say that that definitely applies to the nonprofit I'm involved in. It is certainly not my role as a board member for my fund portfolio companies because we have rejiggered two or three of my portfolio companies and made them into one, and we took one and made it into four, and so on. So the best thing to do for those businesses from the point of view of value maximization might not be perpetual existence. My job as a board member is to execute on the goals that are built into my job as an owner, which are to buy a company, to increase its value and to sell the company. Those steps accomplish the goal of the owner, which as a private equity owner has a certain time horizon.

Deborah Midanek: Well, perhaps health is a better word. One of the things that others in this conversation who've serve both public and private equity held companies have observed is that there's a joy in being on the board of a private equity company because the goal is so clear.

Paul Halpern: Yes, you can tell when you've won. That is a very nice thing about my business.

Deborah Midanek: There's clarity along the way as to how to decide between one path and another because you know where you're trying to go. That's a much harder thing in a public company, which does more typically assume a perpetual existence.

What other suggestions do you have based on the three interesting and different models you have outlined of how boards function? How can we close this conversation with a compelling thought from Mr. Halpern?

Paul Halpern: The learning that I would take from my board experiences is that establishing clarity of the board's responsibility and the resources available to accomplish it can be transformative. I would say that when there is a weakness at a public company board or a lack of direction or stability at a private company board, it can ultimately be traced to a lack of clarity about the role and responsibility, the mission of the board in that context. And that clarity can be transformative if and only if it is honest.

Deborah Midanek: Right. And honest of course covers a multitude of subtexts.

Paul Halpern: Yes. Exactly.

Deborah Midanek: I think that there's been a continuing theme in your remarks about leadership. Even though you haven't used the word leadership, the question of where that clarity comes from is important. It can come from the CEO and perhaps shouldn't, but it can. It can come from the fund manager if they are in the control position. It can come from the board chairman. It can come from the mission and history of the organization.

Paul Halpern: Yes. But where it needs to come from is from the person who is recruiting the board member.

Deborah Midanek: Ah, now that's a very good point.

Paul Halpern: A person who's hiring the board member is giving that person a job to do, and compensation for doing it, and needs to spell that out, and then the board member needs to, as part of due diligence, find out if that's true. If the story is, we want you to join this board to represent the interests of shareholders, all the board does is watch management to make sure they are increasing shareholder value. That's your job, right? Maybe I want to be on that board. Maybe I don't want to be on that board.

But then my due diligence requires that I sit down with the CEO and the CFO and the other board members and the chair of the board and find out if that's what they're actually looking for in a board member. If they've got a more complicated or nuanced view or a simpler view about selecting and supervising and supporting the CEO, then you want to find out if that's actually what they're looking for.

I don't think that the job needs to be the same in every public company. I certainly don't think it needs to be the same in every private company, nor in every non-profit. There are certainly non-profits where the role of the board is to serve as a fulcrum for supporting giving to that non-profit. That's a great thing to do but if you go on that board thinking your job is to put management under the microscope and steer them when they're wandering off and change them out when they can't wander back, then you're on the wrong board. So I would say that, while no one can dictate a standard answer to this question, everyone on a successful board will know the answer, and it'll be the same answer to that question.

Deborah Midanek: Then there's another piece of that which is, in addition to the person doing the recruiting, what is the type of person they're looking for?

Paul Halpern: And is it consistent with what the parties think they're looking for? Because if you're looking for someone that is not a compliance-driven, well-trained, independent director, but you go out and recruit in that pool, your likelihood of success might not be that high.

Deborah Midanek: Thanks so much, Paul, and it was a great pleasure to talk to you.

Chapter 14
None of us has the monopoly on wisdom

Paul Washington

Paul Washington, Director of the ESG Center of The Conference Board, is a leader in corporate governance with a distinguished career in the ESG arena. Before joining The Conference Board ESG Center, he served as Senior Vice President, Deputy General Counsel, and Corporate Secretary of Time Warner Inc. He also served as Chief of Staff for the company's Chairman and CEO. Prior to Time Warner, Washington practiced law at the firm of Sidley & Austin and served as Vice President and Corporate Secretary of The Dime Savings Bank of New York.

Washington's career also includes extensive work in public service. He served as a law clerk for former Supreme Court Associate Justices William Brennan and David Souter, and for Circuit Court Judge David Tatel. He was the principal staffer on tax matters for former Congressman Stanley Lundine and, later, his principal speechwriter, when Lundine served as New York's Lieutenant Governor. Washington has served on the boards of numerous cultural, civic, and professional organizations, and is a former Chairman of the Society for Corporate Governance.

Paul graduated from Yale College and Fordham University School of Law, where he is a Resident Fellow and has taught corporate governance for over a decade.

Deborah Midanek: Thank you, Paul, for taking the time to speak with me. I am struck by the breadth of your background. Can you start by giving us a sense of where you come from? How did you come to be?

Paul Washington: I'll give you a little bit of my personal background and then we'll talk a little bit about my professional background. I grew up in Woodstock, New York, which was an extraordinary place to grow up because it was a town, and still is a town, of 6,000 people. It's a small community where people know you, you feel supported and it's got all the good advantages of a small town. It is also a place that has been an arts colony since 1902, a place where people have come from all over the world for a variety of reasons, whether they came to work at IBM or they came to be artists or they came to open shops or whatever. It had a lot of the virtues of a small town, but it wasn't a place where people peered from behind their lace

https://doi.org/10.1515/9783110670004-015

curtains and looked askance at anyone who was different. It offered both the support of a small community and the openness of a place that was part of a much broader world. I felt very lucky to grow up in that environment.

I'm not sure how much that has shaped what's come afterward, but I think the combination of being grounded in a particular place that was open to broader influences may have led to what I've done with my career. It also prepared me for the world of governance, where one often has a solid grounding in one area, while being open to a variety of perspectives. If you think about what good governance requires, you need to approach it with a solid framework that also allows you to take into consideration a whole lot of viewpoints and a whole lot of information, while remaining grounded in certain principles.

I spent a lot of time in government initially and thought I might make a career in government. I interned for two US senators, Senator Javits of New York, and Senator Huddleston of Kentucky. After college I worked for the mayor of Hamden, Connecticut, which is right outside New Haven. Next, I ran the scheduling and advance operation on a nationally targeted congressional campaign, which was really interesting. I returned to Capitol Hill, working for Stan Lundine, who was a congressman from upstate New York, which included working on the tax reform bill of 1986, which was really fascinating.

I went with him to Albany, where he was the first Governor Cuomo's Lieutenant Governor. I became his speech writer and principal policy person for a number of years and worked on an affordable housing task force with Harry Albright, who was chairman of the Dime Savings Bank and co-chaired the task force on affordable housing. Harry wanted someone to come down and be his chief of staff. I moved to New York, worked for the Dime Savings Bank, first with Harry and then with CEO Dick Parsons. I became secretary to the board while going to law school at night. Following law school I clerked at the DC Circuit, then the Supreme Court, and spent a little time in private practice. Dick Parsons then brought me to Time Warner to work again with him. I had a 20-year run there, first as an in-house litigator and then, after the AOL merger, I worked with the board of directors from 2001 until 2018.

Along the way, I had the pleasure of teaching corporate governance at Fordham Law School for about 15 years. I have experience in the public sector, private sector, and nonprofit sector, plus some insight into the academic world. All of that naturally led to my current position here at the ESG Center at The Conference Board.

Deborah Midanek: How great that you had all that variety before you took that role at Time Warner, because typically people in those roles do not have that varied perspective.

Paul Washington: It also helped that I worked for seven or eight years before I went to law school. It helped me do a better job in law school and then let me do a much better job as a clerk, because I had some real-world grounding before I clerked and entered private practice. That early work experience was enormously helpful.

Deborah Midanek: Having worked while going to law school at night, you then got the great opportunity to engage in pure life-of-the-mind activity in clerking for the Supreme Court.

Paul Washington: One of the great things about clerking at either court was the ability to take as much time as you needed to make something as close to perfect as you could. There were no billable hours, there were only all the hours in the day and night to do it. You could really work on getting it right, which involved figuring out exactly what you wanted to say, and then getting to work with really brilliant co-clerks and extraordinary judges. We gave them a semi-okay draft and they turned it into something extraordinary. That was a really great experience.

Deborah Midanek: That must have been wonderful. Then 20 years of longevity in another place because until then, you really hadn't had a lengthy perspective on one organization.

Paul Washington: I was delighted to have that depth of experience. One of the things that came through in clerking at the DC circuit court that served me well in governance was the practice it gave me in applying the law in a way that is consistent with the facts and many levels of other court opinions. When you're working as a clerk at the appellate level, you are looking for an answer that works; that's consistent with Supreme Court precedent, consistent with your own circuit court's precedent, and that takes into account other circuit court opinions. That is what applying the law to a particular set of facts in light of all these other factors – sister circuit precedent, your own precedent, the Supreme Court's precedent – requires.

That's very much what you try to do when solving an issue in corporate governance or sustainability. You're trying to solve this specific issue; trying to drop a plumb line through what works for investors, what works for the board, what works for management, and what works for multiple stakeholders.

And you have to do this based not only on principle but also with an awareness about the real-world impact of what the court's decision means. The challenges and dynamics you face when you're working in a corporate governance role at a company are similar to those I experienced in applying the law as a clerk.

Deborah Midanek: What you're trying to do in each role is remain true to timeless principles while also trying maintain constant 360° vision about the perspectives of all the different parties who have a stake in the outcome.

Paul Washington: That's right, it has to work in every way. Your decision has to work institutionally for the court; you can't be overstepping its bounds. Similarly, a decision you are recommending to the corporate board has to be within the company's jurisdiction. It has to work in terms of the company's business and its identity. There is a multiplicity of factors to take into account along with what the law says in both arenas.

Deborah Midanek: You took those broad and very particular skills and worked both with Albright and then Parsons, at Dime and then Time Warner. When did your interests become specifically focused on governance per se?

Paul Washington: It really developed while I was at the Dime. I joined the Dime in September of 1989 and, shortly after my arrival, the stock market crashed. Not long thereafter we came under intense scrutiny from federal regulators – the Office of Thrift Supervision and the FDIC. What the Dime had done, which made a lot of sense at the time, was to avoid the interest rate risk issues of the early 80s by investing heavily in adjustable rate mortgages.

We loaded up on adjustable rate mortgages, a novel product. The bank offered low-documentation or no-documentation loans based largely on the appraised value of the property and the downpayment. When the real estate recession hit, the bank was, therefore, hit very hard. The regulators thought the board wasn't doing a great job and we were, at one point, quite close to insolvency. I had the opportunity to work with an extraordinary board and CEO, Dick Parsons, during that time. Within a year and a half, we took the bank from being on the brink of insolvency and seizure by the government, to having the highest possible rating from the regulators. That was due to the recapitalization of the bank, but it was also due to changing the way the board operated.

We really enhanced the quality of the materials that went to the board. They got all the materials in advance, and we sent a cover note with each of the briefing books that explained what we were asking the board to do, why, and what the major risks were. We also adopted policies approved by the board that covered all of the bank's operations. I learned then that relatively modest changes in the way the board operated could make a significant change in the board's performance, which could in turn have a cascading effect on the institution's performance. I saw that what might seem unimportant, such as minor changes in process, can help a really good group of directors do an even better job as a board and have an extraordinary impact on the organization. I got hooked on governance there and then. It only deepened with my going to law school, because I was fascinated by constitutional law and I realized that corporate governance was basically constitutional law for corporations.

Unlike constitutional law in the government sphere, however, there is no single authority in corporate governance. The allocation of power and responsibility among shareholders, board, and management was intellectually fascinating. You've got the SEC, the stock exchanges, your investors, your board all exercising different kinds of authority. In corporate governance, if you work at a company, you get to create and maintain and oversee changes in the constitution for your corporation. It is as if you're a perennial founder, which is an engaging role to be in. You have to answer to a lot of masters, but you also have a fair amount of freedom in helping to craft what works for particular companies.

Deborah Midanek: What I was doing in 1989 was having my second child and working for Drexel Burnham. Off on maternity leave, I could see that the firm was sort of in liquidation during that period. On February 13th, 1990, which is when the company filed for bankruptcy protection, I was sad, but Drexel had said to come back for the first quarter; and April 1, we'll put you in business. Instead, I ended up organizing the shareholders, all but one employees, to get recognition by the bankruptcy court, and was elected chairman of the resulting equity committee.

In that role, I negotiated a restructured board of directors which put independent directors in the preponderance for the first time. As the consensus candidate, I became de facto the lead director in the middle of the Drexel Burnham Lambert Group Inc. bankruptcy. It was a fascinating trial by fire in terms of learning and just as you said, it was rivetingly interesting. I felt like I had come home because I intuitively understood the timeless principles of it. I fell madly in love with governance, but nobody else wanted to talk about it then. I mean there were six people talking about it and two of them were over at the Dime, right?

Paul Washington: Right. This was the era when governance thinking was really nascent. There were the General Motors principles out there.

Deborah Midanek: There was the Treadway Commission.

Paul Washington: But that was just scratching the surface. If, however, you were doing governance right at the time, it's not that much different from doing governance right today. There are a whole lot more rules out there now than there ever were before. But at its heart, then *and* now, the task requires figuring out who is responsible for what, helping the board and management fulfill their fiduciary duties within a thoughtful framework of allocation of responsibilities at the three levels: management, board, and shareholders.

Deborah Midanek: That takes us right to the key question, which is what is the role of the board of directors? I actually think that there's a timeless answer to it, but there are an amazing range of answers that people give. What's the legal responsibility?

Paul Washington: Its legal responsibility is to act faithfully and with due care in overseeing or, if it chooses, actually managing the corporation in the best interest of the corporation. And let me elaborate on that. Picking up on Jay Lorsch's book, *Back to the Drawing Board*, he identified multiple roles of the board: the board decides, the board oversees, the board advises. I would add that now the board engages. I think it engages not just with investors, but it engages management. Increasingly, it engages either directly or indirectly with other stakeholders. Though the board has multiple roles that it fulfills, its core duty remains the same. It's there to make sure that the corporation is run well and run responsibly.

Deborah Midanek: Responsibly, now that's an interesting one. How do we make that real and practicable?

Paul Washington: What's involved in running a company responsibly may vary a little bit by company and by industry. In my view, a company, and a public company in particular, is given a measure of the public's trust by virtue of its charter. You always, therefore, need to run the company in a way that is consistent with the public interest.

Deborah Midanek: So every company operates by the grace of the government.

Paul Washington: That hasn't changed since the Dutch East India Company was chartered in 1602. Corporations are given a license by society to operate. They need, therefore, to operate in a way in which they are conscious of their responsibilities to society. At a bare minimum, it means operating in accordance with the law. It means operating in a way that is ethical in your dealings not just with investors, but with competitors, with suppliers, with employees, with the public, obviously with the government, with regulators. It calls corporate leaders to a higher standard of behavior than simply complying with the legal requirements. I don't think that's changed. I think expectations have changed, but the core responsibilities of directors and officers of a corporation have remained the same. People may have been blinded at different times along the way.

Deborah Midanek: At about the time that you and I were cutting our teeth in this arena, our economy was dealing with the impact of prolonged high inflation. Inflation drove a number of things that changed the thrift industry and that created the interest rate swap market. It brought us the pronouncements of Milton Friedman on the purpose of business, and it drove growth of the market for the leverage buyout. The related spate of hostile takeovers also brought us the rise of independent directors.

Paul Washington: I would say that it's not surprising that as an economist, Milton Friedman looked at business purpose through a financial lens. We are, however, all people first. Having studied history as an undergraduate, I look at corporations and corporate governance through a different lens. I think most people look at the subject of corporate governance through a broader lens than simply an economic one. We are now seeing investors working to apply a broader lens.

I think that if you were going to decide to invest in a company in the 19th century, before the development of public markets as we know them now, your considerations were likely not purely economic ones. You thought it was going to be run by people who knew what they were doing. You thought that a valuable product or service would result. You were most likely not investing in a remote enterprise. You were more likely investing in a local opportunity, maybe run by your neighbor. You were investing in their enterprise and it was going to have an impact on your community. Those factors were all taken into consideration in prior centuries of investment. I think that, now, multiple factors of impact on the community, impact on employees, impact on society and the environment are coming into play in investment decisions. This wider focus is in some ways only a return to what was part of the consideration set before people started to look at investing on a purely economic basis through the public markets.

Deborah Midanek: So we are coming full circle? Interestingly, it's the institutional investor and their rise that has driven us toward this prevalent thing called short-termism. But it's also the institutional investor and their increasing scale and the fact that they in many cases have no choice but to remain invested in our public companies, whether through index funds or not, that bring them to the realization that there's a lot more than tomorrow's stock price we need to be thinking about.

Paul Washington: I agree with that. And that goes along with any number of other factors that are encouraging a greater social consciousness within companies and regarding companies.

Deborah Midanek: We are at an interesting juncture as there are a couple of major trends that we haven't confronted until fairly recently. These include a remarkably high proportion of our capital markets being invested in index funds, which has driven deeper engagement with companies, and we have a small number of big financial intermediaries. A related trend is that while we've got many, many corporations and businesses, given our pluralistic system, we now also have a small number of dominant mega companies on both sides: a handful of very big companies and very big investors. While aspects of that are frightening, to me that means there's an opportunity for real dialog.

I'm interested in the New Paradigm for Corporate Governance, put together by Marty Lipton and the World Economic Forum in Davos. It explores ways for longer term investors and companies to make common cause. It is not defined this way, but one effect could be to head off the short-term activist raid impact. Do you think that we can find common cause between investors and companies in terms of long-term thinking?

Paul Washington: It's going to be easier to do in principle than it will be in practice because companies cannot hide behind the stakeholder model to avoid being held accountable for underperformance, and investors will continue to feel pressure to outperform their competition.

Those commitments are going to be harder for companies to fulfill when an activist shows up, and they will continue to do so. I think it's not only possible, but necessary, to have agreement on a certain set of principles that promote long-term overall performance of corporations in the best interest of their investors, in the best interest of their employees, in the best interest of their customers and their suppliers and of society. In order to be able to focus on the long-term best interests of all of those stakeholders, it is going to take an agreement primarily between companies and the major investors.

You also need government at the table because if they're not and they're setting a different set of rules, it can undermine that compact. And similarly, if the other constituencies aren't at the table, those other constituencies, including employees, may be demanding short-term action that could actually hurt the long-term future of the corporation. Everyone represents their own interests, and I think all of them need to come together to agree on what is expected of a corporation.

Deborah Midanek: Now you're talking about something that requires a very nuanced set of judgments to be made and made again and then made again. To develop that wisdom, how do we populate the boardroom? How do we arm the directors to be able to think that way? You have worked with some really effective boards, and I'm sure you've seen a number that are not so effective.

Paul Washington: Let me give you an example of when a board did a really good job with a broader consciousness of its role and its responsibilities. In the summer of 2014, right after Time Warner spun off Time Inc., we received an unsolicited offer from 21st Century Fox with a headline value of $85 per share. A substantial portion of the offer's consideration was in Fox stock, and we believed that their stock was inflated by guidance that they were highly unlikely to meet.

There were good, purely economic reasons to reject the offer. We believed, given their financial profile and what we thought we were worth on our own, that there was no way Fox could ever offer us enough money to make it worthwhile. We responded with a statement, pretty bold at the time, to the effect that we not only reject your offer, but we feel that there's no point in even talking because you can't pay us enough. What went into our consideration was that we looked at what it might mean for our employees to be part of 21st Century Fox. They were a family-run company that had significant reputational and regulatory issues due to the phone hacking scandal in the UK. We also considered what it could mean in terms of the quality of the content to be created by the Time Warner portion of what would then have been a combined company. These issues would have serious impact on the ongoing value of the company after completion of the transaction.

We looked at the possible impact on not just the financials but on our shareholders, on our employees, on our public, and on the mission that our company believed in. All of those reasons argued in favor of rejecting the offer and, after not too many weeks, we prevailed. We later did a transaction not for what the Fox offer was worth, which was about $70 per share, but two years later for over $100 per share. To me, that was a good example of the board operating for the right reasons in a way that was in the best interests of the corporation and all of its constituencies. Many of the people who wanted to create television shows and movies for Warner Brothers, for Turner, for HBO, might not have wanted to create the same quality of work for 21st Century Fox. If they didn't want to create it first for us, maybe they'd go somewhere else, maybe that content would not have been created. It could have been bad for Fox and for everyone who enjoyed the content that we created if we had combined.

Deborah Midanek: So if that approach were made today, what would happen?

Paul Washington: I think the same thing should happen. I think boards may be even more comfortable taking into consideration matters beyond purely economic ones. Delaware law is clear: You have got to care about price. But a number of factors go into determining the value you're receiving. If, for example, you're being paid partly in stock by the acquirer, you're allowed to look beyond the closing date to see what this would mean for anyone who would hold onto the stock of the combined company thereafter. These considerations can come into play in a takeover situation like that.

Deborah Midanek: One of the mechanisms that has been helpful to the courts in being able to support decisions like that has been the role played by the independent director, simply because a management director cannot be believed to be supervising himself. In other words, how can the public have confidence that an arm's length analysis of what's best for the corporation has been done when management has a considerable amount of value at stake?

Paul Washington: I would challenge that actually. Management owes exactly the same fiduciary duties to the company that an independent director does. The duty of care and the duty of loyalty. They do have more at stake financially than the director does, although that depends on the financial circumstances of the director and on how much they've invested in the company's stock. So you can have directors whose financial well-being is very much tied to a corporation. As a matter of theory and as a matter of law, you shouldn't have a big divergence between management directors and independent directors on any of these issues. As a matter of practice, however, independent directors tend to have, as a general rule, more at stake in their reputation than their financial situation. That's not to say management doesn't have its reputation at stake as well. But directors' concern about reputational risk does provide a natural brake on risk-taking by an organization. Companies may shy away from excessive risk taking because directors have their reputations at stake and don't want to do something that could wind up looking foolish.

Deborah Midanek: Regardless of the reasoning as to why, then, we have nonetheless seen a huge move, a really radical move to independent directors being in the ascendancy. I've lost track of the specific percentages, but it's a high percentage at something like 90% of public company directors are independent.

Paul Washington: I think that the emphasis on independent directors was really spurred by Sarbanes-Oxley and the stock exchange listing standards that required you to have a majority of independent directors, and many investors have argued in favor of a supermajority. I think that did it even more than Delaware law.

Deborah Midanek: So going back to look at this question of the nuanced thinking that the board needs to do to try to determine the best interests of a wide variety of people, in having now a majority and in most cases a supermajority of independent directors seated, what we don't have then is native knowledge of the company. We don't have people with native knowledge of each other. In other words, directors come together infrequently, whether it's 4 times or 10 times a year or in between, in a fairly ritualized set of circumstances. In order for that group of people to make those kinds of decisions well, a very special kind of leadership is required to draw out the opinions and views of a variety of people, who do not naturally know and trust each other.

Paul Washington: It is a particular kind of person who should be on a board, and it's got to be someone who understands that they as an individual director do not have any power, unless it is given to them by resolution of the board. That can be a hard adjustment for a lot of people, especially if you're a CEO, if you're an entrepreneur, if you've run your own shop. All of a sudden you're in a situation where you don't call the shots. So it takes a particular kind of skill set and maybe even personality and perhaps even character to serve as a director. That's why I think that, while there's much to be said for having diversity of experience and diversity of perspectives, what you have in common, the ability to work well and understand the role of a director, is just as important as diversity of backgrounds. You've got to have certain things in common, including an understanding of the role of director, the ability to work well with others, and the ability to handle issues that come up that are outside of your normal wheelhouse.

Deborah Midanek: The question in not just about having diversity in the boardroom, but is about how to get the benefit of that diversity while still supporting the CEO. First, there has to be this thing called respect for all the different people in the room, and if you have the ability to respect the different points of view then you can move towards trust, which allows you to speak in candor.

Paul Washington: I would add into the mix that, from a management standpoint, there needs to be transparency, and that transparency builds trust with the board. So, trust and transparency go hand in hand, and only enhance each other over time. That's why it's really important for management when they're not just talking to the board, but talking with the board, to say this is what we know and this is what we're going to try. These are all the things that could go wrong and this is what we just don't know. They need to be candid, and ask if anyone around the table has thoughts on how we might enhance the upside and mitigate the risks on the particular venture, or even whether it should go forward, with management regarding the board meeting a bit more as a seminar and a little less as a lecture is I think a very healthy approach.

That transparency makes a big difference. That transparency and the related trust allows that board to deal with really challenging situations that arise much more effectively than they can if simmering doubts vis-à-vis management or among the board members vis-à-vis each other are allowed to persist. I agree with you that it takes a particular set of skills from the chair of the board and the chair of the committees to bring out the best of both the commonality and the diversity in the room. You didn't ask, but a CEO can have those skills as well. To me, it is not impossible for one person serving as both chairman and CEO to be able to orchestrate that.

What it does require is for the person who holds both the CEO and the chair position to check their CEO ego at the door when they're in the boardroom. If they can wear the CEO hat in providing information to the board, but then check the ego associated with, "I'm the leader," once that is done and really focus on their role as the chair, they can be effective. The CEO shifts into being the conductor, the orchestrator of the discussion, the person who gets the best out of all the different instruments in the room, so they can be successful together. It takes someone who's got flexibility to shift gears like that.

Deborah Midanek: It takes a lot of self-confidence to do that.

Paul Washington: Such self-confidence that you don't need to prove you're the smartest person in the room when you walk into the room.

Deborah Midanek: Exactly. There's another piece of it. There needs to be recognition that the work of the board and the work of management are very different. The process of building the fabric of the board and the ability of people to speak candidly with each other and the ability to run the seminar as opposed to simply review the quarterly financials takes a lot of work. Sometimes the CEO just does not have time to do that.

Paul Washington: I would take a somewhat different view because I don't think there is a really bright line between the board and management. Again, going back to the Jay Lorsch point, boards decide, boards oversee, boards advise, boards engage. That's exactly what management does. They do it at different levels, but a well-run management should actually resemble a board a little bit more than it does in the traditional top-down pyramid. A well-run management elicits the best views from people within the organization at a variety of levels. A well-composed management will have a diversity of views and a diversity of experiences, so orchestrating management is not that different from orchestrating a board. When it comes to certain subject matter areas such as strategy or, increasingly, environmental and social issues that are dealt with at both the management and board level, it's not entirely clear who has what responsibility in those areas. On strategy, how much depends on management and how much on the board can vary over time as to who plays the leading role.

For a well-run company in a stable industry, maybe there's more that rests with the management than with the board. Or in certain crisis situations, who's closer to it than management? In a crisis situation, maybe management should be even more in charge than in a run-of-the-mill kind of time. But you're right, it's not going to be a clear line. That's why I think we need to provide fluidity between roles regardless of what your governance policy has provided. There's fluidity between the role of the board and management. The one thing that is a clear constant is that it is the board's responsibility to decide where to draw that line and when to move the line. That to my mind is a clear distinction in the role of the board and management, because even though I believe the distinction can shift, the board gets to draw the line.

Deborah Midanek: I was just having a similar conversation yesterday regarding a board on which I sit. I was talking with the CFO and asked, "Sitting here at a distance, I hear a very different tone at the company now. There's a sense that everybody is hitting on all cylinders. Can you tell me what made that happen?" And he said, "Actually, I *can* tell you, we have done several things very deliberately this year and it all has to do with emotional intelligence. We have gone on several executive team retreats, in which we have worked very hard to learn what emotional intelligence is so that we can support each other instead of competing with each other. We have offered mentoring and coaching that the company pays for to the top 50 people and that has had a huge impact. And we have done advanced planning for any major project in which we all get in the room and brainstorm about how can this thing fail? When the product is done, we always create an after-action report, asking ourselves what did we learn from this that we can use for the next project?" It was just music to my ears.

Paul Washington: I think that's really smart because one thing that is pretty clear is that if your company is going to go through a crisis, one of the biggest factors in determining the outcome is the ability of your management team to work together well. You can have great outside advisors – and we certainly did over time at Time Warner – but you have to have a cohesive management team because your outside advisors are not that familiar with the company. The decision makers are within the company and need to work together well.

What drives good emotional intelligence in working with your colleagues is understanding where your colleagues are coming from, what makes them tick in a way that's nonjudgmental. One of the best projects I ever did, just within my governance team, resulted from a personality survey of all the members of the group. It was not only really interesting to figure out who was ambitious, who wasn't, who was an extrovert, who was an introvert, who was impetuous and who was a planner, but it was very helpful in building a strong group.

When you understand where each person is coming from, who'd like to be included in other projects and who'd like to be working independently on their own, for example, it is possible to play to their strengths. If you found out that one of your colleagues really just likes to work independently, you didn't get upset when they didn't want to be part of a team. You understood that that's how they were and who they were. Building both the general emotional intelligence and the knowledge of your colleagues in a nonjudgmental way can really help a management team work a lot more effectively. What you're getting into here is something that I think is one of the next frontiers of governance. Sure, there's stakeholder engagement, which is something that companies are doing a whole lot more of, but I think that another area that is worthy of further exploration is governance within management.

You don't want to have a whole bunch of rules that hamstring management, but what are the right processes to have in place? The answers will vary by company, but what are some of the right processes and the right allocation of authority within a company to help companies make effective decisions within the management level? Because we know that most of the big mistakes, while they ultimately involved board action or board inaction, really were driven by management. So I think that there's a lot to be said for the governance profession helping at the senior management level and not just focusing on the board and shareholder levels.

Deborah Midanek: Shall we call that systemic governance? It seems that you are pretty bullish on the future of governance broadly; the engagement of the board and the management with each other, as well as the board and management with the shareholders and the stakeholders and the governments. Now we add engagement among management levels and top management and the board. This has been an inspiring conversation. I have one final question for you: when is your book coming out? You have an interesting and lively perspective that includes what many others have said, and adds original ideas valuable to a broader audience.

Paul Washington: If I didn't have a full-time job, that might be in the offing, but for now I'm happy to work with others on their books as I am with you on yours. And on being bullish on governance, I am. I think, though, there's a big challenge. There is going to be a generational shift on boards. At some point people who are in their 40s and 50s now are going to be joining boards. That's a new generation. We are at the tail end of the boomers, and we will soon be bringing Gen X and then millennials into the boardroom. I do think we want the different generational perspective, but the hard-thought and hard-learned lessons in the corporate governance world need to be passed on to the next generation of board members.

We want to avoid generational hubris. I'm not singling any generation out, but every generation has some degree of hubris and thinks that they've got the right answers and that prior generations have failed. I think what's sort of incumbent on companies and anyone in the governance field is to make sure that the concepts that are timeless are passed on from generation to generation. I think that's going to be an important challenge. If we do that right, then I am quite bullish on governance, but if we don't, the response from the next generation of directors may be okay, boomer, out of the way. And they may be doomed to repeat some of the mistakes that have been made in the past.

Deborah Midanek: It's going to mean a number of new directors arriving within a very short period of time, unless we keep appointing old people to fill old people's slots.

Paul Washington: We have certainly faced boomer hubris, especially with the older side of boomers. The great business leaders from earlier generations had a different view of corporations and then in came the boomer generation, with their strong convictions. I think taking a bit more of a historical perspective and looking at governance from a generational perspective might be interesting. I do think one of the challenges is to make sure that succeeding generations benefit from the learnings of prior ones.

Deborah Midanek: I think we're just about ready to conclude here, but do you have any other parting comments you want to be sure that we include?

Paul Washington: None of us has the monopoly on wisdom. I'm deeply grateful for the opportunity to talk with you and I look forward to the result.

Deborah Midanek: Well, thank you. Thank you for a fabulous conversation.

Conclusion: Developing the corporate director's creed

We have heard interesting and candid views from a cross-section of remarkable and experienced people. What strikes me is the overall harmony of their views. While it is hazardous even to try to summarize, here is my distillation of the points upon which we can act. Inevitably, I will have missed some, or misinterpreted, but I hope to offer a synthesis that is useful as we strive to build ever more effective governance systems, and declare the Corporate Director's Creed.

- Directors help corporations endure by embracing not only the desire to earn a profit but purpose beyond profit. Directors and companies alike behave in accordance with values they espouse. They understand that there is no one-size-fits-all model and government would not be well served by seeking to impose such. Instead, directors dedicate themselves to discerning the purpose of the company they serve in accordance with its particular circumstances and helping to define its values.
- Directors cherish procedural justice, the establishment of an environment in which decision-making processes are seen and believed to be fair and balanced, with attention to all voices. This concept must become the foundation for every governing body in order for the resulting decisions to be honored.
- Board service is not a passive role, but a role that demands the best of those who choose to accept a seat. Similarly, the most useful motives of directors in choosing to serve include a desire to serve not only the enterprise itself, but to serve the public good.
- Rigorous evaluation by and of each director, committee, and board is imperative for continuous improvement, as is modeling the ethical behavior we expect of all.
- Clarity and agreement as to the specific vision and purpose not only of the company but of the board itself is important to building effective decision-making bodies systems. Focus on flexibility and forward movement even as we monitor the past and present.
- Each director invests in earning and cultivating respect among board members, and between board members and management, shareholders, and other stakeholders as an essential element of building a strong and trusting team. This is especially important as participants with diverse points of view continue to increase. Respect can lead to trust, and trust to candor, in a virtuous cycle.
- Directors contribute to the result while subordinating individual ego, including that of the CEO, to the goals of the team and to continuous exploration, learning, and improvement.
- The board actively cultivates awareness of current issues and trends to avoid insularity. It enriches board discussion by allowing time for unstructured conversation

https://doi.org/10.1515/9783110670004-016

and mining perspectives offered by independent directors. It invites discussion with stakeholders. The board as a listening organism has much to learn from members of the workforce; from investors, customers, regulators, academics, technologists, farmers, visionaries and futurists; youngsters and oldsters; and beyond.

- The board recognizes that intangible assets – people and processes as well as brand values – represent the preponderance of public company value today and directs significant attention to those areas. Directors embrace opportunities to build their own capacity to interpret technology, people, and other risks and rewards.

- Each director and the board recognizes that active development of engaged board leaders who are excellent thinkers, honest communicators, and skilled facilitators dedicated to drawing out and harmonizing the many views expressed by diverse players inside and outside of the boardroom is imperative. Directors commit themselves to helping management and the board to discern the best possible path for the enterprise.

Several phrases deserve additional emphasis before we close. Those leaders must proceed with humility and courage as well as moral principle and character. And the rest of us must recognize those who do that well and revere their service as we do the public service of our judges.

In a world characterized by constant change, we look to ideas that are timeless. We must prepare ourselves as corporate leaders to follow the teaching of Aristotle: Rigorous thinking in that part of the world that is not constant requires imagining possibilities and choosing the one for which the most compelling argument can be made. Again, and again.

Index

https://doi.org/10.1515/9783110670004-017

CPSIA information can be obtained
at www.ICGtesting.com
Printed in the USA
FSHW022056111020
74726FS